Washington-Centerville Public Library
Centerville, Ohio

WHAT OTHERS ARE SAYING ABOUT THIS SERIES OF BOOKS...

"Fran's broadly generational approach to today's kids is very nicely executed. While he's familiar with youth up close and has a voracious appetite for interesting facts, he also sees the big picture. I learned a lot. There are things in here that I didn't know and I make a living doing this!"

> – NEIL HOWE, co-author of *Generations* and *Millennials Rising*

"Fran Kick presents a thoughtful and research informed approach to engaging youth, packaged in a lively and vital way. His work recognizes not only that getting kids involved is beneficial, but that making it fun and meaningful is essential to making it happen. *What Makes Kids KICK* is filled with good advice for coaches, educators, parents and anyone else who works with kids."

> – RICHARD RYAN, Ph.D., Professor of Psychology, Psychiatry & Motivation at the University of Rochester, NY and co-editor of the *Handbook of Self-Determination Research*

"What fantastic books!!! I gave my sister, who is a high school counselor in Scottsdale, the *What Makes Kids KICK @ HOME* one. Your graphics are always so stunning and they are on this book as well. I really enjoyed *What Makes Kids KICK*. Positive, well thought-out and researched, lots of good ideas, fun to read, plus great resources. Covers all the ground of *Millennials Rising* and more, but in a more accessible way. I like the size and shape. It's a home run!"

> – CLAIRE RAINES, author of *Connecting Generations* and co-author of *Generations at Work*

"Fran Kick knows kids inside out, and he gives real-world practical ideas for those seeking to parent and teach them. This book provides a wealth of amazing resources and usable tools to KICK IT IN with kids of all ages!"

> – ERIC CHESTER, Founder & President of Generation Why, Inc. and author of *Getting Them to Give a Damn: How to Get Your Front Line to Care About Your Bottom Line*

"Fran Kick is a genius. He can relate to an entire generation like no other. In *What Makes Kids KICK*, Fran's take on motivation is so right on the button. Motivating today's ! Read this book to unlock the mystery."

> – JIM CANTERUCC

D1311606

"I constantly hear kids voice two complaints about the adults in their life – 'they don't listen' and 'they don't understand.' By helping us listen and understand, Fran Kick opens doors for positive communication with the kids we know, love, and long to lead into healthy adulthood."

– WALT MUELLER, President
of the Center for Parent/Youth Understanding

"Fran Kick has given us a tried-and-true blueprint-of-success to positively focus the efforts and energies of our youth. *What Makes Kids KICK* is a compilation of cutting edge research closely linked with real world experiences. You and your students will be the benefactors of Fran's insightful writing and keen awareness of what makes young people tick and KICK. In the world of adolescent behavior patterns, Fran Kick stands as one of the select professional leaders who continues to open new realms of possibilities for our students, our schools, our communities, and ultimately our future. Satisfaction guaranteed and even more!"

– TIM LAUTZENHEISER, Attitude Concepts for Today, Inc.
and Director of Education for Conn-Selmer, Inc.

"Fran Kick addresses the many factors that influence children today, which in turn makes students today unique. I have brought Fran into the Diocese of Buffalo for many years and his presentations with students, teachers, and parents always get rave reviews. I feel after reading this book, Fran has researched the material for the book as much as he has for his presentations. This book puts together in an entertaining manner, the research and the practical observations that he has seen while making his presentations across the country. It includes many references to books and web sites to give further information to the reader. *What Makes Kids KICK* is a 'must read' for all parents and educators."

– TOM PETERS, Assistant Superintendent
Department of Catholic Education Diocese of Buffalo, NY

"*What Makes Kids KICK* is a wonderful book. Based on the latest scientific knowledge and clearly written, it will benefit parents, educators, and everyone interested in children's emotional growth. I commend Fran for producing this up-beat and encouraging work."

– EDWARD HOFFMAN, Ph.D., author of *Future Visions:
The Unpublished Papers of Abraham Maslow*

"Fran Kick not only knows what makes kids kick, he understands what kids today need to be the kind of self-motivated, self-reliant everyday heroes the world will soon need them to be. Helping today's generation of children to think for themselves demands a new adult-child level of communication that's positive, unambiguous, and constructive. This book offers parents, teachers, and anyone else who works with today's youth a clearer perspective of the strategies and skills most helpful in diminishing an over-dependence on the approval-driven choices of others. Guiding a more internally directed generation of kids who won't fall victim to an externally manipulative world, *What Makes Kids KICK* can serve as your resource of resources."

> – ELISA MEDHUS, M.D. Author of *Hearing is Believing: How Words Can Make or Break Our Kids*

"Fran Kick hits the nail on the head with *What Makes Kids KICK!* Instead of focusing on the negative and theorizing like arm-chair philosophers, he is out there doing and seeing. By doing and seeing he understands that raising children and guiding a generation in society cannot be McDonaldized. It's not a one size fits all world. This book helps us understand the importance of taking the time to learn 'what makes kids kick' (or just be interested in learning). There isn't one set methodology or a single seven-step system for today's generation of kids. We need to set aside what works for us or what it was like 'when we were their age' and try focusing on what works for them and how we can engage and interact with kids today without turning them off. Fran does a great job helping us do this."

> – SHAWNA GFROERER, Director of Member Services & Events for Business Professionals of America

"I believe these books have real merit for us with our staff as part of their professional development. I was impressed with the breadth of Fran's research and the broad applicability of his work in the school setting. It is a very kid-centered work that appropriately places the emphasis on 'who' we teach rather than 'what' we teach."

> – TERRY RILEY, Associate Superintendent Centerville City Schools, OH

"Fran Kick's series of books on *What Makes Kids KICK* are a breath of fresh air and should be required reading to those of us who are parents or teachers. With 37 years as a high school teacher and having 6 children and 13 grandchildren I was thrilled to read Fran's insights and amazingly thorough research concerning today's youth.

Being of the Boomer generation and having taught through three generations of students I was delighted by the way Fran dissipated the clouds of confusion about what makes our current young people tick. As a music teacher who has watched things progress from LP vinyl recordings to 8-tracks, to cassettes, to CDs, DVDs, mini-discs, MP3s, iPods and memory sticks, I can say it's nice to have these books to use as a resource when dealing with today's young people and their parents. You will find them a wonderful tool for understanding what motivates drives, distracts, and frustrates our Millennial young people. Fran's conclusions are laser guided and definitely on the mark."

– WALT LOVELL, teacher at Elko High School, NV

"WOW! Double WOW!! As an associate professor of Leadership at a large, suburban university and as a seasoned corporate leadership development coach/trainer/consultant, I am compelled to say those emotional words about Fran's absolutely wonderful, insightful, energizing, refreshingly written, on-target book. He totally nails what motivates and ignites the passions driving the Millennial generation. I have consulted with Baby Boomer and GenXer leaders for many years, and these leaders often say about Millennials 'they just don't get it' when it comes to work. When working with Millennial new hires, they say about their bosses 'they just don't get us'. Well, with Fran's bridge building book so sorely needed by so many leaders in the workforce, all groups can now better understand one another and work more passionately and engaged. Get this book now if you want to 'get it.' I gotta say it again – WOW!"

– SCOTT GRAHAM, Associate Professor
of Organizational Leadership at Wright State University, OH

"Fran has done a great job of writing a useful book that will connect the adult and student populations. As a faculty member, I find the contents very useful for me as I prepare leadership seminars for my students – Millennials. Being a Baby Boomer, I must keep myself current on what inspires and motivates the Millennials in order to be successful as a teacher, coach, mentor, and advisor. *What Makes Kids KICK* does just that for me. I encourage teachers and faculty members to add this book to their collection of useful and practical resources."

– GAREE EARNEST, Ph.D., OSU Leadership Center Program Leader
and Associate Professor at The Ohio State University

"An eclectic blend of thought and content that's strikingly comprehensive – bringing readers up to date on many culturally literate and developmentally essential points. The narrative, as usual, is engaging. I continue to learn every time when reading Fran Kick's 'stuff' or participating in the follow-on discussions. There's particular value in the Chapter Three Appendix on the history of generational theory. The resource listings at the end of each chapter are notable as excellent resources in themselves."

– J. COOPER ACKERMANN, M.Ed., Adjunct Faculty of Educational Leadership at Wright State University, OH

"In a short and easy read, Fran has not only given us a great insight on what makes today's kids tick, but also a historical perspective of where we came from! So find yourself a comfortable chair, start reading, and get a KICK out of this book!"

– PAUL LABBE, Vice-President of Operations at CompuNet Clinical Laboratories, OH

"The perfect handbook for anyone seeking to connect and communicate with today's youth. Fran's keen understanding of today's teen intellect combined with his experience and training makes him the model practitioner for helping young people to find and choose successful pathways. His seamless combination of depth and breadth allows for the reader to join him with ease as he reflects both on the past and the future of our next 'greatest generation.' Through the author's unique perspective, you will understand the awesome combination of power, strength and unique optimism contained within the Millennial generation. *What Makes Kids KICK* should be a must read for anyone who works with young people!"

– SCOTT LANG, Synergy Leadership Endeavors

what

makes

kids
kick @Home

inspiring
the millennial
generation to
kick it in®

Fran Kick

What Makes Kids KICK @ HOME!
Inspiring the Millennial Generation to KICK IT IN®
by Fran Kick

Special discounts and customized versions are available on bulk quantities of this book
purchased for educational, corporate, professional associations, organizations, and events.

Published by:
Instruction & Design Concepts
441 Maple Springs Drive
Centerville, OH 45458-9232 USA
http://www.whatmakeskidskick.com

Copyright © 2005 Fran Kick, Instruction & Design Concepts

All rights reserved. No part of this book may be reproduced or transmitted in any form or by
any means, electronic or mechanical, including photocopying, recording or by any information
storage and retrieval system, without written permission from the author, except for the
inclusion of brief quotations in a review.

This publication is designed to provide accurate and authoritative information in regard to the
subject matter covered. It is sold with the understanding that the author and publisher are not
engaged in rendering any professional or clinical psychological services. Every effort has been
made to ensure the accuracy and appropriateness of the references and web sites mentioned in
this work, but no warranty or fitness is implied. All information provided is on an "as is" basis
at the time of publication. The author and publisher have no control over and assume no
liability for the material available via the references, web sites and other links.

KICK IT IN® is a registered trademark of Fran Kick, Instruction & Design Concepts.
All other trademarks are property of their respective owners.

ISBN-10, print edition   1-59199-016-5   ISBN-13, print edition   978-1-59199-016-1
ISBN-10, PDF edition   1-59199-017-3   ISBN-13, PDF edition   978-1-59199-017-8

Publishers Cataloging-in-Publication Data

Kick, Fran
        What Makes Kids KICK @ HOME! Inspiring the Millennial Generation to KICK IT IN® /
Fran Kick. – 1st ed. – Centerville, OH: Instruction & Design Concepts, 2005
        p. cm.
        Includes bibliographical references and index.
        ISBN-10: 1-59199-016-5
        1. Parenting
        2. Family – United States
        3. Generations – Intergenerational relations – United States
        4. Youth – United States – Social Conditions – 1980-2000
        I. Title

Library of Congress Control Number: 2005902023

Table of Contents

Acknowledgements..v
Preface vi

CHAPTER ONE: HOMES, FAMILIES AND NEIGHBORHOODS..........1

Homes are different..2
Families are different 4
Neighborhoods are different 8
Books about homes, families and neighborhoods........................13
Web sites about homes, families and neighborhoods.................14
Notes for Chapter One 15

CHAPTER TWO: PARENTS AND PARENTING 17

Parents are different 18
Parenting is different..19
Stressed out and burned out families......................................20
Affluence..22
    Motivating kids with money 24
Production to consumption..30
    More trophy rooms, homes & toys for our trophy kids.........31
Books about parents and parenting 39
Web sites about parents and parenting......................................41
Notes for Chapter Two 42

CHAPTER THREE: TECHNOLOGY MEDIA/TV 24/7/365.................47

The invasion of technology 48
Media..50
What has TV taught kids today? 52
Overscheduled families & kids 61
Books about technology, media/TV 24/7/365 69
Web sites about technology, media/TV 24/7/365........................70
Notes for Chapter Three 72

CHAPTER FOUR: TODAY'S KIDS ARE ACTIVE..............................75

Youth sports 76
Youth in the arts..83
    Strike up the band...and the orchestra...and the choir..........85

Theater, drama, lights, camera, action 89
Gotta dance.. 95
The arts for every kid in America... 96
Youth Groups.. 98
Religious youth groups 98
Secular youth groups, clubs & organizations........................ 104
Scout's honor 105
Youth camps and retreats... 106
Books worth reading about kids' activities................................ 111
Web sites worth visiting about kids' activities 112
Notes for Chapter Four 113

CHAPTER FIVE: INSPIRING KIDS TO BE SELF-DISCIPLINED 121

Discipline 122
Punishment vs. discipline 122
Generational parenting patterns... 124
The parenting approaches and style matrix 128
Responsiveness and expectations.. 128
Permissive to controlling 131
Uninvolved to involved 133
Unaware to aware... 136
Hostility to love... 137
The sweet spot for self-discipline... 139
The 123s of encouraging self-discipline 142
Books about developing self-discipline in kids 148
Web sites about developing self-discipline in kids.................... 150
Notes for Chapter Five 151

RESOURCES AND INDEX

Organizations & Research Sources... 153
Index.. 198
About the author 207

If you have already read the first book:

You'll want to skip the acknowledgements as well as the preface pages and simply start with Chapter One on page one – THANKS!

Acknowledgements

First of all, let me acknowledge and THANK YOU! Yes, *you* – the person reading this right now. The very fact that you're taking the time to explore *What Makes Kids KICK* is impressive in our non-stop 24/7/365 "always on" world and I sincerely appreciate your interest.

As you read, I suggest you keep a highlighter and a pen handy so you can write down your thoughts or mark any items for future reference. Let's face it, there is a lot of information in this series of books and *you* are the best person to determine what's relevant for you. When you do find a reference of interest or a resource of value, star it, mark it, do something so you can come back to it, got to it, or dig into it.

Since this is an acknowledgement page, if you are going to use quotes from this series of books in your own writing or speaking, please remember to cite the original source material appropriately. Anything and everything used here has been painstakingly and professionally sourced so that you can properly attribute who said or did what. Please don't say "Fran Kick said…" when in reality it was 7,000 students in some comprehensive national study who "said it." Now, if you want to mention that you read about the study in one of Fran Kick's books – *What Makes Kids KICK* – cool!

So many people did so much so many times over the years in putting together this material, that a simple acknowledgement seems so inadequate. Please know that all of your contributions, both large and small, directly and indirectly, professionally and personally, have had a profound influence. Certainly all the writers and researchers whose work is cited need to be thanked. Specifically I'd like to acknowledge my appreciation to: Ed Deci, James MacGregor Burns, Frank Gregorsky, Edward Hoffman, Neil Howe, Alfie Kohn, Tim Lautzenheiser, Bill Strauss and the late H. Stephen Glenn for their insightful input early on. Also, thank you to Cathy Simonson and all the reference librarians at the Washington-Centerville Public Library, who went above and beyond the call. I'd also like to thank: Jo Ackermann, Ruth Donlin, Mitchell Kick, Tami Markworth, Tamara May, and Nikki McLaughlin who carefully proofread and thoughtfully reflected with me over numerous versions of this work. A very special thank you to Judy Kick for one KICKin' cover and to every convention, school, college, or camp that KICKed IT IN!

Preface

This series of books is a collection of ideas, research, thoughts and perceptions about kids today. What *inspires* them and what *motivates* them to do what they do. In other words – what makes them KICK. It's not meant to be *the* definitive study on kids. It's just one person's perspective after spending two decades traveling across the country talking with kids and the people who work with them. Toss in a boatload of research, offer opinions of highly respected experts from various fields, provide a number of references for follow up, and you'll soon get a clearer picture as to *What Makes Kids KICK*.

As an eclectic blend of thought from generational influences, psychology, education, motivational theory, parenting, and managing, this series of books attempts to bring you a perspective that's broad and deep. The first book in this series serves as an overview or a "compass of thought" for reaching today's kids – providing an overall framework through which to view kids. It explores the many influences and inspirational factors that are in play with today's kids collectively as a generation. If you haven't read it, you might want to get yourself a copy since it does provide a solid foundation for the material presented throughout the series. This book builds on that overall framework and details what inspires kids specifically at home, while at the same time maps out pragmatic steps you can take to reach them, teach them, and lead them.

Everyone wants an easy-answer, a silver bullet, foolproof, this-will-always-work, one-size-fits-all kind of solution to the problems they face. Reality dictates that when it comes to dealing with people, this isn't possible. Sure, there are some universal truths, underlying common denominators, and cause-and-effect tendencies. But overriding all of these, helping or hurting, supporting or sabotaging, remains the single greatest influence of all – an individuals' perceptions and their own free will to respond.

The language we use impacts our perception and therefore colors the way we see the world and each other. The importance of this needs to be understood up front, so let's define a few things first to clarify and share some perspective before we begin.

A few definitions and some perspective

Before we can look at what works with kids in terms of inspiring them and/or motivating them to KICK IT IN, we need to define what it truly means to "inspire" and/or "motivate." Having studied psycholinguistics (as in the psychological impact words have on people), I tend to be hypersensitive to the fact that certain words have certain meanings for different people. You've probably heard the expression "it's not what you say, but what they hear" or, better yet, "it's not what you say, but what they get!" Sometimes what people hear and what they get are two different things.

Inspire literally means breathing in – and metaphorically speaking this represents what much of this book shares in terms of what today's kids have been breathing in during their lives. *Webster's Dictionary* defines "inspire" as "to influence, move or guide... to exert an influence on... to have an animating effect upon..." When one looks at *Roget's Thesaurus*, the word "inspire" is defined as "to encourage, stimulate" and words like "affect, arouse, be responsible for, cause, excite, fire up, give one an idea, inform, reassure, spark, urge and motivate" are also listed. "Inspiration" is defined as "an idea or stimulus" which is associated with "approach, awakening, brainstorm, creativity, encouragement, enthusiasm, illumination, insight and motivation."

All of these words represent what this series of books can be for you – an eclectic inspiration from a variety of perspectives. A chance for you to stop your world and look at kids today (born 1980-2000± a.k.a. the Millennial Generation) and how we can live with them, teach and learn with them, work with them as well as lead them and manage them. It's a big picture with subtle detail – a collage of ideas constructed by one person who has been working with kids and networking with a diverse collection of people, parents and professionals who also work with kids. Reading this contextual framework of various theories, practices, mind-sets and attitudes about kids today will hopefully guide you to appropriately sift through all the modern rhetoric and research related to kids. Inspiring you to reflect upon your own real-world experience with kids and join in on a more affirmative postmodern discourse about *What Makes Kids KICK!*

❏ ABC's and ✔123s

You'll find a careful balance between theory and practice in this series of books. The goal in sharing both a detailed understanding or perspective (the ❏ ABCs) as well as a few approaches or steps to try (the ✔123s) presents down-to-earth bottom-line information to walk away with as you try to make things happen with kids today. Not being too hung up on semantics, let's define the following as:

ABC's	123s
❏ Theory	✔ Practice
❏ Principles	✔ Application
❏ Thoughts	✔ Action
❏ Perspective	✔ Approaches
❏ Strategy	✔ Tactics
❏ Compass	✔ Map
❏ Foundation	✔ Tools
❏ Planning	✔ Implementation
❏ Goals	✔ Objectives
❏ A frame of reference	✔ A way to connect the dots
❏ Ways of looking at	✔ Ways of dealing with
❏ Questions to consider	✔ Steps to take…
❏ Why to do…	✔ What to do…

Think of the ❏ ABCs as the direction you want to head – a guiding compass of thought, while the ✔ 123s are the steps, path, or road map to get there. Can you take different routes to get to the same place? Sure, and there would be no way to present all the possible "ways to get there" in this book. The hope is to give you enough information and/or perspective so you can figure it out for yourself – which we know is the best way to learn anyway. Throughout this series of books you'll notice there's a heavier emphasis on the ❏ ABCs – especially in the first book of this series. Given that the world currently overemphasizes the ✔ 123s, the idea here is to help you know which tool to try, tactic to take, or approach to apply.

"Strategy without tactics is the slowest route to victory. Tactics without strategy is the noise before defeat."

– Sun Tzu (circa 400-320 B.C.)

B.T.W.F.Y.I.

BTWFYI: (which stands for "by the way for your information") are all the "grayed out" items (like this paragraph of text) providing you further detailed information and knowledge. Whenever possible, you'll find additional facts to consider, books to explore, or specific web sites to visit. Many others – colleagues, friends, writers, historians – have contributed greatly to the thoughts and ideas presented here. You're encouraged to check out any that interest you and/or have application to what you want to know.

Snapshot Examples/Case Studies

Throughout this series of books and especially in the corresponding *iGuides* (as in "implementation Guides"), snapshots are offered as a quick glimpse of what's going on with kids and their world. Just as a real snapshot of your family taken at a given event and time doesn't represent *everything* you are and do, the snapshots used here are simply illustrative and share a perspective. Collectively they allow you to get both a broader view of this Millennial Generation as well as present specific situations they deal with on a day-to-day basis. Some are big-picture panoramic views while others are candid close-up shots, perhaps even slightly out of focus. Some have been professionally developed with research and references while others are anecdotal. Since "actions speak louder than words," different types of snapshots are shared to bring to life both theory and practice in a more real way. In the home and school areas they're referred to as examples, while in the work and related marketplace materials they're referred to as case studies. They're essentially the same – a realistic situation that relates to what's presented.

WARNINGS

WARNING! At times you'll see a warning that appears to be contrary to what you might think appropriate. It could even be an exact opposite to what's being advocated or something that's different from conventional wisdom. Most of the time it's designed to keep you paying attention and thinking, just as any good warning will do. While I have your attention here, allow me to caution you...

LOOK BEYOND AND BEHIND THE NUMBERS

So many people casually use terms such as "research, surveys, studies, polls, statistics, facts, data, theory" and the like when describing kids. Many times it's an attempt to add credibility to "what they've found to be true" or in some cases just a misapplied use of the word itself. The *fact* of the matter is that great confusion exists about how much credibility a certain word implies and when that word is to be used. Some words *do mean* certain things. For example, the term "theory" isn't used as opposed to "fact." And the word "fact" does not mean the same thing as "data." This word usage understanding is important in order to separate certainty from generality. Consider the following words in terms of their meaning:

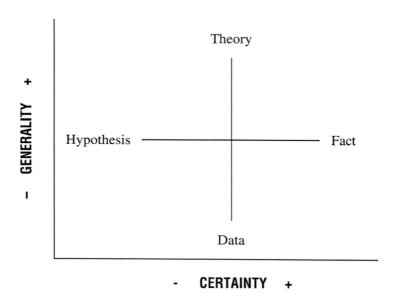

While it would be great if everything presented as "valid" was from the top right quadrant, the reality is a bit messier than that. People actively working with kids, the *practitioners,* tend to know what's real based on their experience – the facts as they observe them or the "here and now" data. Writers, commentators, and the various people analyzing kids today, the *theorists,* tend to hypothesize and theorize about what they see. Add to this the amazing variation in what some consider to be a representative sample, multi-cultural bias, or a socioeconomic bias, and it's no wonder people rarely look beyond the numbers.

Four fast disclaimers

With all the challenges in presenting "valid" research findings about kids and the ongoing practitioner-theorist dilemma, please allow me to state up front a few last-minute disclaimers before we begin. Consider it the fast-talking, fine-print disclaimer always read at the end of an ad or printed at the bottom of the page in micro-sized type.

1. Whether I want to admit it or not, my background *will* bias my beliefs about kids today. As obvious as that might sound, it is important to admit this up front so that no one thinks I'm trying to present some all-encompassing, grand, monolithic narrative about today's kids. Everyone's worldview gets influenced by their experience. My own experience is appropriately disclosed in the back of this book.

2. I consider myself both a reflective practitioner and a relevant real-world researcher who strives to stay on top of current trends and pull together from-the-past-to-the-present real-world research in a casually creative untraditional way. Being someone who has spent most of his life packaging ideas as an informational architect, the goal remains the same: making the complex clear, differentiating between similar yet not identical concepts, and increasing awareness as well as understanding.

3. To all you English teachers out there, this series of books "ain't no high English piece of literature," while at the same time it's not quite as light, layered and linked as webwriting on a blog.

4. As a professional speaker, I'm at a distinct disadvantage communicating via writing. Because communication cues are evident when I'm presenting to people. I can sense when they get it and when they don't. It's hard to do that in a book. It's also hard to capture the energy, enthusiasm, and excitement of speaking live with someone in person. So for those of you readers who have seen me speak and are reading this, *please* don't expect the exact same just-in-time, interactive, back and forth story-filled, activity-driven, dialogue-like quality of my live presentations here on these pages. Speaking and consulting are obviously different from writing and reading. The advantage of a book lies in its ability to present a depth of cited research, resources and material you can consult again and again.

Faster Ways to Read this Book!

People who read books conventionally from start to finish might find this "gray box" a bit strange. Granted, there may not be many people left in the world who literally read a book from start to finish. Time presses everyone. And if you're pressed for time and want to get the most out of this book here are a few approaches:

✔ **Scope out the table of contents** – Chapters one through four share specific perspectives on kids and their world at home.

✔ **Jump to Chapter Five** – The last chapter shares the what to do when it comes to encouraging self-discipline, while at the same time nurturing the self-motivation kids need to succeed on their own. You won't find any "carrot and sticks" to "get kids to do what you want them to do." If that bothers you, you'll want to check out the first book in this series to better understand the generational, developmental and psychological basis for this entire series. Chapter Five does share two important perspectives:

✔ **The parenting approaches and style matrix** – On page 128 you'll begin building a graphical representation of the various overlapping ranges of factors which influence your impact with kids. Be sure to see the "sweet spot for self-discipline" page 139.

✔ **The 123s of encouraging self-discipline** – On page 142 you'll find a checklist of pragmatic practices – things you can do! Parents, teachers, youth group leaders, managers or anyone else who works with kids will find value in applying these approaches as well as understanding the principles behind them.

✔ **Get more information via the resource list** – More specifics and further details can be found thanks to the annotated resource list of organizations and research sources beginning on page 153.

✔ **Find what *you* want via the index** – Want to know out how kids can or cannot be motivated by money? How about doing chores or anything else? Just flip to the index on page 198 and look it up.

✔ **Read the gray boxes** – Items of implementational importance are found throughout the text in gray boxes such as this one. If you simply want to know "what do I do?" – these boxes are for you.

Chapter One

Homes, Families and Neighborhoods

Family households with kids make up over one-third of the approximately 105 million households in the U.S. today. Over two-thirds of these families own their own home. According to the U.S. Census, that's the highest level of home-ownership *ever* and for the first time in our history, more than half of minority households own their own homes. Real median household income reached its highest level ever recorded in 2000 and, despite recession, held up well through 2001 to 2003.

While "family values" have become popular within mainstream America, so have consumer values – and the two don't always reinforce each other. Pop culture is pumped into our homes faster and is more accessible than ever before. The combined onslaught from TV, radio, PCs, the Internet, "lifestyle publications" and lesser media lures away ever more family time and attention. Activities that kids participate in have proliferated. Parents are working more.

So many people seem to be stressing out and burning out. Discipline has become "whatever works," and never mind how a short-term payoff in temporary compliance or short-term results, could become a longtime liability by over-relying on carrots and sticks.

Before we begin, let's admit up-front that the last thing needed on store shelves is another parenting book. Part of the problem with homes today is that too many experts (and so-called experts) already poke their heads into your living room via the TV, news and parenting magazines. Other interventions come by way of well-meaning in-laws, teachers, counselors and friends. Of the books, many are good, filled with lots of perspective and even some how-to advice that helps. But – there's way too much of it! How do you keep up with the latest research? Who's the current talk show guest guru offering their seven steps to super-spectacular parenting? What's the latest parenting style du jour?

Everyone wants an easy answer – a silver-bullet, fool-proof, this-will-always-work, one-size-fits-all kind of solution to their parenting puzzles. Rather than hand out the answer (which by the way usually begins with "*it depends...*"), let's take a calm look at the influences today's kids have experienced, along with what will inspire them to KICK IT IN at home in the future. The goal is to help you figure out what works best for you and your situation so you can sort through the latest solutions, as well as make better sense of the ones you already know.

Homes are different

Something is vastly different about how kids today are being raised in homes across America. Not one single difference, but a multitude of overlapping influences have fundamentally changed home-life for kids born since 1980. Most of them don't know about the longer-term changes because – well, they weren't around to see how things used to be. Still, their parents know.

"Things ain't what they used to be."

– Duke Ellington

The culminating effect of change has reached a point of cross-generational influence hard to ignore in homes today. Depending on your perspective, these influences could be considered bad or good, yet in reality they just are a fact of how homes and families have been drastically changing ever since the end of the second world war.

"You know... after remaining essentially unchanged for generations, the child-rearing process has undergone more bewildering mutations over the past few decades than Phyllis Diller during a long weekend on Dr. Moreau's island. The heretofore rigidly choreographed parental line-dance has morphed into a chaotic mosh pit where the Cleavers have been knocked to the floor and are being trampled to death by the Bundys."[1]

– Dennis Miller

Even physically and architecturally speaking, homes have drastically changed from one generational cycle to the next. Features that were luxuries for one generation, become standard for the next. In 1940, just half the homes in America had complete indoor plumbing with running hot water, a toilet and a bathtub. Today it's nearly universal. When World War II began, a telephone was a luxury. Now they're in almost every home, with some families having phones in *every* room of the house – including the bathroom! The average size of new homes has increased 50 percent between 1970 and 2000 – from 1,500 to 2,266 square feet. More than half of all new homes today have two or more floors. In 1971 only 20 percent were two or more floors. More new homes have more bathrooms too. New homes with at least 2.5 bathrooms rose from 15 to 54 percent and the percentage of new homes with four or more bathrooms went from 24 percent in 1971 to 34 percent in 2000.[2] Now when you consider the kind of homes today's kids are growing up in compared to previous generations, it's no wonder college campuses are scrambling to change their dorm rooms of the past as well as today's retrofitted residence halls into brand new suite-style apartment/condominium learning and living communities for the future.

Let's take a look at a few of the many overlapping influences which have developed, converged and fundamentally changed family life within today's home.

Homes, Families and Neighborhoods   3

Families are different

Families have changed from "extended" to "nuclear" to one inexperienced biological relative having custody one night a week and every other weekend. Throughout the history of this planet, and up to World War II, "family" meant more than just mom and dad, brother and sister. It meant aunts and uncles, neighbors who were considered close friends of the family, cousins, nieces, nephews and grandparents living in the next town, perhaps down the street, right around the corner, or even living in the same home. The 1940 U.S. Census reported that 70 percent of all households had at least one grandparent living in the home. Today that number is under 2 percent.

When all those World War II G.I.s came home, got married, and started families, a housing shortage created the need for lots of homes. Fast! So *voila!* The birth of the suburbs! Taking the mass-production assembly-line approach, places such as Levittown, New York and thousands of communities like it were popping up all over America. With these new homes came new realities in raising kids. Extended families became *over*-extended to the point of being occasional visitors versus the constant network of support they historically had been. Mom and Dad were in many cases on their own with the kids struggling to make the nuclear family more than just a cold-war metaphor.

It was Abraham Levitt and his sons Alfred and William who started building post-World War II suburbia, turning 4,000 acres of Nassau County farmland on Long Island into 17,447 concrete-slab Cape Cod style houses. What started in 1946 continued through the 1950s and 1960s with similar communities outside Philadelphia, Pennsylvania, and near Willingboro, New Jersey. "The three Levittowns and other subdivisions built following World War II appealed overwhelmingly to young, white families with small children. The Levitts refused to sell houses to African Americans through the mid-1960s, and realtors handling resales were quietly discriminatory."[3] Critics say this as well as the "cookie-cutter" architectural sameness created a homogeneous suburbia that in some places still exists outside large metropolitan areas even today.

By the time John Kennedy was elected President in 1960, the G.I. Generation, big business, superhighways and cheap mortgage money had done their work. As a social and economic proposition, for many the concept of "family" had changed drastically from the Depression years.

Okay, now fast-forward and toss in skyrocketing divorce rates from the mid-1960s into the 1980s, more farms being plowed into subdivisions while at the same time many inner-cities becoming ghost towns, many dual-income households struggling to keep up with the Joneses, and by 1990 you're looking at a whole different kind of family in America. Another three decades of riptide and upheaval.

Today's families make up over one-third of all households in the U.S. Where do kids live today?

68% of all kids live with 2 parents…

> 11% of all kids live in a home where dad works
>   and mom stays home
> 25% of all kids live with both biological parents
> 36% of all black kids live with 2 parents
> 64% of all Hispanic kids live with 2 parents
> 74% of all white kids live with 2 parents
> 64% of married couple families with kids under 18
>   are dual-income homes[4]

27% of all kids live with 1 parent…

> 23% of all kids live just with mom
>   4% of them because Dad died
>   22% of them because Mom and Dad separated
>   34% of them because of divorce
>   40% of them because Mom never married***
> 4% of all kids live just with dad***

Five percent of all kids live with their grandparents. And while almost half of these kids also have their mothers living there too,*** 2.4 million grandparents are the primary caregivers to a grandchild.[5]

***These three family settings have been the fastest rising type of household over the past five years. During the same period of time the divorce rate has stabilized – although still historically high.

Families have fragmented into different versions of families faster than TV sitcoms can keep up with them. From the Cleavers, to the Bradys, to the Huxtables, to the Bundys, to the Simpsons, to the Barones and the Wilkersons. *The* American family no longer exists. *Many* American families have evolved, mutated, and blended into the fabric of our diverse society.

During all of this fragmentation many suggested that more and more families were "dysfunctional." Perhaps what they meant was that families were no longer functioning the way they used to, but they were functioning. In fact the breadwinner-homemaker model of *Ozzie and Harriet* never really was the norm. Most historical scholars consider it unusual: Primarily a white middle-class phenomenon occurring twice in our country's history – during 1860 to 1920 and again right after World War II.[6]

From the earliest colonial days up until 1860, fathers and mothers both worked to make ends meet. Farming their land, tending to animals, taking care of their homes, working a trade, Dad, Mom and even the children all took part in doing what they could do to contribute to the family financial situation. They had to. Raising children was a tag-team situation for mothers and fathers, grandparents, aunts, uncles, as well as neighbors. Teachers jumped in the mix for most kids after the mid-1800s. Horace Mann, considered the father of public education, helped pass the first compulsory-attendance law for elementary school age children in Massachusetts. The goal was to establish common schools and with them the very beginning of a state-supported universal education for all kids.

"There is nothing so costly as ignorance."

– Horace Mann

Parents have *always* been concerned about the kind of world in which their children were growing up. Many farmers and blacksmiths of the 1820s worried about their kids making it through the Industrial Revolution, just as today's parents are worried about their kids making it through the digital information revolution[7]. In an age of rapid social change, with obsolete-tomorrow kind of product life-cycles, constant job-hopping and high divorce rates – it's no wonder parents yearn for the good old days. Even if those days are, for the most part, a fantasy portrayed on TV.

Yet parents today *do* have something to be concerned about. There continues to be a rise in the number of kids who live in single-parent households, as well as a rise in the number of kids who have two parents working jobs outside the home. Both situations feed the same problem: Parents without the time and attention to tend to parenting, and/or one parent having to carry out the roles of two.

Both single-parent and dual-income households face the same set of obstacles, critical factors and/or concerns:

- Extremely limited immediate and extended family network of support for most kids has forced parents to rely more and more on outside resources.

- Few meaningful roles for their kids to assume in home-life situations because too much is done *for* them versus *with* them.

- Not enough on-the-job training/experiences (where kids are actively learning about life via hands-on involvement and tangibly contributing to the home/family kind of experience as opposed to watching it on TV or being done *for* them).

There's also the reality of income inequality that tends to compound the above factors and impact people whether they realize it or not. Researchers state that changes in the labor market and household composition have affected the long-term trend toward increasing income inequality. Between the rich and the poor the middle is being pulled in either direction depending on circumstances. Yes, in 2000 the U.S. poverty rate hit the lowest level since 1979 and unemployment reached a 30-year low, but there are some areas of concern even according to the U.S. Census and the Center on Budget and Policy Priorities.[8] "For example, one in every two children under age of six who lives in a female-headed family – 50.3% of such children – lived in poverty last year [1999]." International comparisons indicate that the overall child poverty rate in the United States remains higher than the rate in many western European countries and Canada.

BTWFYI: For more detailed information about the generational changes, societal influences on kids over the years and how families have been changing, check out: *Raising Self-Reliant Children In a Self-Indulgent World* by H. Stephen Glenn & Jane Nelsen, *Raising*

Adults by Jim Hancock, *The Rise & Fall of the American Teenager* by Thomas Hine and *Millennials Rising* by Neil Howe & William Strauss.

Neighborhoods are different

Even as the world becomes more interconnected, the very notion of connecting with our neighbors becomes less and less realistic. As homes and families have changed, so have our neighborhoods. More dual-income working parents have kids in day care and preschool. Weekends are packed with even more activities and shared-custody situations resulting in kids moving back and forth from one parent to the other. Lots more after-school commitments for older kids whether in activities or on the job which sometimes prevents a big sister or big brother from being able to baby sit younger siblings and assume a more active role in maintaining the home.

All have contributed to ghost-town neighborhoods being created across America. With the exception of a few occasional rush-hour moments, many neighbors don't have a chance to connect anymore. My G.I. Generation mother-in-law, Loretta (whose linen closet is nearly famous), noticed one week during the school year a strange quietness of our kid-infested neighborhood during the day. "Where are all the kids?" she asked. "No one's outside playing?" Even after school lets out, many kids are still in adult-led organized activities or simply jump into an after-school daycare van. Cookouts with the family next door, shooting hoops with a father and son across the street two on two, and even just sitting on the front porch chatting with neighbors passing by all seem like quaint old-fashioned neighborhood traditions today. Adult relationships with kids outside their own family rarely have the impact they used to.

True, Millennials have unbelievable opportunities for horizontal socialization via their sometimes over-organized and over-scheduled activities after school. When they do get home, AOL buddy lists and IM chat connects dozens of kids in a way that's probably not too good for developing a focused concentration span on homework. On the other hand, what about the vertical socialization that comes from ongoing exchanges with adults other than harried teachers or power-wielding parents. Think of Gus the Fireman, who used to help Theodore "Beaver" Cleaver think through his dilemmas. Can we encourage this during a time filled with fears of child abuse? What's your guess? While we used to count on a concerned teacher, a caring neighbor, or the Catholic priest to be pseudo-members of our extended family – today they're all unfortunately suspect.

"Recently, Colin Powell and I had a conversation about the human information network in our neighborhoods growing up. We had more aunts than our mothers and fathers had sisters. At any given time, our aunties might be on the stoop or at the window, from one end of the neighborhood to the other. Nothing under the sun was hidden from our aunties. If you got into trouble on one end, the news was at the other faster than you could run. Kids today have the Internet. But in my neighborhood, and General Powell's, we had the Auntie-Net."[9]

– Ken Blackwell, speaking to the Urban Institute May 4th 1999

While most adults in any neighborhood across America would agree with the belief that it's important we connect with kids, that it "takes a village" and all that can be gained from a pseudo-extended family of neighbors – most don't act on their beliefs. A recent first-of-its-kind nationwide survey found that just one in 20 adults are actively engaged in promoting kids' healthy development within their neighborhood. Most of the adults surveyed actually agreed overwhelmingly on the top ten actions they "believed to be important." But when asked whether they "actually did it," the gap between what they say is important and how they act on that belief reveals a great deal:

Beliefs neighbors say are important	% believe it	% do it	% gap
Encourage success in school	90	69	21
Expect parents to set boundaries	84	42	42
Teach shared values	80	45	35
Teach respect for cultural differences	77	36	41
Guide decision making	76	41	35
Have meaningful conversations	75	34	41
Give financial guidance	75	36	39
Discuss personal values	73	37	36
Expect respect for adults	68	67	1
Report positive behavior	65	22	43

– From the Search Institute's *Grading Grown-Ups* Study[10]

As neighbors, it's obvious we don't walk our talk. Consider the top four biggest percentage gaps: Reporting positive behavior, expecting parents to set boundaries, teaching respect for cultural differences and having meaningful conversations. While most neighbors seem to have no problem telling parents when their kids are misbehaving, how about when they do something positive? The presumption of kids getting into trouble still remains strong in our backyards and around the corner. Maybe that's why many parents would rather keep their kids inside? Watching TV, DVDs, or videos, playing video games or surfing the net at least keeps them from "bugging the neighbors." Besides, kids get enough exercise with all the adult led youth sports programs – right? Well...we'll talk about that later.

Perhaps most neighborhood adults have a "Well, they're not my kids!" kind of attitude that keeps them from saying anything. And who has time to have "meaningful conversations" with the kids in the neighborhood, when most people have a tough time finding the time to have them with their own spouse and kids.

As for respecting cultural differences, while the 2000 Census does document the increasing diversity of America, diversity within a given neighborhood may not quite measure up. Within supposedly diverse metropolitan areas like Chicago, Gary, New York, Newark, Milwaukee, and Philadelphia, many individual neighborhoods remain racially segregated. Despite fair housing laws, civil rights marches, and multi-cultural education initiatives, whites tend to live in their neighborhoods, blacks tend to live in their neighborhoods, and Hispanics tend to live in their neighborhoods.[11]

Sure, schools have done more and more to help instill a message of tolerance, acceptance and racial understanding. Schools are no doubt increasingly more diverse today. Many schools are even more diverse than the various individual neighborhoods that feed kids into it. "But where kids live can still lead to a separation that even a diverse school cannot bridge. For example, at Teaneck High School, a racially diverse school in New Jersey, the doors of opportunity are literal. There are three main entrances at the school, and kids refer to them as 'the black door,' 'the Latino door' and 'the white door.' Originally, the nicknames came from the fact that those were the doors the various groups entered when the buses dropped them off; even though Teaneck has become more integrated, the terms have stuck, and each group continues to hang out by its respective door."[12] These kids aren't prejudiced or anti-diversity. It's just their neighborhoods aren't diverse and that's "the door" the buses bring them to and from school.

In fact it's neighborhoods that many times keep schools from being as diverse as many would like. Even 50 years after the Brown v. Board of Education ruling declared segregated public schools unconstitutional, a disturbing trend still remains. The Civil Rights Project at Harvard University recently found that while desegregation has succeeded in many places, in others it is being abandoned.[13] "More white children go to overwhelmingly white schools and more minority children go to predominantly nonwhite schools."[14] The Harvard University Civil Rights Project acknowledged that many inner-city schools lose their best and their brightest to magnet schools and charter schools. School integration actually hit its peak in the 1980s and since then has slid back a bit due to demographic shifts in neighborhood populations and court-ordered busing laws expiring.

There is hope that, in the next 20 years, we're going to see a huge change within neighborhood diversity because polls show kids have moved beyond their parents' views of race. Today's kids say "race is less important to them, both on a personal level and as a social divide, than it is for adults." This more racially accepting attitude reflected in a 1997 Time/CNN poll is all the more remarkable given the fact that researchers conducting the polls noted "black teens and white teens most often live in separate neighborhoods and sometimes, it seems, separate planets."[12]

But watch out! Those planets are colliding demonstrated by a quiet yet dramatic increase with inter-racial marriages. Ben Wattenberg, senior fellow at the American Enterprise Institute for Public Policy Research in Washington, DC, reminds us that "Demography is a very intimate deal. It's not about what activists say; it's about what young men and women do. And what they're doing is marrying each other and having children." It is projected that by 2050, 21 percent of the U.S. population will be multi-racial versus approximately 7 percent today.[15]

There's a culminating effect of change in homes, families and neighborhoods across America today. A kind of change that's vastly different for today's generation of kids compared to what previous generations experienced when they were kids. While this statement might have been uttered throughout history, today we've reached a significant point of cross-generational influences that are increasingly harder to ignore. Faster and faster the speed at which today's changes occur challenges kids, parents and the parenting process.

BOOKS ABOUT HOMES, FAMILIES AND NEIGHBORHOODS

Tag, You're It! 50 Easy Ways to Connect to Young People
by Kathleen Kimball-Baker

All Kids Are Our Kids: What Communities Must Do to Raise Caring and Responsible Children and Adolescents
by Peter Benson

What Kids Need to Succeed
by Peter Benson, Judy Galbraith and Pamela Espeland

What Teens Need to Succeed
by Peter Benson, Judy Galbraith and Pamela Espeland

The Way We Never Were: American Families and the Nostalgia Trap
by Stephanie Coontz

The Way We Really Are: Coming to Terms With America's Changing Families
by Stephanie Coontz

The Intentional Family: Simple Rituals to Strengthen Family Ties
by William Doherty

Ties That Stress: The New Family Imbalance
by David Elkind

I Swore I'd Never Do That!
by Elizabeth Fishel

Domestic Revolutions: A Social History of American Family Life
by Steven Mintz and Susan Kellogg

Tough Times, Strong Children: Lessons From the Past for Your Child's Future
by Dan Kindlon

What Young Children Need to Succeed
by Jolene Roehlkepartain and Nancy Leffert

At-Home Mothers	http://www.athomemothers.com
Community Associations	http://www.caionline.org
Community Research	http://www.cairf.org
Contemporary Families	http://www.contemporaryfamilies.org
Divorce Magazine	http://www.divorcemagazine.com
Executive Working Moms	http://www.bluesuitmom.com
Families and Work	http://www.familiesandwork.org
Families Worldwide	http://www.fww.org
Family Fun	http://family.go.com
Family Relations	http://www.ncfr.com
Family Research Project	http://gseweb.harvard.edu/~hfrp/
Family Support America	http://www.familysupportamerica.org
Generations United	http://www.gu.org
Grading Grown-Ups	http://www.search-institute.org/norms/
Grandparents	http://www.civitas.org/grandparents.html
Grandparenting Foundation	http://www.grandparenting.org
Grandplace	http://www.grandsplace.com
iGrandparents	http://www.igrandparents.com
Neighborhoods Online	http://www.neighborhoodsonline.net
Neighborhoods USA	http://www.nusa.org
Search Institute	http://www.search-institute.org
Single Mothers	http://www.singlemothers.org
Single Parent	http://www.singleparentusa.com
Stepfamily Foundation	http://www.stepfamily.org
Stepfamily Magazine	http://www.yourstepfamily.com
Strong Families	http://nuforfamilies.unl.edu
Working Women	http://www.9to5.org

NOTES FOR CHAPTER ONE

1. Miller, D. (1998). *Ranting Again*. New York: Doubleday.

2. Armas, G. C. (2003, February 2). "Home Sweet (Big) Home" full of fixtures, phones. *Dayton Daily News,* p. 4.

3. Reef, C. (2002). *Childhood in America: An Eyewitness History*. New York: Facts On File, Inc.

4. U.S. Department of Labor's Bureau of Labor Statistics. (2000). *Employment Characteristics of Families Summary* [Online]. Bureau of Labor Statistics. http://www.bls.gov/news.release/famee.nr0.htm

5. U.S. Census Bureau. (2003). *Grandparents Living With Grandchildren: 2000*. Washington, DC: U.S. Department of Commerce.

6. Footlick, J. K. (1990, January 1). What Happened to the Family? *Newsweek, 115,* 14-20.

7. Kantrowitz, B., Wingert, P., Nelson, M., Halpert, J. E., Lauerman, J., Weingarten, T., et al. (2001, January 29). The Parent Trap. *Newsweek, 137,* 49-53.

8. Center on Budget and Policy Priorities. (2000). *October 10, 2000 Press Release* [Online]. Center on Budget and Policy Priorities. http://www.cbpp.org/9-26-00pov.htm

9. Blackwell, K. (1999). *Kenneth Blackwell's Remarks to the Urban Institute* [Online]. U.S. Census Monitoring Board. http://govinfo.library.unt.edu/cmb/cmbc/speech-archive/050499.asp

10. Scales, P. C., Benson, P. L., & Roehlkepartain, E. C. (2001). *Grading Grown-Ups: American Adult Report on Their Real Relationships with Kids* [Online]. Lutheran Brotherhood and Search Institute. http://www.search-institute.org/norms/

11. Orfield, G. (2001). *Schools More Separate: Consequences of a Decade of Resegregation*. Cambridge, MA: The Civil Rights Project at Harvard University.

12. Farley, C. J. (1997, November 24, 1997). *Kids and Race* [Online]. Time Reports. http://www.time.com/time/classroom/psych/unit7_article1.html

13. Orfield, G., & Lee, C. (2004). *Brown at 50: King's Dream or Plessy's Nightmare?* Cambridge, MA: The Civil Rights Project at Harvard University.

14.   Crary, D. (2004, February 29). Desegregation Still Affecting Schools: Historic Brown ruling remains a work in progress. *Associated Press/Dayton Daily News,* p. A6.

15.   Stanfield, R. L. (1997). The Blending of the United States. *National Journal*(September 13, 1997).

Chapter Two

Parents and Parenting

Given how the world has changed, there's no question that parents and parenting has changed as well. When you consider the level of intelligence and affluence more parents today possess combined with the nonstop 24/7/365 informationally overloaded world we live in – it's no wonder more parents are stressed-out and burned-out. Toss in the fact that kids today are consuming more and more of *everything* than ever before, parents are striving to give their kids the best of the best, and a world that seems to be saying "grow up faster," and you can understand why some parents consider raising kids today a contest to be won versus a process to be nurtured. This chapter looks at how parents, parenting, stress, affluence, and our sometimes overly consumeristic – and competitive – world have influenced "the game" for kids, parents and their families in America today.

Parents are different

Parents today are the oldest most educated parents the world has ever known. That's both good and bad. "Good" in terms of being highly educated, planning ahead, preparing adequately, taking care of health issues, and overall being more informed during pregnancy as well as the child birth experience. "Bad" in terms of waiting too long to have kids, being overeducated to the point of being too-smart-for-their-own-good, obsessively-compulsively over-preparing, over-stimulating, over-medicating, over-scheduling, and in general overseeing *every* detail of their kids life. Many hyper-parents[1] are spoiling childhood.[2]

Smarter parents help make smarter kids – right? No question they help make kids safer. Infant mortality rates, child death rates and accidental teen deaths are all down. Overall the educational attainment of Boomers and Xers make moms and dads today more informed and demanding when it comes to their Millennial kids. And demanding they are! From prenatal care, through child birth, past toddler play dates, to enriched preschool programs, K-12 schooling and higher education, *all* have been influenced by higher parental expectations for their kids. Parents know what they want for their kids and if they don't – they know how to find out what they *should* want. With the same kind of zeal that many of them completed college and even graduate school for that matter, today's parents are voracious consumers of how-to books. They know what to expect when expecting,[3] how to develop healthy sleep habits,[4] all the touchpoints and challenges to child-development,[5] what happens in the first three years of life,[6] and the list goes on and on.

With all that reading, the advanced education attained by parents, a continuation of the I-want-more-for-my-kid-than-I-ever-had kind of attitude, smaller family size, or a booming economy which allowed parents to enrich their kids lives like never before – kids today are smarter (and safer) than you think. They've also been spoiled more than you think and are stressed-out more than you may believe.

BTWFYI: For more information on the spoiled and stressed-out situations some parents create in their attempt to do more for their kids, check out: *Hyper-Parenting* by Alvin Rosenfeld & Nicole Wise, *Spoiling Childhood* by Diane Ehrensaft and *Time Bind and She Works/He Works* by Arlie Hochschild.

Parenting is different

With kids, homes, families, parents and the world in general being so dramatically different from 1960 or even 1980, it's no wonder that parenting has changed as well. Some detect a fundamental shift in parenting across the socioeconomic landscape of our country. Generations ago, "it was the goal of parents to raise good people, men and women who became upstanding citizens and good parents and spouses themselves. But today the goal seems to revolve around training children to achieve."[7] This acceleration of achievement and pressure to perform increasingly becomes more and more apparent earlier and earlier in life for kids today. Today's Mom and Dad mean well. What parents wouldn't want what's best for their child? After all, the world is very competitive and if you want your kid to get a head start in life… well?

Perhaps we've just gone a bit *too* far. Boomer parents thinking sooner, faster, bigger, better, and Xers taking parenting (like they took sports) towards the extreme – combine to create a pervasive pressure to provide more, and more, and more…

- *In utero* music lessons – For $70 pregnant moms can enroll their fetus in Newark New Jersey's Community School of the Arts.

- Black and white geometric baby-stimulating mobiles.

- Organized toddler play-groups with phone-tree calling lists.

- Pre-Pee-Wee sports leagues of all kinds, some starting as young as three years old.

- Computer software or lapware for toddlers to point and click their favorite cartoon characters into story lines they can't even read anyway.

- Videos that promise to develop intellectual skills and boost IQ.

Has everyone's attempt to bring better and brighter kids into the world actually changed parenting? Erik Erikson in his 1950 book *Childhood and Society* explained that, over time, each generation of parents slowly evolves to deal with society's changing needs. Maybe our hyperlinked, hurry-up, fast-paced, culture has inadvertently made parenting all of that too? Toss in two somewhat paranoid generations of parents always concerned and consumed about doing the right thing along with a whole lot of experts telling them what they're doing wrong and it's no wonder that we forgot Dr. Spock's primary premise: "Trust yourself."

Parents of Millennials question everything. Certainly marketers and the media have tapped into this big-time! During the past 20 years there have been more books, more magazine articles, more workshops, more parenting advocates, more parenting experts, more proponents, critics, and commentary about parenting today, that it's become an industry unto itself. Now, overall – that's not bad. Good information about parenting and access to that information exceeds what previous moms and dads had available to them.

It's when all of these informational points of reference collide on the average couple trying to deal with their kids that we get into trouble. *What do we do? Who do we listen to? What sounds best? We'll do it all or at least a little bit of everything!* In the process, millions of families are crossing the line of what's appropriate – creating stress and burnout for everyone involved.

Stressed out and burned out families

Stressed-out and burned-out are two results from parents knowing so much and kids doing so much. Alvin Toffler must have had a crystal ball when he described "information overload" and "decision stress" in his 1970 book *Future Shock.* When you consider the combination of smart parents who want what's best for their kids, lots of experts (and so-called experts) telling them what they need to be doing, an economy that affords them the opportunity to do so much, along with more information and choices, and less time to do it – it's no wonder families are stressed-out!

Talk to day-care providers, teachers, coaches, all the way up to the college admissions people at Harvard University who have seen first hand an increase in the pressures being placed on kids today![8] Many echo the same concerns – too much, too fast, too early, and too often. We seem to be making big bets on the importance of preparing kids much earlier, much better, with so much more. It is certainly a stark contrast to what was going on with Xers when they were kids. Then, parents were doing too little for their kids. Today we seem to be doing to much *for* them and *to* them.

You've heard the quote before, "I want to be a human *being*, not human *doing*" and yet perhaps we're all influenced by Nike® more than we'd like to admit. Some have suggested that in spite of all our increased education, advances in technology, level of affluence, increasing life spans and overall health, the family is having to deal with more changes, faster changes, and less down time to just *be* "a family."

- Families have experienced a 33% decrease in the number of dinners they have with one another as a family.[9]

- When families do eat together, they spend less time doing it[10] and 60% of the time the TV is on.[11]

- Having friends of the family over for a visit is down 45%.[9]

- Unstructured free time for kids just playing inside the house is down 25%, and outside is down 50%.[10]

- Household conversations are down 34%.[10]

- Number of families taking family vacations is down 28%.[9]

- Kids today spend more time out of the home and more time in structured settings.[12] This can be bad or good depending on what "home" is like.

Family down time is down – so much for "sharpening the saw!"[13] – KICKin' back and just talking with Mom or Dad. Everyone seems to be in such a hurry these days doing what they do that they never have any time just to be. Hurried parents are raising the hurried child.[14] It's actually gotten to the point in America where the first week of October 2000 was "National Eat Dinner Together Week" – the fifth annual, in fact. Getting families to stop their world and sit down at the table together for dinner all at once is becoming a big deal.

"Raising children today is like competing in a triathlon with no finish line in sight. Days are filled with a mad scramble of sports, music lessons, prep courses and battles over homework. We only want what's best for them, but our kids may not be better off. What families risk losing in this insane frenzy is the soul of childhood and the joy of family life."[15]
    – from "The Parent Trap" article, *Newsweek*, January 29, 2001

BTWFYI: If you're looking for more information about prioritizing, reducing stress and creating more down time for your family check out: *The 7 Habits of Highly Effective Families* by Stephen Covey, *Take Back Your Kids* and *The Intentional Family* by William Doherty. You might also visit http://www.puttingfamilyfirst.org a group of citizens building a community where family life is an honored and celebrated priority.

Affluence

Affluence in America is currently at a record high. At no time in the history of America have families experienced the kind of prosperity available in today's economy. Real median household income reached $40,816, the highest ever recorded by the U.S. Census Bureau.[16] Sure, some would state that increasing income inequality is an issue along with the number of female-headed families with children living in poverty,[17] but by and large more people are getting and spending like never before.

"Because of the affluence in this country, there is a part of the population – not everybody, but more people than ever before – who can make a decision about what they want to do and what they don't want to do, when they want to do it, and when they want to stop doing it."[18]

– Richard Saul Wurman

If you haven't ever considered yourself affluent, perhaps you might consider a few of the questions Stephen Glenn and Jane Nelsen pose in their book *Raising Self-Reliant Children In a Self-Indulgent World:*[19]

- Do you have more than one pair of shoes?

- Do you have more than one choice about what you will eat for each meal?

- Do you have access to your own means of transportation?

- Do you have more than one set of underwear?

If you said "yes" to three or more of the above questions, then you would be considered affluent based on overall standards of financial well-being in the world.

"We talk about which pair of shoes to wear when a third of the people of the world have never owned any shoes at all. We talk about what to eat today when a major cross section of the world population wonders if it will eat more than once during the day, and is grateful for the same food every single day. We talk about securing our own means of transportation, even buying cars for our children, when at least half of the people in the world walk everywhere and can only fantasize about having a vehicle at their disposal. Because these advantages have come easily to us, we have no respect for them. And by providing so much for our children without teaching them the means of achieving these things and respect for those means, we might be literally threatening their chances to survive."

– H. Stephen Glenn

There's an old adage that says money cannot buy happiness and yet people tend to measure so much of life by the money they have, the things they possess, the influence they can buy, or the bottom line. Don't get me wrong, we certainly have a great deal to be thankful for in today's world. The available resources and long term strength of our economy can afford us many wonderful things to occur in our society. And they have. Medical research, scientific discovery, a cultural boom, educational access, technological advancement and at least 100 other positive trends have made our world a much better place.[20]

And yet, as Alfie Kohn would point out our pursuit of affluence may have a high price.[21] Others too have suggested that parents today may be using their affluence to buy their child's love, make up for the fact that they're not around much, or simply to help parents feel less guilty about something.[22] Sure, G.I. Dads in the 1950s ladled out the goodies, especially at Christmas, to perhaps make up for their emotional distance from young Boomers. At least today's fathers, Boomer and Xer alike, *are* overall more responsive emotionally with their kids – when they're with them.

BTWFYI: Check out these books on the impact of overindulgent parenting in today's affluent world: *Beyond the Cornucopia Kids* by Bruce Baldwin, *What Do You Really Want for Your Children* by Wayne Dyer, *Punished By Rewards* by Alfie Kohn and *Raising a Happy, Unspoiled Child* by Burton White.

MOTIVATING KIDS WITH MONEY

Obviously money matters to kids today, because they live in a world
– and more specifically during a time – when money seems to matter
more and more. Rightly or wrongly, the pervasively extremist view
of having or not having seems to hit kids hard in the face of reality.
Millennials have grown up, for the most part, during a period of
prosperity few generations get to see so early in their lifetime.
Today's parents, wanting what's best for their kids and wanting to
prepare them to live as best they can, use money to manage their kids
more than any previous generation of parents. Bribing them with it,
threatening them to be without it, sometimes even making them the
products of it – might ironically gyp them out of the financial
literacy they'll need for the future. Motivating kids – or for that
matter anyone – with money may extrinsically create a short-term
gain in both productivity and compliance. It might even cause them
to be initially more engaged in doing something they don't want to
do.[23] But the long-term costs associated with using money as the "be
all and end all" ultimate motivator in life are huge – especially with
kids.

*"I learned about money the hard way – by earning it and spending
it. We can empower our children to have true wealth – the freedom
to have jobs they are passionate about, the financial ability to
support causes they care about, and the security to see themselves
comfortably into retirement – if thy are taught by doing, at a young
age."*[24]

   – Lori Mackey, author of *Money Mama & The Three Little Pigs*

According to *Parenting Magazine*, 88 percent of all parents they
surveyed in 1995 said you should require your child to earn an
allowance by completing assigned household chores. Twelve percent
disagreed saying family responsibilities shouldn't have a price. Well
they're both right. Some regular "citizen of the household" kind of
chores like making the bed, putting dirty laundry away, setting the
table, doing the dishes, taking out the trash, and picking up toys, are
the normal household duties that are everyone's personal
responsibility. Think about it in terms of the natural and logical
consequences involved. Kids make their beds because they sleep in
them. They help set the table so they can eat. They help clean up
because they ate and dirtied the dishes. They put their cloths in the
dirty laundry because they wore them, they dirtied them, and they

need cleaning. *No!* A five-year-old should *not* be tossing things in the washer and dryer! But a fifteen-year-old? Sure. Why not? Again, consider developmental appropriateness and the capabilities of your child. You and I both know a few 18-year-olds who could have used a few years of practice doing laundry before they ended up on some college campus with a roll of quarters thinking "UHhmmm?"

As a member of any family kids – just like everyone else – share in a certain amount of responsibility to make things happen in the home. Anne Ziff, a family therapist in Westport, Connecticut, suggests: "Children should understand that doing chores is part of membership in a family. In healthy families, all members contribute and all contributions are valued." She explains. "The grownups don't get paid for doing family chores – why should the kids? And a share in the family income is an entitlement, just as food, clothing, and shelter are entitlements to any family member." Chores can actually begin earlier than an allowance. Kids as young as two can begin to learn that we put our toys away. Not because we'll get paid to do it or an allowance for doing it! But because that's what we do when we're done with something – we put it away. Every family member has responsibilities and obligations around the home – whether we get an allowance or not.

Besides, most people give an allowance to help their kids learn about the value of money, managing money, saving, investing, spending and sharing money. Giving kids an allowance teaches them something *different* than doing chores does. If *you* don't do your chores around the house, they don't get done. If you don't work, you don't get paid. Ah yes, the magic work/money, job/paycheck, cause and effect relationship. It *is* very important to teach *that* lesson too, but just not with an allowance. That's work, or a job, and we'll get to that aspect of "motivating kids with money" in just a second. But for now, stay with me on this allowance lesson.

Webster's defines allowance as "a sum regularly granted or provided for expenses."[25] Some would suggest that any child old enough to spend money is old enough for an allowance. Many preschool math programs even introduce pennies, nickels, dimes and quarters to bring early math lessons more in line with the real world. As soon as kids start to realize that when something needs to be purchased at the store money is required, that's a good sign they're ready for a small allowance. Or as one mother put it, as soon as they're "old enough not to eat it!"[26] Certainly around first grade kids start to understand the concept of adding things up, putting off an impulse purchase in order to save for something else, and the hard "cold cash" fact that spending money involves making choices. Learning the difference between needs and wants, prioritizing, and saving first, are all difficult lessons everyone must understand in life.

How much money do kids today get for an allowance? Depends on who you ask and who's doing the asking. According to a Nickelodeon/Yanlelovich survey back in 1996, kids ages...

6 to 8	years old received	$2.77 per week
9 to 11	years old received	$3.72 per week
12 to 13	years old received	$7.08 per week
14 to 15	years old received	$8.91 per week
16 to 17	years old received	$10.74 per week

Sound low? Sure it does. But remember that was back in 1996 when first-wave Millennials were turning 16. In 2003, that same survey found kids ages six- to eight-years-old averaged $4.95 a week and for kids nine- to ten-years-old the average was $7.41 per week. Many parents start the allowance game paying between fifty cents to one dollar per week for each year of the child's age. Ohio State University surveyors at the Center for Human Resource Research looked at what teenagers typically received for an allowance. They reported $50 on average per week. Their number is based on the 1997 National Longitudinal Survey of Youth, a federally funded survey of 8,984 randomly chosen kids ages 12 to 18. It's important to note that almost half of the teens surveyed got *no allowance* at all.[27]

A USA Today/Channel One Teens & Money Survey in 1999 found 45 percent of the 193,224 students they asked didn't get an allowance either.[28] Merrill Lynch found in their 2000 Teen Poll that fewer teens received an allowance – only 38 percent.[29] Teenage Research Unlimited found "most teens get money from their parents, but only one in four gets an allowance. Interestingly, teens benefit more from as-needed handouts than from regular allowances. More than half of all teens – 55 percent – report receiving as needed money from parents."[30] Here's the kicker: on average teens spend more than $100 per week! Where do kids get all that money? Well as they get older obviously their sources of income diversifies:

55 to 83% of teens receive money from parents when needed
31 to 45% of teens receive money from gifts
29 to 72% of teens receive money from doing odd jobs
22 to 29% of teens receive money from working part-time
24 to 38% of teens receive money from allowances
1 to 6% of teens receive money from working full-time
1 to 2% of teens receive money from their own business

Perhaps we should call kids today "Generation $,"[31] Millennials'
spending power, as compared to Boomers back when they were teens
and adjusted for inflation, is five to six times as large.[32] As a group,
they are the richest in history. And why not, growing up during one
of the longest economic prosperity periods in U.S. history, Mom and
Dad certainly have passed out a few bucks over the years. Girls do
tend to get more than boys from their parents and universally by the
time kids get into their teen years they rely less on allowances and
more on earnings from work.

Working a job, earning money for doing something, starting kids in
on the American capitalistic work ethic – now *that's* an allowance!
No. Actually that's a paycheck. It's work, *not* chores. If you
differentiate between which responsibilities are expected to be done
as a contributing member of the family – chores – and which jobs are
available to earn extra income – work – you'll save yourself lots of
hassles. How you ask? Imagine what happens if you tie allowance to
chores and your kid decides he or she doesn't need the money this
week. Grandma may have just dropped a crisp $20 bill in a birthday
card and well… "I just don't feel like making the bed, doing the
dishes, or vacuuming my room this week." What do you say? "Fine!
Then no allowance for you!" Remember, your kid made a choice
based on the fact that he or she didn't need your money – they've got
Grandma's gift. Smart kid and the older he or she gets, earning more
and more money outside the home – say after-school babysitting –
the fewer and fewer chores will get done. Is that what you want?

Hopefully, when your kid "leaves the nest" they'll know *both* how
the nest works and what it takes to pay for the nest – and all the
things they'll want to go inside that nest as well. Sure, if you just
give kids all the money they want, they will develop an entitlement
attitude. Help them learn how to make a buck, save a buck, grow
some bucks, share a buck, and spend a buck. Otherwise, they'll be in
your nest longer than you'd like, always asking you for a buck!

A few other items about kids and money to keep in mind when it comes to motivation:

- In 2002, teens spent more than $170 billion and that's 38 percent higher than they spent in 1997.

- Allowances have been rising almost twice as fast as inflation since 1995.

- 70% of undergraduate students in college have at least one credit card and half of all college students have *four or more*.

- The average college student in America graduates with $19,400 in student loans and $2,748 in credit card debt.

- "Not having enough money" is the #2 biggest complaint for teens about everyday life. #1 complaint is "stress."[30]

- 59% of parents tie allowance to household work or chores according to an American Savings Education Council survey.

- Although today's kids spend more, they also save more. When asked what they would do with an extra $100 if they had it, more teens said "save it!"[30]

- Growing up in an excessively consumer-based society has made them very savvy shoppers.

- Teens today on average typically have $19.76 in their pocket at any given moment.

WARNING! Not *all* kids are walking around with $20! Keep in mind that even though the poverty rate in America fell to a record low in 1999 to 16.9 percent of kids under 18, overall children were more likely to be poor than any other age group. The 1999 poverty rate for 18-to 24-year-olds was 17.3 percent.[33] Granted, since then both the poverty rate and the number of kids under age 24 living in poverty has gone up.[34]

Regardless of your place on the socioeconomic scale of life, money matters and yet we all admit money can't buy happiness. Although we've all seen some parents try to buy some peace and quiet around the house with it: "Here kid. Take this and get out of here!" Motivating kids with money might actually negatively impact their ability to be happy in the future. So what's a mom or dad to do when it comes to developing some healthy financial habits in their kids when it comes to money?

✔ **Differentiate between household "chores" and "work"** – Understand that *doing chores* is simply what we do as members of a family to make things happen day-to-day in the home. No one gets paid for that! *Work*, especially the kind you might even be willing to pay someone outside the family to do (i.e. perhaps mowing the lawn, painting the garage, digging out a new flower bed, cleaning the kitchen cabinets or washing the windows), could all be *jobs* available to earn extra *income*.

✔ **Pay kids to work, *not* to do chores** – Compensation or income earned from work is not an allowance and it's not a reward for doing chores.

✔ **Give an allowance to learn about money *not* to do chores** – Motivating kids to do their chores by bribing them with money is not what allowances are for. Think of an allowance as money you'd be giving to your kids anyway. When they're very young it's some change each week for a little purchase they'd like to buy. First lesson taught – the power of saving. As they get older it's a few dollars for stuff they'd like to give as birthday gifts for friends when they're invited to a party – lesson: budgeting. In middle school it might even cover lunch money. By high school it could be enough for clothing. Develop an increasing level of appropriate experiences with money.

✔ **Help kids learn the difference between "needs" and "wants"** – This might be the toughest lesson when it comes to modeling this money matter for your kids. The world makes it too easy to buy lifestyle on credit. Clark Howard and many others would suggest this might be a poor lesson to pass along to your kids when it comes to using credit.

✔ **Prioritization is the key to financial success** – Helps kids realize they need to save some, grow some (i.e. invest), share some (i.e. charitable giving) and spend some. Preplanning and budgeting, while at the same time giving yourself a cushion to fall back on in emergencies, are important lessons to be learned with an allowance.

✔ **Bottom line** – Keep chores separate from allowances. Keep work and money earned from jobs separate from chores and allowances.

BTWFYI: Consider these resources for further information regarding
finances and kids in today's affluent world:
Coalition for Personal Financial Literacy http://www.jumpstart.org
The First National Bank of Dad by David Owen
Hands on Banking http://www.handsonbanking.org
Kids' Money http://www.kidsmoney.org
Practical Money Skills for Life http://www.practicalmoneyskills.com
Prosperity4Kids http://www.prosperity4kids.com
Rich Kid Smart Kid http://www.richkidsmartkid.com
Save For America http://www.saveforamerica.org
Young Money http://www.youngmoney.com

Production to consumption

Families have shifted from production to consumption and in the
process kids have lost their place. Over the past 200 years our
country has moved from agrarian to industrial to service-based.
Perhaps that's an oversimplification, but it illustrates the sequence
during which time the role of the family (and by default members of
the family) has shifted.

Back when most of America's families lived on farms, family size
was a heck of a lot bigger than today's average family size for two
very important reasons: More kids meant more help on the farm and
some of them would die before they reached adulthood. As more and
more workers moved off the farm and into the factory, kids still had
a very important and needed place at home. They'd have chores to
do, brothers or sisters as well as grandparents or even great-
grandparents to help take care of, and in many cases as they got older
even help run a family business or work in the factory themselves.
For a majority of families during a significant portion of history in
this country, parents considered their children as an active,
meaningfully contributing, important asset in helping to support the
family and making things happen at home.

Today that last sentence doesn't necessarily apply for most families.
In the eyes of too many people, kids aren't seen as assets but rather
as recipients of their parents' hard work and financial resources. Or
worse, they're perceived as liabilities that only incur costs to be paid,
denting a parent's ability to buy things for themselves.

For a few parents, kids have even become more of a status symbol to acquire than a member of the family to love. Talk about a consumer mentality! *U.S. News* actually ran a cover story on March 30, 1998, about "The Cost of Children" which had a subtitle "Of course they're cute. But do you have any idea how much one will set you back?" This "hardheaded inquiry" detailed a typical child's "unit cost" for various income bracketed families, "acquisition costs" as well as all the other "liabilities" (oh… and don't forget about lost or "forgone wages") involved in raising kids today. Bottom line – just in case you're curious – in excess of $1.4 million from conception to age 22 per child![35]

Certainly our society's consumer mentality has been fueled a great deal by our affluence. And our affluence which has made our lives easier and faster may have inadvertently caused our kids to "get in our way" to the point that they really have no place to significantly, meaningfully and actively contribute as important members of our family. Rather than being assets in a family where their contribution of effort creates a strong bond of interdependent responsibility and belonging, kids have become recipients of our material affluence, consuming more of what we have or objects that we display to the world as trophies, luxuries, and status symbols. Okay, so that might be a little harsh. But, you and I both know there are parents who act that way and, even worse, treat their kids that way. I think the phrase is…Trophy Kids?[36]

MORE TROPHY ROOMS, HOMES & TOYS FOR OUR TROPHY KIDS

American kids today have grown up in a world designed and built for them perhaps more than any other previous generation in history. And for most, it all begins in their bedrooms. Starting in the early 1980s kids were coming home from the hospital and moving into rooms *designed* for them like never before. It was no longer acceptable to simply have a baby's room painted pink if you were expecting a girl, blue if you were expecting a boy, or yellow if you didn't know. Parents of the Millennial Generation seem compelled to create a special world just for their kids, designing the perfect personal place for their child, and parents have spared no expense.

"Babies are the BMWs of the Nineties"[37]

– Stanley Fridstein

Don't stick them with traditional kid colors. Why not pale heliotrope, shades of celadon green, or any one of the 56 different colors that Connecticut designers Alexander and Meagan Julian used in choosing the color pallet for their children's rooms. "You can't pander to the child. You have to expose them to sophisticated colors," says Alexander. But *do be careful* warns designer Sasha Emerson. "Children's rooms should not be a decision departure from the rest of your house." Designer Celia Tejáda states that above all, "It's important for kids to *love* their rooms to feel that they have a sense of ownership into the space."[38] Don't ask an expectant mother "what color are you painting the baby's room?" Ask: "What will be the theme or color pallet scheme for your child's décor?"

Need some furniture for your kid's room? Then check out Orange, Marne Dupere's lively and unique furniture store in Los Angeles.[39] Opened in 1997, her shop sells vintage retro-style furnishings from the 1950s and 1960s. She admits creating a "great store to shop at for parents because it has great colorful pieces with fantastic finishes that are durable, practical, and fun." Her advice to parents? "I think that when parents are decorating their children's rooms they should take into consideration their *children's* needs. Obviously you need to do a bed, a dresser, and storage, but I think it's important to ask them about what *they* need, what would *you* like?"[38] The furniture industry certainly understands that and furniture retailers too – Bombay Kids, Pottery Barn for Kids, IKEA, and the list goes on and on. "The whole juvenile category has really gone through a huge transformation."[40] That's according to Steve Benidt, cited in *Kids Today*™ – the news magazine of the juvenile furnishings industry. While fashion retailers lead the charge with babyGap, Ralph Lauren for Babies, Limited Too, Talbots Kids, GapKids, and the like – many furniture retailers are now doing the same.

Even entire homes are being designed today with a more kid-friendly, family-friendly approach. "It's not designed for kids, it's not designed for adults, it's really designed for us as a unit." Architect David Hertz and Stacy Fong included their kids in the building process every step of the way. "We felt that would really give them a real sense of ownership and a certain sense of pride." While the resulting multi-level, sophisticated, ultra-modern, contemporary house in Venice, California may appear at first as anything but kid-friendly – an amazing amount of Xer-style pragmatism prevails.[41] "One of our goals with our kids is trying to teach them to become as independent and self-sufficient as possible. Like our son who can get his own diapers. We've got them in two different places and they're about a foot off the ground *and* he knows exactly where to find them," Stacy proudly shares.

Outside the home, even the simple swing-set has been upgraded. What was reserved for the neighborhood playground park, now finds itself smack dab in the middle of many Millennial kids' backyards. Drive through most suburban subdivisions and you'll see multi-level swing sets with climbing walls, slides, rope ladders and a fire pole. Simple tree houses have transformed into custom play structures and houses of all shapes, varieties, and genres. Forts are now castles, with moats, bridges, and even pirate ships! Barbara Butler creates custom kid playhouses for parents who *commission* her as an artist/builder. Since 1987, she has been creating and building unique customized, site-specific play structures that run from just under $3,000 for a simple playhouse to over $87,000 for "Le Grand Fort" assembled and installed.[42]

BTWFYI: You can find out all the latest and greatest in kids bedroom design as well as their influence on our homes at:
The Family Home: Relaxed, Informal Living For All Ages
by Joanna Copestick
Play Equipment for Kids: Great Projects You Can Build
by Mike Lawrence & Gwen Steege
In My World: Designing Living & Learning Environments For The Young by Ro Logrippo
Kids Gardening http://www.kidsgardening.com
House Beautiful: Kids Live Here Too Video available from
A&E http://store.aetv.com/html/product/index.jhtml?id=42666

When it comes to production and consumption in a kid's affluent world, there's one thing that's hard to ignore – toys! Toy sales topped $22 billion in 1997 according to the Toy Industry Association.[43] Some suggest often that money is spent "unwisely because of our misconceptions about toys and play."[44] Chances are you've experienced seeing this firsthand when a gift you thought would be really neat for a kid ended up being played with less and less – while the box it came in was played with more and more. Playing is what kids are wired to do. It consumes a young mind's attention, engages them, and developmentally enhances their cognitive, emotional, physical and social growth. "Many people think play is trivial, but it isn't," says Stevanne Auerbach (a.k.a. Dr. Toy). "Play is vital for the developing mind because it allows children to extend their imagination, resourcefulness, social interaction, problem-solving skills and resilience."[45]

"It is a happy talent to know how to play."

– Ralph Waldo Emerson

Yet as Joanne and Stephanie Oppenheim point out: "Over the last two decades of reviewing products targeted to kids, we've noted that the expectations of what a toy does have changed radically, although not always to the benefit of children and their play-lives."[46]

In the toy world, 50 to 75 percent of the 300,000+ products every year are brand new. "Finding out what children will want to play with still takes a lot of work,"[47] says Tom Neiheisel, who has been researching and marketing toys since 1982. His company, Youth Marketing Solutions sees things constantly changing every year. Oh sure the classic toys maintain and the gender divide still remains huge (ever notice how bicycles now come in two distinctive color ranges: boy or girl). But over the past twenty years toys – like many things in the marketplace – have splintered into differentiated product lines by age, area of interest, cartoon character franchise, movie marketing tie-in, top-40 music sensation, TV sitcoms and series.[48]

Obviously one of the biggest changes involves the explosion of sophisticated technology in toys. A lot of that technology has created amazing toys with huge educational capabilities that would have never been possible a generation ago. Toys from companies like LeapFrog Enterprises with their Turbo Twist®, LeapPad®, and iQuest® series of products create interactive learning experiences kids "play with."[49] It's almost hard to call them "toys" when in reality they're so "educational." In fact, VTech even calls their line of toys "electronic learning products."[50] The influence is everywhere even Lego® partnered with MIT's Media Laboratory "the Vatican of techno-evangelism"[51] to wire their classic interlocking plastic bricks into the Mindstorms™ Robotics Invention System.[52]

Lego® is actually one of the few toys which over the past 70 years has managed to skip the onset of a toy generation gap. They've maintained what toy aficionado Mickey McGowan calls a "generational continuity that exists in the pattern of toys."[53] It's a continual cyclical marketing of memory, nostalgia, redesigning and repackaging even *quasi*-classic toys for the next generation of kids. Boomers were the first to have Slinkys and Silly Putty when they were kids growing up. Xers played with Rubik's Cube, Transformers, Shrinky Dinks and Cabbage Patch Kids. Hasbro even brought back a high tech version of Simon recently and called it Simon2. It now has seven games to test your reflexes and memory, instead of the original three in 1978. Brian Goldner, president of Hasbro's U.S. toy group says: "You just focus on what made the toy so fun, and then build on that with technology."[54]

Classic toys however don't need to be "brought back" since they've always remained on the market. Items such as Crayola Crayons, Tinkertoys, Lincoln Logs, Radio Flyer wagons, Yo-Yos, Legos, Play-Doh, John Deer tractors and Tonka trucks survive year after year. Games like Sorry, Monopoly, Chutes and Ladders, Scrabble, Candyland continue in both their "classic" format as well as some newly revised more modern versions. Sometimes however with mixed results. Take for example the new version of the Easy Bake Real Food Oven. Sure sounded cool for a reminiscing mother who brought it home for her Millennial daughter only to hear her say, "Why wait 30 minutes to make mac and cheese? Why not use the microwave?"[46] So much for a mother-daughter generational connection – more like a generational misconnection!

In spite of the increased educational capabilities technology brings to toys today, the application and appropriate use of these high tech "learning products" concerns some. Educational experts note that many times the best part of a toy or game involves being "open-ended" – giving the child many different ways to play with it. When well-meaning companies try to "modernize" something such as Fisher-Price's nesting cups by putting computer chips in them so they can talk? Well... "It undermines the process [of] having the child find an interesting problem they can solve with the cups – for example, which cup can hold the most water?" suggests Diane Levin, professor of education at Wheelock College in Boston. "When you have nesting cups that talk to you and tell you what the goal is, you can't do that anymore. The child doesn't find their own problems to solve."[44]

There's a trend in toys and among many well-meaning adults to spoil kid's playtime by intentionally loading it up with specific goals, lessons and experiences. It starts early when some parents see to it that they schedule as many play-dates for their young toddler as possible. While some of this is good – especially for Mom – too much can be bad. Kids need time to pursue their own individual interests, at their own pace, without having the experience meticulously choreographed for them. There's actually a tremendous amount of learning that occurs when children entertain themselves. They need an opportunity to just putter around, explore, and figure things out for themselves as they play. If everything is always set up *for* them, how will they learn to do things on their own?

Lesson laden games and so-called "smart toys" sometimes stretch their developmental appropriateness well beyond reason. Remember toy manufacturers want to appeal to the broadest possible market so that more people will purchase their product. Why start preschoolers and kindergartners on the periodic table of elements, when phonic sounds will do just fine? Gear 'em up! Get 'em ready!! Get 'em used to it!!! Starting kids earlier and earlier ties in with this same concern. There's a growing pressure being placed on kids to learn more, faster, and earlier, regardless of their readiness. Most of the time, the only thing a kid learns when *pushed* too soon is frustration. And that's *not* fun. And toys are supposed to be *fun*. So don't buy into the misguided marketing myth that "sooner is always better."

"Pushing kids to do things that are developmentally inappropriate delivers a powerfully negative message that colors how kids think about themselves as competent, able doers. Parents bombarded with the 'smart toy, smart child' message, may also wonder if there's something wrong with their toddler who's incapable of rhyming in three languages or spelling unicorn by age three!"
— Joanne & Stephanie Oppenheim

Believe it or not in our quest to upgrade toys making them more interactive, more educationally enriching, and more technologically driven, we might be taking the *fun* out of toys. With playhouses that create rain-like sound effects while telling kids to close the window – we're essentially eliminating their need to pretend. Why bother making something up when the toy will do it for you? With toys becoming more literal in creating play for kids, the kids become more like passive observers participating in something created by someone – or something – else. That's not what playing is supposed to be for kids. Imagination, creation, interaction, and proactively bringing fun to life – that's play!

MIT's "Toys of Tomorrow"[55] and the "LifelongKindergarten"[56] projects provide some interesting examples as to the future of toys, play and learning. Even the Toy Symphony[57] will bring music to your ears. The one thing these and many other technologically infused toys can't do is create live, human-to-human, face-to-face, spontaneous, physical, mental and social interactivity. Maybe that's why there's been a recent surge of concern about childhood obesity. Kids are "sitting and getting" *way* more than ever before! Playing outside might actually start making a comeback, planting a kid's garden, running through the sprinkler, jumping in the leaves piled high, and sledding in the snow. It could happen! In 2000, the scooter craze hit big and Razor Scooters were everywhere. Before that, and admittedly not quite as physical, Cosmic Bowling was all the rage. Originally intended for adults, the spinning lights, smoke machines and glow-in-the-dark bowling under black lights to loud music actually caught on with kids more than adults.

But why do *that* when you can 3-D simulate it and so much more on your very own PlayStation® or Xbox®? It's okay to "live in your world" but "play in ours," advocates Sony. Grab your Nintendo GameBoy or jump online to experience a virtual multi-player Internet game and you're ready to *really play*. With more and more broadband access coming online directly into many kids' rooms across America – thanks to Mom and Dad – Internet gaming could really "boom 66 percent a year." That's according to Jupiter Communications, who says that the #1 activity for kids – beating email, chat, and homework – is online Internet game playing.[58] While a generation ago, Mom and Dad used to punish their kids by yelling at them: "Go to your room! I don't want to see you or hear you the rest of the day!" Today's older kids are doing just that. The younger ones are still all over the house, making *lots* of noise with all those toys – so many more than we ever had before!

BTWFYI: You can find lots of great information about today's toys and the importance of developmentally appropriate play from:
Oppenheim Toy Portfolio Book by Joanne & Stephanie Oppenheim
Dr. Toy's Smart Play Smart Toys by Stevanne Auerbach
American Specialty Toy Retail Association http://www.astratoy.org

Association for the Study of Play http://www.csuchico.edu/phed/tasp/
Dr. Toy http://www.drtoy.com
Fun Play, Safe Play from the Federal Citizen Information Center
http://www.pueblo.gsa.gov/cic_text/family/toysplay/fpsp.html
Games Kids Play http://www.gameskidsplay.net
Oppenheim Toy Portfolio http://www.toyportfolio.com
Play to Learn – Learn to Play http://learn2play2learn.com
Playing for Keeps http://www.playingforkeeps.org
Playing Throughout the Day http://www.civitas.org/play.html
Toy Industry Association http://www.toy-tia.org

That old adage, "Kids should be seen and *not* heard" no longer seems to apply with today's generation of kids. Ever since we announced to the world we had a "baby on board," society seemed to begin gearing up and rolling out the red carpet wherever there were products to be consumed. With a record level of affluence, parents bought into buying their kids "the best of the best" whenever possible. In so doing we just may have created the most consumer-oriented generation ever to receive an allowance. And with that allowance in their pocket, today's kids are an economic force to be recognized.

With the Millennial Generation currently filling the U.S. teen market, they actually represent almost one-fourth of all teen spending *worldwide*.[59] Collectively as they age, they will "max out" their teen presence on this planet around 2010 when there will be a record 33.5 million kids ages 12 to 19 in America.[30] More important than their affluence and consumption, they are – and will be – the greatest influence on fashion, culture, and so much more worldwide. Just as the Boomers changed many aspects of American life as they aged through their life course, so too will the Millennials. Except this time it will be global. Make no mistake about it, the Millennial Generation will be *"seen* and *heard"* around the world in ways we can't even begin to imagine. Independently and collectively their level of affluence, consumption and production will surpass any previous generation in history.

BOOKS ABOUT PARENTS AND PARENTING

Beyond the Cornucopia Kids
by Bruce Baldwin

Kids Are Worth It! Giving Your Child the Gift of Inner Discipline
by Barbara Coloroso

The 7 Habits of Highly Effective Families
by Stephen Covey

Raising a Responsible Child
by Don Dinkmeyer, Sr. and Gary McKay

Take Back Your Kids
The Intentional Family
by William Doherty

What Do You Really Want for Your Children
by Wayne Dyer

Spoiling Childhood
by Diane Ehrensaft

Raising Self-Reliant Children In A Self-Indulgent World
by H. Stephen Glenn and Jane Nelsen

Raising Adults: Getting Kids Ready for the Real World
by Jim Hancock

Time Bind
She Works/He Works
by Arlie Hochschild

Raising America: Experts, Parents, and a Century of Advice
by Ann Hulbert

Tag You're It! 50 Easy Ways to Connect to Young People
by Kathleen Kimball-Baker

Too Much of a Good Thing
by Dan Kindlon

I'll Be the Parent, You Be the Child
by Paul Kropp

Hyper-Parenting
by Alvin Rosenfeld and Nicole Wise

Parenting from the Inside Out
by Daniel Siegel and Mary Hartzell

Our Babies, Ourselves:
How Biology and Culture Shape the Way We Parent
by Meredith Small

Anxious Parents: A History of Modern Childrearing in America
by Peter Stearns

What Kids Really Want That Money Can't Buy
by Betsy Taylor

Proactive Parenting: Guiding Your Child From Two to Six
by the Faculty of Tufts University's Eliot-Pearson
Department of Child Development

Raising a Happy, Unspoiled Child
by Burton White

WEB SITES ABOUT PARENTS AND PARENTING

Child & Family WebGuide	http://www.cfw.tufts.edu
Child Caring	http://www.ciccparenting.org
Child Magazine	http://www.child.com
Child Study Center	http://www.aboutourkids.org
Civitas Parenting	http://www.civitas.org/parents.html
Developing Capable People	http://www.capabilitiesinc.com
Dr. Bill & Martha Sears	http://www.askdrsears.com
Dr. Spock	http://www.drspock.com
Fathers4Kids	http://www.fathers4kids.org
National Parenting Assoc.	http://www.parentsunite.org
Families with Disabilities	http://www.lookingglass.org
Family Life First	http://www.familylife1st.org
Family Research Project	http://gseweb.harvard.edu/~hfrp/
Fatherhood Initiative	http://www.fatherhood.org
The Fatherhood Project	http://www.fatherhoodproject.org
Hyper-Parenting	http://www.hyperparenting.com
iParenting	http://www.iparenting.com
National Parenting Center	http://www.tnpc.com
Parenting Journal	http://www.parentsjournal.com
Parent Soup	http://www.positiveparenting.com
Parent's Toolshop	http://www.parentstoolshop.com
Parenting Magazine	http://www.parenting.com
Parenting Resources	http://www.ncjrs.org/viewall.html
Parenting Teenagers	http://www.parent-teen.com
Parenting Toolbox	http://parentingtoolbox.com
Positive Parenting	http://www.positiveparenting.com
Stay at Home Mothers	http://www.athomemothers.com

NOTES FOR CHAPTER TWO

1. Rosenfeld, A., & Wise, N. (2000). *Hyper-Parenting: Are You Hurting Your Child by Trying Too Hard?* New York: St. Martin's Press.

2. Ehrensaft, D. (1997). *Spoiling Childhood: How Well-Meaning Parents Are Giving Children Too Much - But Not What They Need.* New York: Guilford Press.

3. Eisenberg, A., Murkoff, H., & Hathaway, S. (1991). *What to Expect When You're Expecting* (Revised ed.). New York: Workman Publishing.

4. Weissbluth, M. (1987). *Healthy Sleep Habits, Happy Child.* New York: Fawcett Columbine.

5. Brazelton, T. B. (1992). *Touchpoints: Your Child's Emotional and Behavioral Development.* New York: Addison-Wesley Publishing Company.

6. White, B. L. (1995). *The New First Three Years of Life.* New York: Fireside.

7. Hart, B. (2001, June 8). High-powered kids: Modern parenting's dubious achievement. *Dayton Daily News,* p. 9.

8. Fitzsimmons, W., Lewis, M. M., & Ducy, C. (2001). *Time Out or Burn Out for the Next Generation* [Online]. Harvard University. http://adm-is.fas.harvard.edu/timeoff.htm

9. Putnam, R. D. (2000). *Bowling Alone: The Collapse and Revival of American Community.* New York: Simon and Schuster.

10. Hofferth, S. L., & Sandberg, J. F. (2000). *Changes in American Children's Time, 1981-1997.* Ann Arbor, MI: Population Studies Center at the University of Michigan.

11. Kaiser Family Foundation. (1999). *Kids & Media @ The New Millennium.*

12. Hofferth, S. L. (1998). *Healthy Environments, Healthy Children: Children in Families* [Online]. University of Michigan. http://www.isr.umich.edu/src/child-development/fullrep.html

13. Covey, S. R. (1997). *The 7 Habits of Highly Effective Families.* New York: Golden Books.

14. Elkind, D. (1981). *The Hurried Child: Growing Up Too Fast Too Soon* (3rd ed.). Reading, MA: Addison-Wesley.

15. Kantrowitz, B., Wingert, P., Nelson, M., Halpert, J. E., Lauerman, J., Weingarten, T., et al. (2001, January 29). The Parent Trap. *Newsweek, 137,* 49-53.

16. U.S. Census Bureau. (2000). *Poverty Rate Lowest in 20 Years, Household Income at Record High* [Online]. U.S. Census Bureau. http://www.census.gov/Press-Release/www/2000/cb00-158.html

17. U.S. Census Bureau. (2000). *Income Inequality (Middle Class) Narrative* [Online]. U.S. Census Bureau. http://www.census.gov/hhes/income/midclass/midclsan.html

18. Wurman, R. S. (2001). *Information Anxiety 2*. Indianapolis, IN: Que.

19. Glenn, H. S., & Nelsen, J. (1989). *Raising Self-Reliant Children In a Self-Indulgent World*. Rocklin, CA: Prima Publishing.

20. Moore, S., & Simon, J. L. (2000). *It's Getting Better All the Time: 100 Greatest Trends of the Last 100 Years*. Washington, DC: CATO Institute.

21. Kohn, A. (1999, February 2). *In Pursuit of Affluence, at a High Price* [Online]. http://www.alfiekohn.org/managing/ipoa.htm

22. Marchant, V. (2001, January 29). Parents Who Give Too Much. *Time, 157*.

23. Kohn, A. (1998, March/April). Challenging Behaviorist Dogma: Myths About Money and Motivation. *Compensation & Benefits Review*.

24. Mackey, L. (2004). *Money Mama & The Three Little Pigs*. Agoura Hills, CA: P4K Publishing.

25. Mish, F. C. (Ed.). (1991). *Webster's Ninth New Collegiate Dictionary*. Springfield, MA: Merriam-Webster Inc.

26. Provenzano, F., & Bodnar, J. (1998). *Allowance Guidelines for Parents* [Online]. National Mental Health and Education Center. http://www.naspcenter.org/adol_allow.html

27. Welsh-Huggins, A. (1999, December 21). Weekly allowance on rise. *Dayton Daily News*, p. 2A.

28. Chatzky, J. S. (1999, May 2). Young, Rich, Smart: Nearly 200,000 Answer USA Weekend's 12th Annual Teen Survey. *USA Today*.

29. Merrill Lynch. (2000). *2000 Teen Poll*. New York.

30. Zollo, P. (2004). *Wise Up to Teens: More Insights into Marketing to Teenagers* (3rd ed.). Ithaca, NY: New Strategist.

31. McGregor, J. (2003, April 23). Teach Your Children Well... *Smart Money*.

32. Youth, Inc. (2000, December 23). *The Economist, 357*, 9.

33. U.S. Census Bureau. (2000). *Poverty in the United States* (Online). Washington, DC: U.S. Census Bureau.

34. U.S. Census Bureau. (2003). *Poverty in the United States* (Online). Washington, DC: U.S. Census Bureau.

35. Longman, P. J. (1998, March 30). The Cost of Children. *U.S. News*.

36. Goodman, E. (2002). *'Trophy' kids create grist for satire* [Online]. The Detroit News. http://www.detnews.com/2002/editorial/0211/29/a09-20528.htm

37. Gubernick, L., & Matzer, M. (1995, February 27). Babies as dolls. *Forbes, 78-82.*

38. Demeecki, S. (1999). *House Beautiful: Kids Live Here Too.* In D. Stein (Producer): Actuality Productions, Inc. http://store.aetv.com/html/product/index.jhtml?id=42666

39. Orange Furnishings and Design. (2003). *Orange Furnishings + Home Design* [Online]. http://www.orangefurniture.com

40. Kitchen, J. (2003). *Teens, tweens stir up creativity in youth* [Online]. Kids Today. http://www.kidstodayonline.com/UPcloseTEENS.shtml

41. Hertz, D. (2003). *McKinley Residence* [Online]. Syndesis, Inc. http://www.syndesisinc.com/arch/mck-main.html

42. Butler, B. (1996). *Barbara Butler Artist-Builder, Inc.* [Online]. http://www.barbarabutler.com

43. Beck, R. (1998, November 27). Toy Business Not Child's Play. *Associated Press.*

44. Strauss, V. (2000, December 12). Learning Lessons in the Toy Store: High-Tech Innovations, Parents' Misconceptions Can Interfere With the Serious Work of Children's Play. *Washington Post*, p. A24.

45. Auerbach, S. (2004). *Smart Play SmartToys: How to Raise a Child with a High PQ (Play Quotient).* Rancho Dominguez, CA: Educational Insights.

46. Oppenheim, J., Oppenheim, S., & Oppenheim, J. (2003). *Oppenheim Toy Portfolio: The Best Toys, Books, Videos, Music & Software For Kids.* New York: Oppenheim Toy Portfolio, Inc.

47. Braddix, D. (1999, November 8). Toys may be consultant's business, but they're still fun. *Cincinnati Enquirer.*

48. Hamilton, M. M. (2001, February 14). Toy Story: Demographic Changes Boost Spending on Toys. *Washington Post*, p. E2.

49. LeapFrog Enterprises Inc. (2004). *LeapFrog* [Online]. http://www.leapfrog.com

50. VTech. (2004). *VTech* [Online]. http://www.vtech.com

51. Shenk, D. (1999). *Use Technology to Raise Smarter, Happier Kids: Behold the toys of tomorrow* [Online]. The Atlantic Monthly. http://www.theatlantic.com/unbound/digicult/dc990107.htm

52. LEGO. (2003). *Mindstorms Robotics Invention System* [Online]. http://www.mindstorms.com

53. Templeton, D. (2000). *What are our toys trying to tell us?* (From the November 30-December 6 issue of Metro - Silicon Valley's Weekly Newspaper) [Online]. Metroactive/Metro Publishing Inc. http://www.metroactive.com/papers/metro/11.30.00/gift-0048.html

54. Barker, O. (2001, December 7). Nostalgic GenXers can find slick updates of fave toys. *USA Today.*

55. MIT Media Lab. (2002). *Toys of Tomorrow* [Online]. Massachusetts Institute of Technology. http://toys.media.mit.edu

56. MIT Media Lab. (2003). *Lifelong Kindergarten* [Online]. Massachusetts Institute of Technology. http://llk.media.mit.edu

57. MIT Media Lab. (2003). *Toy Symphony* [Online]. Massachusetts Institute of Technology. http://www.toysymphony.net

58. Byrnes, N. (2000, March 13). Babes in Virtual Toyland. *Business Week,* 62-64.

59. Moses, E. (2000). *The $100 Billion Allowance: Accessing the Global Teen Market.* New York: John Wiley & Sons, Inc.

Chapter Three

Technology Media/TV and Life 24/7/365

The influence of technology has reached into kids' lives beyond their toys. Today's 24/7/365 "always on" world brings with it both good and bad influences. All the hyper-parenting during an unprecedented period of prosperity has – as some might say – spoiled childhood with more technology, more media, more TV, more toys, more access, more and more and more of so much more! Or maybe not. Perhaps today's kids are better prepared to deal with, interact with, create with, manage, manipulate, and in short, be motivated by the technology, media, TV and overscheduled lifestyle of today's 24/7/365 world. Let's hope so. Our future in this so-called postmodern era may just depend on it as there seems to be no end in sight to the continued, sometimes spam-like, invasion of technology.

The invasion of technology

Technology has invaded our homes at an unprecedented rate. You don't have to be a rocket scientist to see that the average way of life in American homes has been substantially changed by the increased use of technology. Major shifts in how we communicate with the outside world and the amount of information from the outside world that inundates homes today is truly mind-blowing.

In the 1970s, the kind of instantaneous communication that cell phones and pagers allowed was reserved only for the very wealthy. Now entire families can have a family-plan package with shared minutes during the weekdays and unlimited talk time on evenings and weekends. Preschoolers have pagers. Elementary and middle school/junior high students want better computers at home than Mom and Dad have at work. High-school and college kids have personal digital assistants. Practically every kid in America goes to school where there's Internet access. College students expect it, if not in a computer lab or cyber-café, then in their room or, better yet, via laptop with wireless network access campuswide.

We've got microwaves that can auto-cook and will soon know what you're putting into them – refrigerators that auto-shop (via a web browser on their doors) and they'll soon know what you're taking out of them. There are lawn mowers and vacuum cleaners already doing their jobs without you having to push them around. Answering machines are being replaced by voicemailboxes with caller ID for every member of the family. Cable television access, high-speed DSL Internet access, and satellite dishes connect homes to the outside world beyond the levels which governments of small countries could possess just a couple decades ago.

Convergence of all this technology has also impacted families. Consider the power of video phone conversations via your computer/the Internet/telephone/TV or some other combination thereof. The power of email has already been combined with pagers and cell phones to give us IM as in Instant Messaging. Ford and Maytag teamed up to create the ultimate minivan of the future – Windstar Solutions, which has a refrigerator-like cooler, microwave, trash compactor, heated and/or cooling cup holders, a vacuum cleaner as well as a clothes washer and dryer.[1]

Even the family pet has been turned into the latest technological gadget. Sony created AIBO the first entertainment robot. The word AIBO in Japanese means "companion" and in our acronym-hyped world AIBO also happens to stand for "Aritficial Intelligence RoBOt." But, according to Sony, it's not a toy! It's a lifelong friend and companion, complete with instincts, emotions, developmental stages, desires, who will learn from your praise and never mess your carpet.[2]

Much of this invading technology has brought about great access to more information (certainly both good and bad). It has saved us time mostly in terms of doing domestic housework as well as making all kinds of communication faster and more instantaneous. Thanks to technology we have more information, and more time and can do things faster than ever before. That's the good news!

The bad news is we don't always see it that way. Most people believe family life has gotten more complicated with two people working, commuting, car-pooling to the kids' activities, running lots of errands, and overall just struggling to keep up. Overworked American[3] families have become in some respects slaves to the technology and their schedules. Every family seems to struggle with a time crunch[4] – doing more and doing things more quickly as well as simultaneously. Dr. Geoffrey Godbey and Dr. John Robinson, co-authors of *Time For Life* would call this "time-deepening." They would argue that American's sense of this "time famine" is in part due to the increased emphasis on the consumption of experiences. Their studies with the *Americans' Use of Time Project* show that the bigger issue is pace of life not the amount of time.[5]

BTWFYI: If you're looking for an eye-opening, fact-filled book that profiles the influence of technology on kids and families today check out: *Growing Up Digital* by Don Tapscott. For a more critical perspective read *Computers and Children: A New Report* available at http://www.allianceforchildhood.net

Media

Media rode into American homes on the coattails of technology bringing with it the information age whether we liked it or not. More people know more, about more things than ever before. TV started it, the Internet changed it, and when those two technologies truly merge – watch out! Many would debate the kind of impact media has had on families today, but none would debate that it does have tremendously more impact than it ever did before – mostly because it's everywhere. Adults actually spend more time consuming media than kids. The typical American kid spends an average of more than 38 hours a week – nearly five-and-a-half hours per day (5:29) – consuming media outside of school, according to a major national study.[6] That amount is even higher – nearly six and three-quarter hours per day (6:43) – for kids eight and older.

Historically speaking, adults have increased both TV watching and Internet surfing, while kids have seen a dip in TV watching as they go online more and more. Like it or not families today have made media one of the central focal points, not only in our living rooms, but also in our lives.

Just 25 years ago, TV stations routinely signed off the air sometime late at night by playing the National Anthem, which gave way to a few hours of test-pattern color bars until the next morning's programming would begin. Not today! The media business is a 24/7 operation competing around the clock for audience share. Add to that the growing number of individual stations, the fact that we now have seven broadcast networks (ABC, CBS, NBC, FOX, PBS, UPN and WB) nationwide, the reality of cable TV's explosive growth from just under 7% of American homes in 1970 to over 65% in 1999, satellite TV subscribers growing at an annual rate of 25% in each of the past six years[7], and you can begin to understand why TV appears to be so aggressive these days. Media outlets are literally beating each other up for viewers like you.

WARNING! Some of this diagnosis may seem to be sketching the problems of today, while at other times simply presenting the realities of a modern age. Whichever your perspective – they are important. Then again, maybe I'm simply a classic Xer parent, wanting to bring back the 1950s after a Crisis Era passes! Some would call this "generational yearning." The idea is based on the theory that each generation longs to see the type of era they were born too late for. That might explain why much of this chapter so far sounds anti-1990s or like a suppressed longing for a kind of pre-colorless world such as in the movie *Pleasantville*.

Is that good or bad? Well, it depends. What are you watching? What are your kids watching? Do you even care? Many parents do not exercise a whole lot of control over their kid's media use. Among children ages 8 to 18, many (61%) say their parents have set no rules about TV watching and parents watch TV with their kids in this same age range only 5% of the time.[6] TV today is higher quality in the sense of informative, educational, culturally enriching kinds of programming. At the same time, it serves up some of the lowest, most violent, sexually stimulating, graphically depicted junk ever broadcast. Like so many things in life, you've got to take the good with the bad. Or do you?

Ever since television first came into existence, people have been fretting about its content. Congress has been involved since the early 1950s and, over the half-century since, organizations such as the American Academy of Pediatrics, the American Medical Association, the American Psychological Association, the Group for the Advancement of Psychiatry, the National Commission on the Causes and Prevention of Violence, the National Institute of Mental Health, and the Surgeon General's Scientific Advisory Committee have *all* produced landmark reports on the subject.[8] Based on the extent of viewing, correlation studies, experimental studies, field studies, quantitative and qualitative data, there's little doubt that media has tremendous impact on society. Positive or negative influence certainly depends on the individual,[9] but no one can question that more and more kids are being exposed to more and more media.

"The media dominates our lives."
> – Walter Cronkite 9/11/95 on CNN's "Larry King Live"

BTWFYI: If you're looking for insight from a media scholar who actually writes books that are fun to read, check out:
The Disappearance of Childhood, Amusing Ourselves to Death and *How to Watch TV News* by Neil Postman.

What has TV taught kids today?

Okay perhaps that's an unfair question when you consider that you wouldn't ask, "What has the telephone taught our kids today?" In reality it's not about what TV has taught our kids, but rather what the content of TV has taught our kids. On the plus side, television has brought the world into our homes. That's the good news – as well as the bad news. In addition to wonderful programming, the average kid by the age of 18 sees…

- **360,000 commercials** – and when you add on product placements during programs, cross programming promotion, event marketing tie-ins, etc. – it's no wonder kids of all ages say "gimme!" Commercials make up to 30% of what you watch on TV. Admittedly, people don't really pay attention to them like they do to the rest of the programming, but they're there.

- **252,000 overt sexual references** – and *only* 2,700 of those deal with sexual responsibility. A recent study found that three out of four prime time shows include sexual content, while only one out of ten addresses safe sex.[10] Dr. Ruth is still peeved![11] In addition, among shows that contain sexual material, there are an average of 4.1 scenes per hour with sexual messages. During the 1997-98 TV season, 56% of all shows had sexual content. By the 1999-2000 season, 68% had sexual content.

- **200,000 acts of violence** – 16,000 of these are murders. Research over the last 20 years shows kids who view excessive TV violence do become less sensitive to the pain and suffering of others, are more fearful of the world around them, and may be more likely to behave aggressively toward others. During the weekday evening prime time hours TV has on average five acts of violence per hour compared to an average of 26 violent acts per hour during Saturday morning TV.

- **100,000 alcohol commercials** – all before kids even reach the legal drinking age. Kids today know why this Bud's for you, which tastes great, and is less filling, what weekends are made for and "Wasssssup!"

- **More pharmaceutical commercials** – all reinforcing the message that there's a pill to help you physically, emotionally and even sexually. In 1997, when the FDA revised restrictions on pharmaceutical TV advertising, an already rapidly growing two-decade trend produced an avalanche of commercials.

- **More junk-food ads** – 9 out of 10 food ads on Saturday morning TV are for sugary cereals, candy, snacks, fat-filled fast food and generally unhealthy junk food. Add that to the fact that kids who watch a lot of TV aren't doing other more physical activities and it's no surprise TV and obesity in kids many times go hand in hand.[12]

And we wonder why people today are concerned about kids being overweight, overly materialistic, and talking more graphically about sex? Thinking that acts of violence, drinking and self-medicating are the way to solve problems? Hmmm… go figure! Toss in our instant-fast gratification model to miraculous solutions without much effort by the end of each episode and *voila!* How many times have *you* seen TV teach virtues of patience, deferred gratification, hard work, personal initiative and responsibility? Not many? A few?

Now since TV's the #1 after-school activity for 6- to 17-year-olds and the average kid will spend more time in front of a TV than with a teacher (and *far more* than with a parent), perhaps looking at and limiting what kids are watching as well as how much they're watching wouldn't be such a bad idea. Even younger kids ages one to three have been found to watch three or more hours of TV per day.[13] For many families, TV has become an addiction and you won't see too many "Just say no" ads for that particular addiction on TV.

In her book *Glued to the Tube: The Threat of Television Addiction to Today's Family*, Cheryl Pawlowski presents how television has even become a member of the modern American family.[14] In many families the TV has become one of the most influential role models. Think about it – in many homes television influences or even dictates our schedules, serves as our cultural compass in terms of what's really happening in the world, teaches us, emotionally reaches us, and many times keeps us company when we're lonely. Television has moved from being a baby sitter to being the third parent for kids today.

Recently there's been a great deal of debate over the system of TV ratings designed to help parents sort out what's on TV:

E / I   Educational or informational.

Y   Children's programs designed for any age child.

Y7   Children's programs designed for ages 7 and older.

G   General programming for all audiences.

TV PG   General programming with parental guidance suggested.

PG 14   General programming for people 14 and older.

TV MA   General programming designed for mature audiences.

Then there are even sub-codes for the above ratings...

FV   Fantasy violence

V   Violence

L   Offensive language

S   Sexual Content

D   Derogatory language

The ratings are not shown for all programs and when they do appear it's only for the first five to ten seconds of the show. Even the new V-chip rating system offers mixed results. So what's a parent to do when it comes to TV? Here are a few suggestions:

✔ Set age limits appropriately.

✔ Start early developing good viewing habits.

✔ Monitor your own viewing habits and the example you set.

✔ Encourage planning what to watch in advance versus just "vegging on TV."

✔ Don't assume the ratings are accurate or that anything on PBS/Disney is kid-friendly to your standards or their age.

✔ Know what your kids are watching.

✔ Watch TV with your kids.

✔ Discuss stuff you see on TV with your kid.

✔ Balance TV watching with a variety of programming (art, sports, educational, comedy, fantasy, etc.).

✔ Consider videos from your public library or video store and preview them.

✔ Don't let TV cut in on book reading, recreation, studying and other activities.

✔ Don't use TV as a reward for good behavior.

– Center for Research on the Effects of Television[15]
and the Center for Media Education[16]

Based on current research, by the time today's kids are 70 years old they'll have spent about 10 years of their life watching TV! That's a decade of television's influence and education 24/7/365. Parents and kids themselves have the power to decide how and what that influence and education will be for them. Recognizing that they are addicted to television motivates many families to adjust their viewing habits, but it's hard.

In one study, researchers "attempted to train parents to control and severely limit children's TV viewing. This turned out to be very difficult to do. Parents like television themselves, and they also find it an extremely convenient baby sitter. In fact, parents from the poorer inner-city neighborhoods often say that they would rather have their children home watching television than out on the streets confronting various dangers."[17]

"Then shall we allow our children to listen to any story anyone happens to make up, and so receive into their minds ideas often the very opposite of those we shall think they ought to have when they grow up?"[18]

– Plato, *The Republic*

Television airwaves today *do* provide some amazingly positive and constructive lessons for young kids today. When you think back to what was referred to as "children's television" prior to the late-1970s, most of it served as Saturday morning cartoons, with only PBS airing *Sesame Street*, *Mr. Rogers' Neighborhood*, and *The Electric Company*. Today there are entire networks built for kids 24/7/365: Disney, Nickelodeon, Nick Jr., Noggin, PBSKids, and the list goes on. Many of these networks support substantially better television programming "than when we were kids" and the lessons they share might mean much more to Millennials when they grow up. Consider some of the following shows, their stories and the lessons they share:

Teletubbies™

- Conceived to address the anxiety of growing up in an increasingly technology-dependent world.

- Characters speak with sounds based on phonemes to help toddlers develop language skills.[19]

- TV screens on the characters tummies help them relate to each other. Kids recognize that interacting with technology is a vital component of life.[20]

Bob the Builder™

"Can we fix it? Yes we can!"
"Bob and the gang have so much fun,
working together to get the job done."
"Muck to the rescue! Spud's on the job! No prob, Bob!"[21]

- Bob sees "good-as-new" where others simply see junk.

- The show defies gender-based assumptions: Muck the bulldozer is female, does hard physically demanding work and loves mud.

- Bob's a hard working, stand-up-for-his-friends kind of guy.

- He's equally adept to "blue-collar" construction trade work as well as "white collar" office jobs.

- Bob's always polite, even to the occasionally snobby upper-class clients who hire him.

- Wendy and Bob have certain strengths that complement the other's weakness and neither one ever rubs it in.

Barney & Friends™

"I love you. You love me. We're a happy family."
"There are lots of things we can do to be nice."
"Remember please and thank you."
"Anything is possible if you use your imagination."[22]

- This purple dinosaur comes to life each episode by the strong-willed imagination of children – helping them to use their imagination, think creatively, learn something new, and solve problems effectively.

- Each episode reportedly has "over 200 teaching moments designed by educational experts."[23]

- Drs. Jerome and Dorothy Singer from Yale University's Family Television Research & Consultation Center reported that the show "helps children be better prepared to enter a structured learning environment. According to the study, episodes in this series were especially strong in dealing with pro-social behaviors and with emotion."[24]

Bear in the Big Blue House™

"Welcome! Welcome! Welcome!"
"Things to do, fun for you!"
"Seems like we've just begun when suddenly we're through."

- Bear is a gentle, caring, loving father-like-figure who likes to have fun.

- He is always filled with civility and concern for others.

- Deeply reflective at the end of the show recapping what he did that day with his friend Luna the moon – a glowing and wise sage-like personality who often provides new perspectives on the day's events.[25]

Stanley

"Always ready to learn about something new."
"Come help him figure out what life is all about."
"No problem Stan can't solve, having a friend like you."

- Stanley, a curious boy with a big imagination, searches the animal world for clues about life and himself.

- He and his good friend Dennis, who happens to be a goldfish, always turn to the "Great Big Book of Everything with everything inside. To see the world around him the book's the perfect guide."[26]

Dora the Explorer™

"You can lead the way."
"Come on let's get to it, I know you can do it!"[27]

- A seven-year-old Latina heroine takes preschoolers on interactive map adventures. Along the way exposing them to Latino culture and introducing them to Spanish language.

- Dora asks kids to help her out by checking her back-back for things they need and watching out for Swiper the Fox.

- Visual, spatial, and problem solving skills used throughout.

Rolie Polie Olie

"Way up high in the Rolie Polie sky is a little round planet of a really nice guy. Small and smart and round, he's the swellest kid around."[28]

- With a family oriented retro 1930s cartoon-look and a 1950s "Leave it to Beaver" attitude – albeit tossed into the future – Rolie teaches kids that friends come in all shapes and sizes.

- Mom and Dad always seem to know all the answers.

- William Joyce, who created the character said: "Everything in Rolie Polie Olie is a robot or a machine. But rather than it seeming cold and remote, I wanted to see if we could make a robot world that felt warm and kind; an almost old-fashioned version of what the future could be."[29]

Sagwa™ The Chinese Siamese Cat

- This show fosters an appreciation of different cultures, as Sagwa and her friends learn how confidence, determination and hard work pay off.

- Sagwa is the middle child, adventurous, curious, independent, tolerant, and she always learns from her mistakes. "She is trying hard to find her place in the world."[30]

- Based on an original story by Amy Tan, it's inspired by her own adventures when she was five years old moving from a very Chinese neighborhood located in the San Francisco Bay Area to a more "mixed area" near Oakland, California.

Between the Lions™

"Come and read between the lions. Come on, come in, begin, the world awaits."

- Kids get "wild about reading" with a special family of lions who live in a library.

- Independent studies show that kids who regularly watch this program even learn key reading skills faster than kids who don't.[31]

Powerpuff Girls™

- These superhero "symbols of strength for the female spirit" combine sugar, spice, and everything nice with incredible power. Living in Townsville, USA, they fight crime, monsters, and the "evil genius monkey Mojo Jojo" using their superpowers.[32]

  WARNING! Some have suggested these five-year-olds resort to violence too many times in solving problems and represent icons of "third-wave feminism." Others don't like the spoiled little rich girl, Princess Morebucks, who's portrayed as a cross-dressing, red-skinned devil, and referred to in the show by the pronoun "Him."

Care Bears™

"Positively anything's possible."
"Do your share of sharing!"
"Love will find a way, and if it doesn't, I will!"
"Have I got a friend for you – me!" "Lucky for you I'm here!"

- The Care Bears live a gentle lifestyle of kindness and empathy. A group of adorable, furry friends each with a special caring mission – helping teach people how to care.

- Each Care Bear wears "a bright-colored tummy picture that tells the world who they are and what is their special area of caring."[33]

Thomas & Friends™

- Thomas the tank engine and all the other trains on Sir Topham Hatt's railway work really hard to be "responsible, reliable, and really useful." Based on the popular "Railway Series" by Reverend W. Awdry.[34]

VeggieTales®

"And so what we have learned applies to our life today."

- Christian vegetables, led by Bob the tomato and Larry the cucumber, share Sunday morning values and Saturday morning fun!

- Hilariously shares a Biblical perspective on modern-day issues by telling stories and singing silly songs.

- They use a computer named Qwerty to help them look things up. (Qwerty is named after the first six letters on a keyboard.)

- Produced by Big Idea Productions, their stated core purpose is to "markedly enhance the moral and spiritual fabric of our society through creative media."[35]

BTWFYI: For addition resources on "what you can do," check out:
The Smart Parent's Guide to Kids' TV by Milton Chen
Stay Tuned! Raising Media Savvy Kids in the age of the Channel-Surfing Coach Potato by Jane Murphy and Karen Tucker
Handbook of Children and the Media by Dorothy and Jerome Singer
Use TV to Your Child's Advantage by Dorothy and Jerome Singer
PTA's "Taking Charge of Your TV" video http://www.pta.org
Children & the Media at http://www.childrennow.org
Media Awareness http://www.media-awareness.ca/english/index.cfm

Perhaps television represents a good example of how something can gradually, unknowingly and sometimes dangerously without advance notice take over our lives. Certainly lots of super educational programming available today on TV never would have seen the light of anyone's living room a couple of decades ago. Kids have certainly seen more good TV than any previous generation. They've also seen more bad TV.

Many parents over the past 10 to 20 years have recognized how "we need to get our kids involved in something so they're not just sitting there all day watching TV!" So they actively encourage them to get involved in some sort of sport, organized youth activity, club, organization, music lessons, dance lessons, Boy Scouts/Girl Scouts, etc… All of this is good, but *too* much of this is bad. In many families, the over-scheduling of too many activities has also gradually, unknowingly, and in some cases dangerously, taken over their lives.

Overscheduled Families & Kids

My dad used to say, "You can do anything you want. You just can't do everything you want." Maybe it was all the time-management emphasis in the 1970s that caused more parents and families in the 1980s and 1990s to believe they could do everything they wanted. Today's families in many cases need a dispatch scheduler to keep everyone everywhere they need to be. Making connections between being dropped off for one activity and picked up at another gets crazier than O'Hare International! Moms and dads create a chaotic flurry of minivans and SUVs getting their kids from one adult-run youth activity to another.

WARNING! Kids being involved in activities in and of itself is a good thing. Research shows that kids who participate in structured after-school and outside-of-school activities have better work habits and are better adjusted emotionally than their peers who do not take part in these activities. It's the over-participation, the developmental inappropriateness, and the over-scheduling that's creating stress for both families and kids today.

"It used to be they would have to drive me around to wherever and take me to places, so they needed to know exactly 'when the taxi can pull in and leave' is what they used to say. They just have so many responsibilities that sometimes they feel they need to take over our responsibilities, when in fact we can do a lot of it on our own. We're supposed to learn, but then we go off to college and you know they've been doing all kinds of stuff for us or making sure we do stuff and then suddenly we're not going to have them there to push us to do things."

– A student interviewed on the Fox-TV special "TeenTalk"[36]

It all starts innocently enough, with toddler play-dates set up weeks in advance and explodes exponentially in all directions. Earlier and earlier, kids are encouraged to get involved. Sports (cheerleading too), music, dance, art, academic enrichment, testing-prep programs, overnight summer camp and all kinds of various activities are starting younger and younger. The resulting "Frantic Family Syndrome"[37] (as John Rosemond calls it) creates calendar chaos in too many families today. Dr. William Doherty calls it a "scheduled state of hyperactivity."[38] Consider these real-life warning-sign examples:

- Family summer vacations get canceled because there is "no time to go" due to increased number of tournament games.

- Homework starts to "get in the way" of activities or begins to create late-night "it's past your bedtime" study sessions.

- Parents have less time for community involvement.

- Mom and Dad rarely get a "night out on their own."

- Sunday-scheduled events create religious commitment conflicts.

- Kids "play just to win" more than they "play just to play."

- Getting the entire family together is a "big deal."

- Parents find a more restful reality at work than at home.

- Bragging about "how busy our family is" to others.

- Playing the parental peer pressure game of "let's keep up with the Joneses' kids!"

Now developmental differences depending on your kids age(s) will influence how many of the above items come into play for you. But, if you said *yes* to all of them, then you may be ready for some of the following solutions marketed to overscheduled families and kids:

WARNING! Please read the next nine paragraphs in the sarcastic tone as intended...

FranklinCovey® has come up with "solutions for all ages" designed to cover "their academic careers – from the first day of preschool through college graduation – with tools and skills to become effective, responsible and self-directed." That's right! Just what every preschooler needs – a day planner! Why not start them young? (Think of the refill order possibilities!) Don't you want to "improve and encourage goal-setting, time-management, higher test scores, more rapid homework-completion and improve home-to-school communication?" Then you'll want to pick up the Primary Journal (geared for ages 4 to 8) or the Elementary School Planner (geared for ages 6 to12) filled with words of the week, daily reading and writing activities, weekly quizzes and monthly learning themes.[39]

Palm Pilots for kids are showing up more and more on college campuses, in high schools and even in the hands of middle school/junior high students. While most of them are not yet wireless-enabled (like Mom and Dad's), they are becoming the Trapper-Keeper of the Millennial Generation. Trapper-Keepers were those colorful plastic ring binders that contained folders to keep class schedules, schoolwork, assignments and paper, with a flap to close it shut so it wouldn't lose anything. Today's high-tech version of the old Trapper-Keeper can do so much more: Take notes, calculate any equation, build reference lists, track lab results, compute GPA, predict class rank and take practice quizzes. These PDAs (that's personal digital assistants, *not* public displays of affection!) are capable of even more when they become wireless communication devices. You can research the Internet, send email, do instant messaging and even map directions via a global positioning satellite system (GPS). Add beaming capabilities and you can begin to see why downloading family members' schedules might be the only way for parents to keep up with their kids.

Two-way radio sets for families have become big sellers over the past number of years. Because they operate on the Family Radio Service (FRS) frequencies – a re-classified band of radio frequencies set aside by the FCC for family and recreational use – these radios require no licensing or service fees for usage. With a range of up to two miles (depending on terrain and conditions) these high-powered walkie-talkies are "ideal for families who want to stay in touch while roaming the mall."[40] Manufactured by Panasonic, Motorola and other name-brand companies, you're sure to see these become family-issued for all non-cell phone toting kids.

Pagers have been a relatively low-cost entry-level way for parents to stay in touch with their kids and vice versa. Compared to cell phones they're a lot less expensive and there are many different options available starting with basic local numeric-only paging for around $7 per month. Two-way paging has caught on big-time and Motorola's TalkAbout pagers are heavily marketed to kids with their Aqua Ice, Razberry Ice, Mystic Blue and Opaque Black color options. With this pager, not only can you send your kids a text message via email or another pager, but they can respond using the pager's mini keyboard. Timex, SkyTel, Motorola and Yahoo even teamed up, dreamed up and beamed up "from web to wrist" a new Internet Messenger Watch. Capable of receiving emails, headline news, sports, weather, alpha-numeric pages with easy-to-read scrolling and silent or sound alerts, this pager-watch combination would have made Dick Tracy salivate!

Cell-phone family plans have sprung up all over the country. AT&T Wireless has their "Family Plan," Sprint has their "Free & Clear Family Plan," Verizon Wireless has a "Family Share Plan," Nextel has "Direct Connect" and SBC Wireless has "Family Talk." According to Teenage Research Unlimited, one out of five American teens owns a cell phone and, among kids who don't, "it's the most-sought-after coming-of-age badge on their shopping lists."[41]

As prices continue to fall and multi-year contracts disappear, cell phones become a more cost effective and convenient way for families to stay connected. Cricket Communications, a Dallas based Lead Wireless service, has "The Around-Town Phone" plan which gives people the ability to make unlimited local calls and receive calls from anywhere in the world for one low monthly price of $19.99! In many areas of the U.S. that's cheaper than adding a second line for the kids.

Want to keep your family close? Then how about a Stay-Close Alarm! Simply attach the transmitter to your toddler-aged child and the receiver on your belt. The receiver will beep loudly when it reaches a set distance from the transmitter. Originally designed to ensure your luggage stays close to you during travels, this easy-to-use personal alarm is also a great way to keep track of small children in crowded areas.

As your kid gets older you may want to give them more freedom, but still want to keep tabs on them. What you need is a Personal Location System. Hey, it works for pets and cars, so why not kids! Companies like Wherify, Locate Networks and Digital Angel all rely on GPS to track their every movement. If they're in trouble they can even press two buttons on the watch-like unit to summon police. Imagine being able to log on to a secure web site and find your kid 24/7/365. Certainly makes "being where you said you'd be" and "getting home for curfew" an excuseless exercise. One company, "Applied Digital Solutions scrapped plans in 2001 to market the device as a subdermal implant for children due to negative public feedback."[42] That changed however in 2002 when the Food and Drug Administration gave the company the go ahead stating that "it wouldn't regulate the implant as a medical device, as long as it doesn't hold medical records."[43]

Now, before you run out and buy any of these products and/or services for your kids, consider a few questions. Does your preschooler really need a day planner when all they can write is their name? Would that PDA be used more for games than grades? Do you need constant two-way radio contact on your family shopping trip or vacation? Has your kid's school banned pagers and cell phones? Are you so unaware of your toddler that you need an alarm to keep them close? Would you really want to track your kid's whereabouts using satellite technology? Have our kids become that overscheduled and our families that under-connected?

Perhaps there are some lower-tech, lower-cost and more stay-in-touch methods we can use to combat over-scheduling families and kids:

✔ **Plan ahead and get organized** – Be smart about leaving a little extra time for the unexpected. Remember "getting ready" might mean something different to your kids versus you. Set a good example and model planning ahead in day-to-day life for your kids as much as possible.

✔ **Create schedules** – Some things need to happen every day, every week, every month, every year. Create a kind of master schedule that can help every member of the family know what's happening when. Remember to plan for some down time to do something "unhurried" every day. Make weekends less structured than weekdays. Maintain family rituals, traditions, holidays and events.

✔ **More isn't better** – Become aware of your motives to "keep up with the Joneses" and squelch or downplay your kids request for more "I want what my friends have!"

✔ **Earlier isn't always better** – Try not to fall into the trap that says if your kid starts earlier in life, he'll be better for it when he's older.

✔ **Leave enough time** – Depending on your kid's age, different things take different amounts of time.

✔ **Do unhurried activities** – Start thinking about doing things that can be unhurried and enjoyed in their "own sweet time."

✔ **Connect with your kids** – If you're always in a hurry, kids can interpret that to mean your thoughts are actually elsewhere. Sometimes kids dawdle *just* to get your attention – it's their way of checking to see if you're still tuned in to them!

✔ **Respect each other's needs** – Rather than always telling kids "what to do and when to do it," respect and encourage their developing sense of autonomy and self-control. This will obviously vary depending on age. Young kids are more "here and now" aware, so planning ahead doesn't come naturally to them.

Give advance warning in simple terms they understand (i.e. "we'll have to leave in five minutes") and look for a good place to stop (e.g. reading to the end of a chapter).

✔ **Talk with your spouse** – Tag-team parenting works best when both of you have the same game-plan. Take the time to plan ahead what limits you want to maintain for your family before the world invades your home.

✔ **Walk the talk** – Like so many things in life actions speak louder than words. Check your own priorities, perspective and the tone you set as an example in doing what you do.

✔ **Create extended family and grandparent time** – Divorce and long-distance relatives have become a norm in our world. Whenever possible, create times when kids can connect with their extended family and grandparents.

– Adapted from YMCA Parent Tips: Beating the Frantic Family Syndrome[44] and Take Back Your Kids by William Doherty[38]

Speaking of grandparent time, there's no keeping up with Grandma and Grandpa these days. Today's grandma is no longer in the kitchen with the visiting grandkids baking cookies. There's no time to go fishing with Grandpa either. They're both emailing their grandchildren and dovetailing travel itineraries with soccer tournament schedules so they can see them play. Not only that, but grandparents are busier themselves – perhaps because they're younger, wealthier and much more active than any previous generation of grandparents.

BTWFYI: Here are a few resources to help connect grandparents and grandkids in today's over-scheduled world:
Contemporary Grandparenting by Dr. Arthur Kornhaber
How to Build the Grandma Connection by Susan Bosak
http://www.civitas.org/grandparents.html
http://www.grandparenting.org
http://www.grandsplace.com
http://www.igrandparents.com

Poor family relationships are related to many of the problems in society. Nick Stinnett, University of Alabama, and John DeFrain, University of Nebraska-Lincoln, are two family researchers who have spent over 25 years looking at more than 17,000 families in the most extensive study of family strengths in the world. They state "spending time together – quality time in large quantities – has been found to be one of the six characteristics in families who seem best prepared to meet the challenges of modern-day living."[45]

Granted, technology should be able to help us better coordinate our schedules giving us more time to share with our families. Computers and television enables us to know more about what's going on in the world. We have higher quality media-based informational resources and entertainment options than ever before in our homes. All of which dominates both our lives and our living rooms – effectively squelching out opportunities for families to spend time together. Rather than meeting the challenges of modern-day living, many families seem overrun by it. The technology, media/TV and our increasingly hurried up 24/7/365 lifestyle dominates most kids' homes. The over-participation, developmental inappropriateness, and increased over-scheduling of activity for families and kids today threaten both the quantity and quality of time they spend together.

BOOKS ABOUT TECHNOLOGY, MEDIA/TV 24/7/365

Computers and Children: A New Report
by http://www.allianceforchildhood.net

Pushed to the Edge
by Donna Corwin

Putting Family First
by William Doherty and Barbara Carlson

Failure to Connect: How Computers Affect Our Children's Minds
by Jane Healy

Stay Tuned!
by Jane Murphy and Karen Carlson

The Flickering Mind
by Todd Oppenheimer

Glued to the Tube
by Cheryl Pawlowski

Amusing Ourselves to Death
How to Watch TV News
The Disappearance of Childhood
Technopoly: The Surrender of Culture to Technology
by Neil Postman

The Over-Scheduled Child
by Alvin Rosenfeld & Nicole Wise

Growing Up Digital
by Don Tapscott

TV Or No TV: A Primer on the Psychology of Television
by Fay Steuer and Jason Hustedt

The Plug-In Drug: Television, Computers and Family Life
by Marie Winn

ACME Media Education	http://www.acmecoalition.org
Alliance for Media Literacy	http://www.amlainfo.org
Center for Media Literacy	http://www.medialit.org
Children's Media Project	http://www.childrensmediaproject.org
Enough is Enough	http://www.enough.org
Family Night a Month	http://www.familynightamonth.org
GetNetWise	http://www.getnetwise.org
Hyper-Parenting	http://www.hyperparenting.com
Independent Media Institute	http://www.independentmedia.org
Just Think	http://www.justthink.org
Kill Your Television	http://www.turnoffyourtv.com
Learning in the Real World	http://www.realworld.org
LimiTV	http://www.limitv.org
Listen Up! Youth Media	http://www.listenup.org
Kids-In-Mind	http://www.kids-in-mind.com
Media and the Family	http://www.mediafamily.org
Media Literacy Project	http://www.nmmlp.org
Media Matters	http://www.aap.org/advocacy/mediamatters.htm
MediaChannel	http://www.mediachannel.org
Mediascope	http://www.mediascope.org
Net Family News	http://www.netfamilynews.org
New American Dream	http://www.newdream.org
ProtectKids.com	http://www.protectkids.com
Putting Family First	http://www.puttingfamilyfirst.org
SafeKids.com	http://www.safekids.com
SafeTeens.com	http://www.safeteens.com
Screen It!	http://www.screenit.com
Software Ratings Board	http://www.esrb.org
Teen Health & the Media	http://www.teenhealthandthemedia.net
The Media Project	http://www.themediaproject.com

ThirdPath Institute	http://www.thirdpath.org
TV Turnoff Network	http://www.tvturnoff.org
Violence on TV	http://www.apa.org/pubinfo/violence.html
Yahooligans Parent Guide	http://yahooligans.yahoo.com/parents/

1.   Healey, J. R. (2000, April 26). Ford makes room for appliances in minivan. *USA Today,* p. 12.

2.   Sony Corporation. (2000). *AIBO Story* [Online]. Sony Corporation. http://www.sony.net/Products/aibo/index.html

3.   Schor, J. B. (1991). *The Overworked American.* New York: Basic Books.

4.   Council of Economic Advisors. (1999). *The Parenting Deficit: Council of Economic Advisors Analyze the "Time Crunch"* [Online]. White House Council of Economic Advisors. http://www.whitehouse.gov/WH/EOP/CEA/html/famfinal.pdf

5.   Robinson, J. P., & Godbey, G. (1997). *Time for Life: The Surprising Ways Americans Use their Time.* State College, PA: Pennsylvania State University Press.

6.   Kaiser Family Foundation. (1999). *Kids & Media @ The New Millennium.*

7.   Fattah, H. (2001, February). Direct Access: Satellite providers dish up new demos for advertisers. *American Demographics, 23,* 30-33.

8.   Murray, J. P. (2001). *Impact of Televised Violence* [Online]. Kansas State University. http://www.ksu.edu/humec/impact.htm

9.   ABC News. (2000). *Should You Let Them Watch?, 20/20.* New York. http://more.abcnews.go.com/onair/2020/2020friday_001020 _violence_feature.html

10.   Kaiser Family Foundation. (2001). *Sex On TV(2).*

11.   Cutler, J. (2001, March 25). Responsible sex still lacking in primetime TV. *Dayton Daily News,* p. 4.

12.   Kaiser Family Foundation. (2004). *The Role of Media in Childhood Obesity* (Online).

13.   McKeown, L. A. (2001). *Even Kids Under 3 Watch Too Much TV* [Online]. WebMD. http://www.my.webmd.com/article/1728.79081

14.   Pawlowski, C. (2000). *Glued to the Tube: The Threat of Television Addiction to Today's Family.* Naperville, IL: Sourcebooks, Inc.

15. Scheibe, C. (2002). *Television in the Lives of Children* [Online]. Center for Research on the Effects of Television. http://www.ithaca.edu/cretv/

16. Center for Media Education. (2003). *Children and Television* [Online]. http://www.cme.org

17. Singer, D. G., Singer, J. L., & Zuckerman, D. M. (1990). *The Parents Guide: Use TV to Your Child's Advantage*. Reston, VA: Acropolis Books Ltd.

18. Bushman, B. J., & Cantor, J. (2003). Media Ratings for Violence and Sex. *American Psychologist, 58*(2), 130-141.

19. Wood, A. (1997). *Teletubbies*. London: Ragdoll Ltd./PBSKids. http://pbskids.org/teletubbies/

20. Rushkoff, D. (1999). *Playing the Future: What We Can Learn from Digital Kids* (2nd ed.). New York: Riverhead Books.

21. Chapman, K. (1999). *Bob the Builder*. London: HIT Entertainment PLC. http://www.bobthebuilder.com

22. Leach, S. (1987). *Barney & Friends*. Dallas, TX: HIT Entertainment PLC/PBSKids. http://pbskids.org/barney/

23. HIT Entertainment PLC. (2001). *Annual Report & Accounts*. London: HIT Entertainment PLC.

24. PBS. (1999). *The Educational Approach Of Barney & Friends* [Online]. http://pbskids.org/barney/pareduc/parents/philosophy.html

25. Kriegman, M. (1998). *Bear in the Big Blue House*: Jim Henson Company. http://www.bearinthebigbluehouse.com

26. Jinkins, J., & Campbell, D. (2001). *Stanley*. New York: Cartoon Pizza Inc./Disney. http://disney.go.com/disneychannel/playhouse/stanley/

27. Gifford, C., Walsh, V., & Weiner, E. (2000). *Dora the Explorer*: Nickelodeon/Viacom International. http://www.nickjr.com/home/shows/dora/index.jhtml

28. Joyce, W. (1999). *Rolie Polie Olie*. Burbank, CA: Buena Vista/Disney. http://disney.go.com/disneychannel/playhouse/rpo/index.html

29. HarperCollins. (1999). *An Interview with William Joyce* [Online]. http://www.harperchildrens.com/catalog/author_interview_x ml.asp?authorid=22151

30. Tan, A. (1994). *Sagwa: The Chinese Siamese Cat*: CinéGroupe Sagwa Inc. http://pbskids.org/sagwa/

31. WGBH (2000). *Between the Lions*. In WGBH Boston and Sirius Thinking Ltd. (Producers). Boston: WGBH Educational Foundation. http://pbskids.org/lions/

32. McCracken, C. (1992). *Powerpuff Girls*: Cartoon Network. http://www.powerpuffgirls.com

33. American Greetings Corporation. (1983). *Care Bears*. Cleveland, OH: American Greetings Corporation. http://www.care-bears.com

34. Allcroft, B. (1984). *Thomas & Friends, Thomas the Tank Engine & Friends*. London: Anchor Bay Entertainment/HIT Entertainment PLC. http://www.thomasthetankengine.com

35. Vischer, P., & Nawrocki, M. (1993). *VeggieTales*. Lombard, IL: Big Idea Productions. http://www.bigidea.com

36. WRGT-TV Productions. (1993). *TeenTalk*. In D. Dodge, F. Kick, B. Kline & L. Short (Producers). Dayton, OH.

37. Rosemond, J. (1996, March). The Frantic Family Syndrome: A family with too many activities does not always indicate good parenting. *Better Homes & Gardens*.

38. Doherty, W. J. (2002). *Take Back Your Kids: Confident Parenting in Turbulent Times*. Notre Dame, IN: Sorin Books.

39. FranklinCovey. (2001). *Student Achievement Center* [Online]. FranklinCovey. http://www.franklincovey.com/promotion/student/index.htm

40. Family-Radios.com. (2001). *FRS Two-Way Family Radios* [Online]. AHERN. http://www.family-radio.com

41. Armstrong, L. (2000, September 25). Mom, Can I Have a Cell Phone? *Business Week*.

42. Gaska, C. L. (2001, June 15). Parent Tech. *American Way, June 2001*, 64-69.

43. Associated Press. (2002, April 5). Applied Digital to Sell ID Chip That Goes Under the Skin. *Wall Street Journal*, p. 6.

44. YMCA of the USA. (2002). *YMCA Parent Tips: Beating the Frantic Family Syndrome* [Online]. http://www.ymca.net/programs/family/ptfrantic.htm

45. University of Nebraska College of Human Resources and Family Science. (2000). *NU for Families* [Online]. University of Nebraska. http://nuforfamilies.unl.edu

Chapter Four

Today's Kids are Active

Talk about a 24/7/365 generation, Millennials really KICK IT IN!
Overall there are *more* activities, *more* participation, and *more*
involvement from *more* kids than ever before. Compared to Xers,
today's youth are making things happen both in school and out of
school with sports, the arts, youth groups, volunteerism, community
service, clubs and all kinds of organizational activities. While it's
refreshing to see so many kids involved, a couple underlying
concerns emerge when you look closely. Many who do partake in
this seemingly endless parade of participation are living at one end of
the socioeconomic spectrum, while kids who don't live at the other.
There's also a growing group of kids showing signs of stress from
over-participating – sometimes at developmentally inappropriate
levels – and over-scheduling themselves to the point that some
would suggest they need help learning how to kick back.

Youth Sports

Perhaps nowhere else in a kid's life has over-participation, developmental inappropriateness and over-scheduling combined to an all-time – and sometimes beyond belief – level than in organized youth sports. Kids today live in a world where:

- T-Ball leagues start kids as young as four and five years old who end up humorously entertaining parents.

- First-graders are playing full contact football in pads and helmets. Their leagues rival the NFL in organizational effectiveness with a pre-season draft and protected players. Two weeks of summer practice 5 to 8 P.M. Monday through Friday. Games every single weekend. (Oh yeah, they have first-grade cheerleaders too – tryouts and all that goes with it!)

- Second-graders "trying out" for an intramural basketball league spend three days in a gym with seven coaches toting clipboards, running drills, and making notes.

- Little League baseball has become a part-time job for elementary kids who "just want to play" – supposedly this kind of mud-level interest requires a ten-plus hour a week commitment.

- All-Star games and tournaments add more time and more travel to the season as well as increased competition.

- Traveling soccer team leagues cover multi-state regions with eight-year-olds practicing two hours three nights a week and one to two games each weekend. Away tournaments can even create four-game weekends with hotel, meal and travel expenses.

- Motocross phenomenon Travis Pastrana started racing motorbikes when he was only four years old and signed with Suzuki when he was eight.[1]

- In Potomac, Maryland, 12-year-old Freddy Adu's mother rejected a $750,000 offer from a renowned Italian soccer club for her son to play for them.

- Ty Tyon, age 17, turns pro and hopes to join the PGA Tour and chase Tiger Woods (who waited until he had attended Stanford University for two years before he turned pro).[2]

Mick Jordan, an American Youth Soccer Organization (AYSO) volunteer commissioner, notes: "When we were growing up, kids didn't have all these organizations and parental volunteers. They just went to the playground and played." He was quoted in the *Palo Alto Weekly* by Mike Naar, who went on to say, "The Little League parent now has been joined by the 'soccer mom' and the volunteer parent – nearly a full-time job in many cases. Throw in piano lessons, an after-school activity or two, multiple practice sessions and you're getting more depreciation on the Suburban than appreciation for what you do. Two kids means doing double-time, and three or more mean you and your spouse have now gone from playing man-to-man to playing a zone."[3]

Best estimates in the U.S. say over 40 million kids play in organized youth sports.[4] Studies have indicated that 70 percent of those 40 million kids will quit by the age of 13 largely due to unpleasant experiences. When you consider win-at-all-cost coaches, overzealous parents, untrained youth league administrators, and a significant lack of sportsmanship being modeled or developed, it's no wonder that:

- 45.3% of kids surveyed said adults called them names, yelled and insulted them in a game or practice.

- 21.5% had been pressured to play when injured.

- 17.5% reported even being physically hit by an adult in a game or practice.

- 8% had been pressured to intentionally harm others.[5]

Maybe that's why the American Academy of Pediatrics issued a policy statement in June 2001 entitled *Organized Sports for Children and Preadolescents*. In it they state "that when the demands and expectations of organized sports exceed the maturation and readiness of the participant, the positive aspects of participation can be negated. The shift from child-oriented goals to adult-oriented goals can further negate positive aspects of organized sports."[6]

Physically, socially, and mentally, youth sports can be both good and bad. Depending on the age of the player and their physical as well as emotional development, youth sports do offer many positive benefits. Physically youth sports should be more than just a fun worthwhile leisure-time activity. With knowledgeable coaches, kids gain higher levels of physical fitness, acquire increased skills and agility. Socially youth sports can provide opportunities to make new friends and offer an ever-expanding social network for kids. Given appropriate parental involvement, organized sports can even bring families closer together, heightening the overall value of the experience. Mentally, kids learn about self-control, taking risks, cooperation, dealing with success, failure and competition. Attitudes about achievement, respect for authority, persistence, motivation, self-discipline, self-esteem, sportsmanship, and self-confidence psychologically influence the "mental side of the game" for kids both on and off the field.

But what about the "mental side of the game?" While most athletes will say that 70 percent of their performance is mental and that 99 percent of all the mistakes or errors they make are mental mistakes or errors,[7] how much practice time is allocated in youth sports to mental skills versus physical skills?

The irony with many of these adult organized youth sports leagues lies in the fact that high-school coaches consider them community feeder programs into their competitive varsity teams. The logic seems to be that starting more kids at a younger age makes the pool of possible players bigger and deeper. These are professional educators who have advanced degrees in education, child development, counseling, psychology and physical education. They know better, but for some reason – and in some cases in spite of their own efforts to curb this early childhood sports abuse – the game must go on.

Why? Isn't the ultimate focus of youth sports supposed to be youth? Have we lost our perspective and become sucked into the game to the point that we're having four-year-olds entertain adults. Is it really "good for the kids?" Is it even what the kids want? So what if "everyone else is doing it." Starting kids early doesn't determine their ultimate level of success on the field or in life. Actually it could do more harm than good.

The game of youth sports has literally become a "machine" where kids, parents and coaches strive for "the edge."[8]

- Participating in showcase tournaments where individual players pay upwards of $1,000 each to play in front of college coaches and scouts. Often the fee includes a player packet containing glowing profiles or scouting reports with statistics, bios, skills and strengths.

- Sports psychologists counseling kids as young as nine years old for $100 to $500 per one-hour session.

- Recruiters scouting out the seven to eight year old "everyone plays" recreation league games for future players in their traveling club teams.

- Specialty coaches teaching kids as young as three years old hitting, jumping, footwork, and other personalized skill exercises for $150 per session.

- Forcing kids to choose a "specialty" sport even before they finish elementary school.

- The number of kids being treated for overuse injuries has been skyrocketing according to the National Youth Sports Safety Foundation http://www.nyssf.org

- The cost of youth sports-related injuries for kids 14 and under went from $581 million in 1982 to $3.78 billion in 1997.

- Traveling club team board members conducting nationwide and worldwide searches for full-time league coaching positions paying salaries as high as $90,000 a year.

All this to reach the "brass rings" of the youth sporting world – winning, being "the best," making the varsity team, college scholarships, fame, recognition, parents who get to live vicariously through their kids' experiences, big time pro contracts, multi-million dollar advertising endorsements – *wait a minute! Time out!* This is youth sports! Isn't it supposed to be about the kids? Having fun? Making new friends? Learning to play? Well, maybe learning to "play the game" so they can "win the game" – apparently at any cost.

Darrell Burnett, Ph.D., from the Center for Sports Parenting, says research shows most kids playing youth sports actually put winning near the bottom of the list in terms of their motivation. Kids were given two scenarios and asked to pick one. First, being on a really good team and not playing very much; and second, being on a team that wasn't so good, but you get to play most of the time. Burnett reports: "90% of the kids picked #2, saying they just want to play!"[9] In other studies, "having fun" ranks as the main reason kids ages 5 to 17 play sports.[10] Other reasons identified over and over again were: activity and involvement, improvement and skill-building, the physical thrill, friendships, social recognition and attention.

Many parents will say, "Well, at least they're not just sitting at home watching television. It's good exercise and that's important." Yes it is and yet, as sports psychologist Shane Murphy would point out, "as a vehicle for sponsoring mass participation in physical activity, youth sports programs are a huge failure. Researchers have not been able to show that early childhood involvement in youth sports promotes a healthy and active adult lifestyle. We encourage our children to get involved in sports in huge numbers, then we keep restricting their opportunities to participate. By late adolescence, only a few are still playing. Instead we train our children to worship the 'great' athletes on television, we teach them to be spectators rather than participants, and we severely limit their chances to play the games they love. Of course, as adults they end up as passive sports followers rather than as energetic, involved athletic individuals. Is this what you want for your child?"[10] Of course not.

"The culture of youth sports in many cases, is out of control. Youth sports have become less about fun and more about pressure."[11]
                                    – Jack Llewellyn, author of *Let 'em Play*

"I have come to realize that youth sports programs in America are in crisis."[10]
                    – Shane Murphy, author of *The Cheers and the Tears* and
          former head of sport psychology for the U.S. Olympic Committee

So what's a concerned parent to do? Well, amazing as it may seem, very few large youth sports organizations, youth sport experts or advocates have come to any conclusions as to what ages are best to start various youth sports, what sports when, or even to guidelines as per the number of practices, games, and time involved. Dr. Chris Carr, sports psychologist explains, "I would be surprised if you found any definitive statements regarding when a kid should start, in what sport, and so on."[12]

Everyone from the PTA, The National Alliance for Youth Sports, the Institute for International Sport Center and the American Academy of Pediatrics offer policy statements on organized sports for children. All of them recommend non-definitive, somewhat generalized, often vague suggestions. No one wants to draw any lines in the sand in terms of recommendations because all kids are different, develop differently and are capable of different things at different points of their childhood. There are however a few guidelines that must be kept in mind with regards to youth sports. Development of young athletes has been studied and certain stages do seem to emerge that require a more sensible approach to youth sports. Even the NFL determined that helmets, pads, and any type of contact were unsuitable for kids ages eight and younger.[13]

✔ **Keep it fun** – Youth sports first and foremost need to be fun! Too many times the pressures on parents and kids squeezes the very fun out of youth sports. The National Recreation & Parks Association with funding from the National Football League commissioned North Carolina State University to develop the *FUN FIRST! Sports for Kids Program.* "Research indicates that parent behaviors have a direct and significant effect on the benefits their child receives from sports and most importantly, the fun they experience through sports participation."[14]

✔ **Consider ages five to twelve an "Exploration"** – Introduce your kid to a variety of sports. Emphasize fun and basic skill development that's age appropriate. Minimize the competitive atmosphere. Look for positive coaching and a playful approach. Remember that kids do have open growth plates – soft cartilage areas near the center of a child's bones – responsible for the growth of growing bones. For kids under age twelve, open growth plates and the surrounding areas are prone to fracture. The younger the player, the greater risk for serious injury. Kids ages five to seven have bones two-to-five times weaker than in late-adolescence.[15]

✔ **Find alternative solutions** – many times there is more than one league represented in an area. Some in fact have started to limit the number of games and practices. In many areas there are even "Saturday Only" leagues.

✔ **Look for NYSCA Certified coaches** – Talk with local school athletic directors and your local parks & recreation directors as they tend to keep tabs on the who and the what in area sports. http://www.nays.org/IntMain.cfm?Cat=3&Page=1

✔ **Wait** – Try not to fall into the trap that says if your kid starts football at age three, he'll be better when he's thirteen. Research doesn't support this and doctors would surely disagree. When a neighbor says "they've got to learn sometime" or "the sooner the better," politely remind them about being certain it's something developmentally appropriate for your kid.

✔ **Start smart** – If you do feel you and your child are ready to (and need to) start sports young (ages 3 to 5) then look for a "parent with child" instructionally based program that teaches developmentally appropriate basic sport skills without the threat of competition or the fear of getting hurt. For information on parents working together with children in a supportive environment to learn all of the basic sports skills like running, throwing, catching, kicking, and batting check out: http://www.nays.org/IntMain.cfm?Page=56&Cat=9

✔ **Everyone plays in every position** – Keep youth sports an all-inclusive experience with everyone playing more than they stand around waiting. Learning the various positions rather than getting slotted into one makes the learning much more valuable.

✔ **Teaching vs. touring** – Progressively learning and getting better, increasing competence and confidence requires more teaching and less touring. Save the weekend tournaments for high school.

✔ **Keep *youth* sports in the proper perspective** – It's supposed to be all about the kids, not the coaches or parents.[16]

BTWFYI: For additional information on the *true* value of sports for kids and some of the many myths from a parent's perspective, check out this thoughtful article at http://www.accta.com/sports.html
Books to read and web sites to visit include:
Just Let the Kids Play by Bob Bigelow, Tom Moroney & Linda Hall
Why Johnny Hates Sports by Fred Engh
A Balancing Act: Sports and Education by Gary Funk
Fair Play by Scott Lancaster

Raising a Good Sport in an In-Your-Face World by George Selleck
The Cheers and the Tears by Shane Murphy
For the Fun of It by Bob Rodda
Way to Go Coach by Ronald Smith & Frank Smoll
Positive Coaching by Jim Thompson
American Sport Education Program http://www.asep.com
Center for Sports Parenting http://www.sportsparenting.org
MomsTeam http://www.momsteam.com
National Alliance for Youth Sports http://www.nays.org
National Recreation & Park Association http://www.nrpa.org
Positive Coaching Alliance http://www.positivecoach.org
Time Out! http://www.timeoutforbettersportsforkids.org
Youth Sports Institute http://ed-web3.educ.msu.edu/ysi/

Youth in the arts

There's an interesting trend that's been happening in the arts education world just as the Millennial Generation emerged. Today more and more research is discovering more and more benefit to arts education. With more and more kids to participate as well, this double crescendo of advocacy and support for the arts has yielded an explosion of participation. In most circles of educated administrators, the arts have moved from "frivolous add-ons to a serious curriculum."[17]

A report based on the analysis of 62 different studies from various areas of art education (music, drama, dance and visual arts) conducted by 100 researchers found "important relationships between learning in the arts and cognitive capacities (thinking skills) and motivations that underlie academic achievement and effective social behavior." The report entitled *Critical Links* went on to suggest "that for certain populations – students from economically disadvantaged circumstances, students needing remedial instruction, and young children – learning the arts may be especially helpful in boosting learning and achievement."[18]

James Catterall, one of the contributing researchers and a professor of education at UCLA, states: "*Critical Links* shows two clear streams of outcomes for economically disadvantaged children. One is a set of effects related to skills basic reading comprehension for children who have in fact been 'left behind.' An added set of effects for these children is increased achievement motivation. Feelings of competence and engagement can impact outlook and approach to studies more generally and research on the arts finds impacts showing both increased attendance and fewer discipline referrals."[19] Specifically, the report found critical links in the following six major areas to arts education:

❑ **Reading and language development** including basic reading skills, literacy and writing.

❑ **Mathematics** by developing spatial-temporal reasoning and understanding relations of ideas and objects in space in time.

❑ **Fundamental cognitive skills and capacities** which engage and strengthen spatial reasoning (the capacity for organizing and sequencing ideas); conditional reasoning (theorizing about outcomes and consequences); problem-solving; and the components of creative thinking (originality, elaboration, and flexibility).

❑ **Motivations to learn** and the attitudes and dispositions to pursue and sustain learning including active engagement, disciplined and sustained attention, persistence, risk-taking, increased attendance and higher educational aspirations.

❑ **Effective social behavior** and growth in self-confidence, self-control, self-identity, conflict-resolution, collaboration, empathy and social tolerance.

❑ **School environment** conducive to student and teacher success.

"While education in the arts is no magic bullet for what ails many schools, the arts warrant a place in the curriculum because of their intimate ties to most everything we want for our children and schools,"[17] Catterall says. He suggested some "might call the arts the Cal Ripkin of American education"[19] due to the long scorecard this compendium of research, studies, and analysis presents. All in all 84 separately distinguishable, valid effects of the arts were differentiated among groups of students who benefit from participation in the arts. In addition, various art forms were found to help students in different ways:

✔ **Music** – Improves math achievement and proficiency, reading and cognitive development; boosts SAT verbal scores and skills for second language learners.

✔ **Drama** – Helps with understanding social relationships, complex issues and emotions; improves concentrated thought and story comprehension.

✔ **Dance** – Helps with creative thinking, originality, elaboration and flexibility; improves expressive skills, social tolerance, self-confidence and persistence.

✔ **Visual Arts** – Improve content and organization of writing; promote sophisticated reading skills and interpretation of text, reasoning about scientific images and reading readiness.

✔ **Multi-arts** (combination of art forms) – Helps with reading, verbal and math skills; improves the ability to collaborate and higher-order thinking skills.

The report, which took two years to produce and was funded by the U.S. Department of Education and the National Endowment for the Arts, benchmarks a new starting place for future research in arts education representing a "comprehensive picture of what research-based knowledge exists."[17] That's according to Gerald Sroufe of the American Educational Research Association. "It's the first to combine all the arts and make comparisons with academic achievement, performance on standardized tests, improvements in social skills and student motivation." While copies of the report were distributed to school leaders across the country upon its release, Thomas Houlihan, executive director for the Council of Chief State School Officers, acknowledged that too many superintendents, principals and teachers are still unaware of the value of arts education.

STRIKE UP THE BAND ...AND THE ORCHESTRA ...AND THE CHOIR!

More kids are playing and singing than ever before. The amazing growth in music education across this country overall since the late 1980s has risen non-stop. The music products industry grew for an unprecedented twelve straight years – from 1989 to 2000. Even in spite of 9/11 and an economic slowdown, the music products industry still experienced two record-setting years in a row ($6.8 billion in 2001 and $7.1 billion in 2000). Half of all households in America have at least one person age five or older who currently plays a musical instrument. Forty percent have two or more. This proportion has been increasing substantially over the 38 and 34 percent respectively that was reported back in 1997.[20] Positive public support for music education continues to crescendo. The Gallup Organization conducted a survey in 2000 and found that:

98% agree that playing a musical instrument provides life-long enjoyment
97% believe school band is a good way for young people to develop teamwork
97% agree that playing a musical instrument is a good hobby
97% agree that playing a musical instrument is a good means of self-expression
96% agree that playing a musical instrument teaches appreciation for the arts and culture
95% of respondents agree music should be a part of a well-rounded education
95% believe it provides a sense of accomplishment
93% feel all schools should offer instrumental music as part of the regular curriculum
93% agree that playing a musical instrument is fun
92% agree that playing a musical instrument helps children make friends
90% agree that music brings the family together
89% agree that playing a musical instrument teaches discipline
87% agree that music is a very important part of life
85% wished they had learned to play a musical instrument
81% agree participation in a school music program corresponds to better grades/test scores
78% agree that states should mandate music education in schools
75% agree that learning a musical instrument helps you do better in other subjects
73% believe teenagers who play an instrument are less likely to have discipline problems

– From *American's Attitudes Toward Music, Music Making and Music Education*[21]

Over three million students participate in school music programs and 90 percent of them go on to college. They're in the top 26 percent of their class academically and represent every community in the U.S. That's according to one of the premiere presenters of music events for high school students – Bands of America http://www.bands.org. Creating "positively life-changing" experiences since 1975, this unique organization annually brings together over 80,000 students participating in more than 25 events nationwide to a collective audience topping 230,000 family members and music enthusiasts.[22]

Why is this significant? Two reasons: First, music students are smart students. Besides going to college at such a higher percentage and sitting in the top quarter of their classes, music students:

- Are less disruptive in class (i.e. number of times in trouble, skipping classes, in-school suspensions, disciplinary actions taken, arrests and drop-outs)[23]

- Score higher on the SAT – up 57 to 63 points on verbal, 41 to 44 on math in 2001.[24] Students in public school music programs scored overall 107 points higher on their SATs than students who didn't participate in 2002.[25]

- Have the lowest lifetime and current use of *all* substances (tobacco, alcohol and illicit drugs)[26]

- Show significantly higher math proficiency by 12th grade[27]

- Are admitted into medical school at a higher percentage rate (FYI: 66% = highest percentage of any group! Only 44% of biochemistry majors were admitted)[28]

- Show significant increases in self-esteem and thinking skills[29]

- Earn more As and Bs as grades in class and receive more academic honors and awards[30]

- Have a larger brain region called the *planum temorale* (related to some reading skills) and a thicker *corpus callosum* (nerve fiber bundle that connects the two halves of the brain)[31]

Second, music students tend to bring more socioeconomic clout with them into the workforce and marketplace. That's true for all of the arts given that the more arts education someone receives, the more likely they are to attend arts performances.[32]

- U.S. consumers spent $9.8 billion on admissions to performing arts events in 2000 and $10.2 billion in 1999. In comparison, the 1999 total was $2.8 billion *more* than consumers spent at movie theaters and $2 billion *more* than they spent for spectator sporting events.[33]

- From 1989 to 2000, performing arts events saw a 47% increase. By comparison during the same period of time, spending at movie theaters grew only 15% and spectator sports grew 45%.[33]

- In 2001, the National Governors Association reported an issue brief on the important role of the arts in economic development in the U.S.[34] In 2002, a second issue brief addressed the important impact of arts education on workforce preparation.[35]

- One in three kids in school today will end up working in an arts-related job at some point during their career.[36]

- According to the 2000 U.S. Bureau of Labor Statistics, more than 2 million people were employed – in primary jobs – as artists. FYI, that's 1.4% of the U.S. workforce. Compare that to elementary school teachers at 1.1%, accountants at 0.67%, lawyers at 0.47% and professional athletes at 0.04%.

- In 2000 the nonprofit arts sector alone was $134 billion.[37]

- The arts are America's second largest export and collectively the arts industry (profit and nonprofit) as a whole contributes over $857 billion per year to the U.S. economy.[38]

- In 2002, the National Governors Association reported an issue brief addressing the important impact of arts education on workforce preparation.[35]

Smart arts organizations know the demographics involved with their events. Bands of America, a 501(c)3 nonprofit educational organization, even conducts independent surveys of their programs. They *know* their audiences. In fact, 70 percent have a household income of over $40,000 and almost 40 percent have an income over $60,000.[22] Interestingly enough, the National Endowment for the Arts reports that "findings indicate that the higher one's socioeconomic status, the more arts education one received."[32] The same research report goes on to caution that "a busier lifestyle reduces one's rate of arts attendance." While there may be "bucks and brains" being in music, being *too* busy limits kids' opportunity to fully realize their musical potential.

"Just as there can be no music without education, no education is complete without music."

– Tim Lautzenheiser

BTWFYI: You'll find more music advocacy resources at:
American Music Conference http://www.amc-music.org
Music Achievement http://www.musicachievementcouncil.org
Music for All Foundation http://music-for-all.org
National Association for Music Education http://www.menc.org
Support Music http://www.supportmusic.com
The MusicEdge http://www.themusicedge.com
VH1 Save the Music http://www.vh1.com

THEATER, DRAMA, LIGHTS, CAMERA, ACTION!

Shakespeare said "all the world's a stage"[39] and there's no question that today's generation of kids has been raised to shine bright in many ways. A colleague of mine who has also spent years in the trenches working with and living with kids suggests this generation "craves the spotlight like no generation before so cast it in their direction and make them a star."[40] Perhaps that's why theater and drama has experienced a growing interest from kids.

"Today's theater offers a world of creative, intellectual, artistic, and physical work for kids who have grown up in the overly easy point and click era." That's according to Gloria Logan, a 30-year high school theater director whose tenure at Plymouth-Canton Education Park in Canton, Michigan (a high school outside Detroit), has both inspired and produced actors, awards and international acclaim. She suggests that kids today are drawn to the beauty of participating in a high school theater program because of the unique opportunity it provides for students to cooperatively meet the challenge of successful creative problem solving. "In Theater production, students achieve success through creative camaraderie. As a member of a Theater family they come to value the work of others as well as their own. They discover first hand that the best way to improve yourself is to improve the achievement level of those around you." Certainly the team-oriented disposition of today's kids connects with both the challenge in "creative problem solving" and the hard working, cooperative, family atmosphere in today's theater. "There is a sweetness in success that requires the whole person to sweat as part of a creative collective. It increases our human sensitivity to the needs of others – which rarely happens at an isolated computer station. Kids learn to use technology as a means to an end rather than as the end itself."[41]

It works for both sides of the spotlight too. Today's "Theatre kids" as Gloria calls them are all pieces of a whole production process rather than the on stage "half" and the off stage "half." Anyone who really understands theater production knows you can't think of them as independent "halves" when they are so intertwined and incomplete without each other. "I think when the adult leadership fosters that sense of unity it creates a happier and certainly more cohesive group and production product," Gloria suggests. "The kids who chose to work backstage exclusively feel just as satisfied and proud of the production as the kids who work visible to the audience. There's a wonderful musical called *WORKING* that has a lyric, 'Everyone should have something to point to, something to be proud of. Look what I did, see what I've done, I did the job.' One of the many positive effects of Theatre work for kids is that they experience how rewarding doing a good job can be without public acclaim, that giving your best to a group creation is reward in itself. Everyone enjoys being appreciated and awarded but the reason kids do all the hard work that producing Theatre requires has much more to do with the joy of belonging to a successful community than standing alone in the spotlight. Whether the sense of success comes from designing a complicated piece of scenery or simply pounding a nail without bending it, there is a true appreciation of contributing to the whole, knowing that the importance of a job lies in the fact that it needs doing – *not* in its level of difficulty."

One of the more unique organizations/events supporting the world of theater and drama education was actually started by someone who knows a great deal about this generation – and every generation for that matter – William Strauss. Besides co-authoring four generational books, Bill Strauss is co-founder and director of the Capitol Steps http://www.capsteps.com. This professional musical-satire troupe has performed over 7,000 shows, three PBS specials, and 50 radio shows for NPR. They've released 22 albums, two books and have performed off-Broadway many times with Strauss in the cast. In addition, Strauss has written two musicals; *MaKiddo* (a comic take-off on Gilbert & Sullivan's *The Mikado*, about gifted teenagers, pushy parents, high school stress over grades, standardized tests and college applications) and *Free-the-music.com* (about high-tech teenagers who like to upload and download songs and a big entertainment company that wants to stop them).

This background suddenly came in handy nearly four years ago, when the atrocities at Columbine High School gave him a chance to spotlight a different kind of high-school awards program. In May 1999, two weeks after Columbine, Strauss offered a U.S. Senate Committee a list of "what we can do" and advised adults to "signal that they value teenage contributions – in realms other than athletics – a little more. When community newspapers across America devote page after page to high-school sports and proms, while saying nothing about high-school arts or letters, they are feeding the Columbine problem. Historically, arts and letters have been the means by which young outcasts could vent their feelings in legitimate, and safe, ways."

Later that Spring, speaking with University of North Carolina student Michael McSwain, Strauss elaborated: "School personnel, parents, and students should try to identify the outcasts and find ways of engaging them more in school or community activities. Theater, music and other creative-arts programs can be important motivators for these kids, and can help connect them with student life."[42]

Bill Strauss began carrying out such a program, starting with 23 high schools in Northern Virginia. Calling on his Capitol Steps experience, Strauss created the "High School Critics and Awards Program" – or *Cappies* for short (as in *Grammys* and *Emmys*). It's cosponsored by the Capitol Steps and the Northern Virginia Theater Alliance, a group of three dozen artistic production companies. "He saw the *Cappies* as a way to counterbalance the negative press teenagers received following the tragedy at Columbine High School in Colorado. He also wanted to give recognition to students in theater arts who often don't have much attention paid to them in relation to sports. "The goal we had was to try to provide more positive community celebration of the great things that teenagers do," he said.

Here's how *The Washington Post* explained the process: "Each school designated one play or musical as its *Cappies* entry. Student critics from other schools reviewed the performances and submitted their work to faculty mentors, who forwarded the reviews to *The Washington Post* and local newspapers for publication, along with photos of the casts. The system not only gave students a chance to get published; it offered them an opportunity to learn from, and make friends with, peers at other schools – something rare in the past, students and teachers said."[43]

Two years later, The *New York Times* reported, "The original program of 23 high schools has grown to include 38 schools in Virginia and the District of Columbia, and the idea has spread to Dallas, El Paso, Las Vegas, Cincinnati and Eugene, Oregon."[44] *Cappies* are also getting started in Detroit, Kansas City, Long Island, Oklahoma City and Broward County, Florida. Washington, D.C., and other areas hold an annual "gala" to hand out awards and allow parts of plays and musicals to be performed.

BTWFYI: Faculty serious about launching a companion effort in their city or region can check out http://www.cappies.com which contains information about the *Cappies* program.

Meanwhile, how does Strauss see all of this activity in generational terms? Remember that, as of 2003, all of the kids in American high schools are Millennials. When I met with him at his Virginia home in August of 2002 for an interview, here's a bit of what we shared:

> STRAUSS: One thing about high-school theater is that it has never been better. Never, ever better. I have a feeling – I don't know this; I know it about theater, and you probably know it more [on the musical side] but – I have a feeling that bands and orchestras are better than ever, because of the skill levels. I suspect there are more kids with lessons [today] and the whole Millennial notion of working as a team must be translating into quality bands and orchestras.
>
> You look at theater, and you have way better instruction than you ever had before – in most places. There are some pockets where they're cutting it too much, but around here [in the D.C. suburbs] it's extraordinary. And you have kids with individual skill levels because they've had training. The perfect-child thing: You can dance – *dance, dance, dance, dance*! So when you get to high school, WOW!
>
> [Two-way laughter]
>
> STRAUSS: And you have the technology – it's the sound and light and other aspects of the theater. The staging that they do... And when you put it all together – kids with the skill levels; the parental support (check-writing and all that); the quality of the teachers; and the technology – every now and then, you walk into a high school, and you see a show that you would've paid fifty bucks to see! It's just really, really, really GOOD!

To anyone who has read his and Neil Howe's books, it's no surprise that Strauss sees theatrical trends paralleling the cyclical pattern of generational theory:

> And what's most interesting about high-school theater [is that] what they're "fixing" is in the exact opposite direction of what

Boomers "fixed" in the '60s. Boomers and Silents in the '60s were minimalizing – they were getting rid of the sets; they were going away from having these grand villages and country scenes. Instead, they had ladders and scaffolds and —

KICK: Right. A stool [laughs].

STRAUSS: Yeah, or a stool. Or they're dressed in black, rather than a grand, ornate costume – all dressed in black leotards. They even stripped harmonies out of singing, and choreography. When you watch Boomers do choreography, it's sort of the David Letterman "I'm hip, so I don't do it that well, and that's better" kind of thing. It's the old *Saturday Night Live* Chevy Chase kinda stuff.

So what do these kids do? *Exactly* the opposite: Big, teched-out, chorus lines, carefully choreographed. Team. Colossal. Colorful.

I saw a local high school do a Broadway review of the 20th century where they did one song from each decade. And it was quite fun because the kids picked it and then they designed the costumes and they directed it. It was totally Millennial culture – no X. And what they picked for the '60s was "Aquarius" from *Hair*.

And of course *Hair* was famous in New York for drawing a cast that couldn't sing because they were mainly looking for a cast that was stoned. Honestly – blue haze in the back. *Hey man! Alright, we'll cast you, alright yeah, so...* And you listen to the original cast album of *Hair*, and it's about at the vocal level of the below-average middle school – they just didn't sing well [laughter]. I shouldn't slander middle-school musicals; they do better than that.

KICK: [Laughs]

STRAUSS: So what they did for "Aquarius" from *Hair* is, where the original song had people in all different costumes kind of grasping and groping, and no choreography at all, they brought out four guys and four girls in identical costumes. They were silver and metallic blue, with gossamer wings – these wingy things under their arms. And they did something that looked like

Esther Williams synchronized swimming. "This is the dawning of the Age of Aquarius..." Perfect blending harmony.

And I thought: "Oh my God, whoever wrote *Hair* would just drop dead to think that, 32 years later, this is how it would be interpreted."

KICK: [Laughs]

Strauss even sees theatrical parallels between today's teens and the upbeat G.I. Generation youth of 70 years ago:

STRAUSS: Busby Berkeley is coming back. And it's true, Busby Berkeley *is* coming back. You look at the first Busby Berkeley movie – *42nd Street*, came out in '32. And it's so uncannily like what you see now – except they do it better now. And you can learn more about Millennial culture by watching the Andy Hardy movies of the late '30s than by watching *Breakfast Club*.

STRAUSS: They [kids today] look at *Real World* and it doesn't speak to them – it's not a world they want to be real. When they're 25, do they want to be mainly concerned with working out and complaining about failed relationships and feelings? No [laughter], that isn't what today's teenagers want to do – or will do.

So what we need to do is to help them develop a culture, and I think that high-school arts programs of all kinds are very important for that. By the time we get to 2010, I think we'll see some major cultural assertions and what the real flowering of their culture will be [during the second decade of this new century]. And so adults who are disappointed in TV programs and movies should be *demanding* that their schools have outstanding arts programs.

"Todays' teenage 'Millennial Generation' truly is America's next theater generation. They're great kids with bright futures, on stage and elsewhere, and they deserve every Cappie award we can give them, and more."[45]

– Bill Strauss, Co-founder of *Cappies*

BTWFYI: You can find further theater education references via…
American Alliance for Theatre and Education http://www.aate.com
Educational Theatre Association http://www.edta.org
Association for Theatre in Higher Education http://www.athe.org

GOTTA DANCE!

Dance education first found its place in the world of K-12 schooling and higher education thanks largely to physical education programs. The University of Wisconsin at Madison approved the first dance major back in 1926 thanks to their Women's Physical Education Department. From then, all the way up to the 1970s, most dance education stayed in gym class. However, following the passage of Title IX in 1972, the Equal Educational Opportunity Act in 1974 and overall a more fine arts emphasis in schools, dance education shifted into an independent department of the performing arts. "More and more dance educators were now being trained in the creative and artistic processes in dance that involved creating, performing and analyzing dance; techniques founded in problem solving, critical thinking skills, deconstruction and reconstruction, critical analysis, comparative and evaluative analysis, etc., as well as in the cultural, historical, social, and artistic contexts of dance. Professional preparation and pedagogy in dance changed dramatically."[46]

In the early 1990s, dance education joined forces with other disciplines in the arts – music, theater and visual arts – creating the very first set of national standards in arts education. The push for national standards actually began in January 1992 – an outcome of the educational reform efforts during the 1980s resulting from *A Nation at Risk* being released in 1983. The National Council on Education Standards and Testing called for a system of voluntary national standards and assessments in the "core" subjects of math, English, science, history, and geography, "with other subjects to follow." The arts were actually the very first of the "other subjects" to receive federal funding. With the passage of *Goals 2000: Educate America Act*, the national goals were written into law, naming the arts as a core, academic subject – as important to education as English, mathematics, history, civics and government, geography, science, and foreign language.[47]

Still, "of all the art forms, dance is experienced the least"[48] and according to the National Assessment of Educational Progress the number of schools offering dance is so small they couldn't even target a sample to study. There are notable exceptions. In Maryland, where the state Department of Education's 2002 fiscal budget included $4 million for arts education, additional enhancement funds of up to $200,000 were also made available to schools thanks to the *Moving America* program through Towson University. This collaborative program provides certified dance educators to teach students and train additional teachers. Baltimore County schools even produced a dance education curriculum with learning goals for *all* K-12 students. The state of Minnesota has a *Dance Education Initiative* for the entire state. An educational support network lead by the Perpich Center for Arts Education, trains teams of teachers to create and deliver dance education in schools across the state. While these examples are still exceptions in dance education, that may hopefully change in future.

BTWFYI: In 2001, the National Dance Education Organization started an extensive research initiative titled: *Research in Dance Education*. The project provided the most cogent body of research and data ever assembled identifying, examining, analyzing, evaluating and supporting dance education. A final report is available at http://www.ndeo.net/research/.

THE ARTS FOR EVERY KID IN AMERICA

"But even as reports like these call for a strong role for the arts in the basic education of every student, several realities of contemporary schooling work against teaching the arts."[49] As schools attempt to address the ever-increasing demands for more subjects to be covered (or at least offered), pressing societal issues, and higher expectations to raise standardized test scores with increased instructional time – something has to give. With many states currently in fiscal crisis and new demands from the Federal level, many arts educators are rightfully concerned. Toss in a growing shortage of arts specialists available to teach and it's no wonder principals respond to another arts education report with: "It'll just collect dust."[48]

There seems to be great disparity between what is supported in principle versus what is practiced by principals. Even though in 1998 ten of the most important and influential educational organizations in the U.S. including the...

American Association of School Administrators
American Federation of Teachers
Association for Supervision and Curriculum Development
Council for Basic Education
Council of Chief State School Officers
National Association of Elementary School Principals
National Association of Secondary School Principals
National Education Association
National Parent Teacher Association
National School Board Association

… stated that "every student in the nation should have an education in the arts." Sadly in practice, most kids spend more time at their lockers than in arts classes.

Throughout the 1990s more and more kids were getting more and more arts, not just in school but *outside* of the school day as well. Visual and performing arts programs expanded across the country in communities big and small. Perhaps it's was a result of all that music *in utero* pregnant moms were playing via those headphones stretched over their bellies. Maybe the black and white geometric mobiles parents hung over their cribs did it, or even the Gymboree® Play & Music[50] as well as the Kindermusik® classes[51] they took. Marketing mania over the "Mozart effect"[52] in the 1990s also helped inspire so many more music and arts opportunities – from commercial vendors to community centers across the U.S. – than ever before for kids. Starting in the late 1980s public opinion increased significantly regarding the value of arts education, more research supported education in the arts, more money was spent on the arts, standards became laws, and *extra*curricular programs became *core*curricular classes throughout the 1990s.

"The arts are windows on the world in the same way that science helps us see the world around us. The arts are not just important; they are a central force in human existence. Every child should have sufficient opportunity to acquire familiarity with these languages that so assist us in our fumbling, bumbling, and all-to-rarely brilliant navigation through this world. Because of this, the arts should be granted major status in every child's schooling."[53]

– Charles Fowler

BTWFYI: If you're interested in more information about how the arts motivate kids and additional arts advocacy resources check out:

Arts Education Partnership http://www.aep-arts.org

American Arts Alliance http://www.americanartsalliance.org

National Endowment for the Arts http://www.arts.gov

ArtsEdge http://artsedge.kennedy-center.org

Americans for the Arts http://www.americansforthearts.org

New York Foundation for the Arts http://www.artswire.org

Business Committee for the Arts http://www.bcainc.org

Iowa Alliance for Arts Education http://www.smartz.org

National Assembly of State Arts Agencies http://www.nasaa-arts.org

NAEP Arts Assessment http://nces.ed.gov/nationsreportcard/arts/

President's Committee on the Arts http://www.pcah.gov

Youth Groups

<u>WARNING</u>! For many there seems to be a split definition to the term "youth groups," so you'll find in this section both a religious based and secular perspective to the world of youth groups.

RELIGIOUS YOUTH GROUPS

Growing up Catholic, the first thing that comes to mind whenever I hear the term "youth groups" are the many once-a-week gatherings which were hosted at various friends' homes. The youth group was affiliated with a beautiful Franciscan seminary chapel located at St. Leonard College. A friend encouraged our family to check out this dynamic, down to earth, funny friar Father Tom Richstatter,[54] who would lead liturgy every Sunday and always provide a smart sermon you could relate to. The cool thing for a middle school/high school-age kid was, that once you got involved in a youth group, you no longer had to go to CCD!

Confraternity of Christian Doctrine, Sunday school, religious education, bible study, call it what you want, but it was the oversized paperback workbooks, led by parent volunteer teachers, who instructed via the "I'm-supposed-to-read-this-to-you-and-you're-supposed-to-listen-to-this," 90 minutes of torture that my adolescent GenXer friends and I disdained even more than doing chores around the house!!! Don't get me wrong, today I'd consider myself a spiritually engaged Christian. Yet if it wasn't for the St. Leonard's youth group experiences, Father Tom's real-world sermons, and Brother Dennis (who let me play my trombone with the choir), I surely would have lost the faith.

Many Xers did lose the faith or at least they lost faith in organized religion. The first generation to be born into a postmodern world, Xers are really the "disconnected generation"[55] when it comes to religion. During our generation's formative years, the exodus from more mainline denominations began, creating less and less exposure to organized religion. "Xers are not resistant to spiritual matters. They're not resistant to the concept of God. But they are resistant to the Christian church. They view church as being separatist, segregated, institutional, irrelevant, judgmental, holier-than-thou, controlling, authoritarian."[56] Sick and tired of the "stained-glass stereotypes," Xers are experiencing – and as parents are creating for their kids – a kind of "generational disorientation"[57] when it comes to the church.

George Barna, who heads a company specializing in research for Christian churches and church-related groups found that: "The biggest transition has been a loss of adherents by the Catholic church, dropping from more than 30 percent adherence among self-described Christians in the early '90s – and as recently as 1997 and 1998 – to just 22 percent in 2000."[58]

Yet the often unseen and untold story about kids today is how spiritual – and yes even religious – they are. Conrad Cherry, director of the Center for Study of Religion and American Culture states: "We're witnessing a new revival of religion. Prayer circles and faith-based groups like True Love Waits or Fellowship of Christian Athletes have proliferated in high schools and college campuses like so many WWJD bracelets; Christian rock festivals and CDs rival their secular counterparts, bringing the message out of the pulpit..."[59] Not just out of the pulpit, but right out of the church. While 78 percent of teens surveyed said that religion was important to them, only half of them said they go to church regularly – a number that's been declining since the 1970s. American Demographics reports that in the late 1950s only 1 in 25 Americans left the religious denomination they were raised in. By 1999, more than one in three had either left or switched.[60]

When it comes to religion, the resulting "relational deprivation"[61] –
provided particularly by postmodern parents – has forced today's
kids and their families to satisfy their spiritual hunger outside the
congregational pews of the past. More and more people are
"shopping for faith"[62] in the "spiritual marketplace."[63] Looking for a
good fit, a good pitch, a good buy, a good way to satisfy their hunger
for something genuinely meaningful. Many organized religious
groups and even churches have gone in some interesting directions to
"sell themselves" to a growing free market of faith:

- Theology-on-Tap, which began in 1981 at St. James Parish in the
  Chicago Archdiocese, reaches out to Catholics in their 20s and
  30s over a beer. The program has spread to over 50 other
  dioceses nationwide.[64]

- Many churches now hold a "Saturday Night Alive" rock and
  gospel music service. This goes *way* beyond the folk guitar
  services of the 1970s. We're talking casual dress, live bands,
  high tech light and sound shows pumped with a PowerPoint
  presentation style. Plugging people into a message that's sure to
  turn them on with lots of laughs too. Plus many promise to have
  you in and out "6:00 to 6:45 P.M."[65] with plenty of time to go out
  to dinner, a party, or even the movies following the service.

- And speaking of the movies, why not "Church at the Movies."[66]
  It makes "church like it oughta be" according to the Mill Creek
  Community Church of Atlanta, Georgia. Every Sunday morning
  at the Mall of Georgia Cinemas – and a growing number of
  movie theaters across the U.S. – churches are finding new ways
  to reach young and old "audiences." Well think about it, lots of
  parking, people already know how to get there, comfy chairs,
  and a cup holder on every seat.

- When all else fails give away some of the collection plate.
  Christian Life Center in Dayton, Ohio, passed out $20,000 to
  members of its congregation in crisp five, ten and twenty dollar
  bills. Kind of a reverse collection that certainly "deconstructs the
  image of the traditional house of prayer."[67] They asked their
  congregation to "take it to the streets" and find someone –
  outside their own family and their own church – who could use
  some help. The idea paid off when over 2000 example cards with
  what people did were turned in following this little ministerial
  outreach project.

- North Coast Church in northern San Diego County[68] combined multiplex theaters with a hint of the modern shopping mall and converted an entire industrial park complex into an *a la carte* retailing approach to religious services. "We have 11 worship options. Experience-wise, each one has its own theme and flavor," says senior pastor Larry Osborne.[69] There's almost a religious street fair feeling surrounding the eclectic combination of boutique-like ministries available to people. Ranging from upbeat contemporary to rock-and-roll edge, even more traditional seeking older-folks have a hymn-filled nostalgic option available as well. Creating various video venues via this multi-site venture enables different people from different generations to worship in different styles, yet all with the same sermon being shared.

- When senior pastor Michael Slaughter first arrived at an original 1860s small brick church back in 1980, it only had 90 members. But don't let an old-fashioned homespun name fool you. Today the Ginghamsburg United Methodist Church has grown and transformed 100 acres of corn into a campus. Multisensory-worship created every week takes parents and kids "beyond virtual Christianity" tuning them in and turning them on to "what God wired them to do."[70] In addition to the Dolby® sound system, a 12- by 19-foot main video screen and dozens of other monitors scattered around the "church," kids are invited to The Avenue. This $3 million cavernous arena has inspirationally entertained over 40,000 youth from around the surrounding area since it was built in 1999.

The list could go on and on with teen masses,[71] chapel coffeehouses,[72] and more. Why all this growing effort to reach today's generations spiritually? Well, according to the Pew Research Center, more Americans say "they never doubt the existence of God" than perhaps ever before.[60] Two-thirds of today's teens report having some interaction with a church youth program over the course of a typical month.[58] A national survey of American youth by the University of Pennsylvania's School of Social Work found that 86 percent of kids ages 11 to 18 believed that religion is an important part of their lives.[73] But wait you say? Hasn't church attendance been declining since the 1970s? Haven't more people been leaving *their* church for another? Welcome to the "post-denomination era of American religion," says Richard Cimino and Don Lattin. "In the post-denomination era of religion, spirituality and experience edge out doctrine and dogma."[60] Postmodern generations like Xers and Millennials are into spirituality, not necessarily a particular religion.

Kids especially seem willing to cross major denominational boundaries, sometimes even bringing their parents with them. At SouthBrook Christian Church, in Dayton, Ohio, family pastor Frank Crockett admits: "Many times the kids will come to a few of our youth events first, then after awhile their parents start checking things out. We even have some families who attend one of the other 'more traditional' churches in the area for mass, and their kids come here for youth group."[74] While Boomers may have left the Catholic church for the Lutheran one up the street, kids today seem very willing to even combine aspects of Eastern and Western religious beliefs. "Teens might cobble together bits of several faiths: a little Buddhist meditation or Roman Catholic ritual, whatever mixture appeals at the time. Many of these teenagers who are picking and choosing are the children of mixed marriages, a growing slice of the American population. About half of all Jews, for example, now marry outside of the religion; the figure for Catholics is nearing 50 percent."[59] For kids today, religion is like a smorgasbord – picking and choosing what works best for them to satisfy their spiritual hunger. And what seems to be working best for kids today are youth groups.

What is it about religious youth groups kids like best? Half of all teens say the experiences, the interaction, and friends. In fact, being with their friends and making new personal relationships outranks other factors by three to one. Other reasons like learning about God (which was mentioned by one out of four kids) and particular events and activities (mentioned by one out of five kids) also made the list. What didn't make the list? "Relatively few teens mentioned the charisma of the youth leader, the music or the opportunity to experience God's presence."[58] In addition, with as many as 60 percent doing some form of community service or outreach work, it appears that "teens are less interested in the good word than in connecting with faith through good work."[59]

In an online poll of youth group leaders, guess how they answered the question "How do you teach your kids spiritual truths?"

23% with experiential activities followed by debriefing
23% with role modeling
22% with small-group Bible study
16% with one-on-one conversation
10% with group discussion
5% with youth talks or lecture

– From http://www.youthministry.com[75]

Yet many, including George Barna, have been quick to point out that it's more than just the choices, the friends and the activities that *keep* kids coming back. Sure, all that might get them in the door along with the music, the snacks and the fun. But when kids are pressed to reveal why they continue being involved with their youth group, it turns out that all of *that* isn't enough unless, as George Barna states, "the church delivers the goods." He goes on to share what kids today really want. In a word: "Substance. Learning practical and credible insights about God was listed twice as often as anything else as the most important reason for returning. The fellowship, the games, the music, the casual and friendly atmosphere – all of those elements are important to getting kids in the door – the first time. Getting them there on subsequent occasions requires those benefits plus solid, personally applicable content."[58]

BTWFYI: If you're interested in additional insight about religious youth groups and how they're reaching kids today, check out:
Arab-American Institute http://www.aaiusa.org
Barna Research Group http://www.barna.org
Children's Ministry Magazine http://www.cmmag.com
Christianity Today Magazine http://www.christianitytoday.com
Group Magazine http://www.groupmag.com
International Study of Youth Ministry http://www.iasym.org
Jewish Education Service of North America http://www.jesna.org
National Federation for Catholic Youth Ministry http://www.nfcym.org
National Network of Youth Ministries http://youthworkers.net
National Study of Youth & Religion http://www.youthandreligion.org
Willow Creek Student Ministries http://www.wcastudentministries.com
Young Life http://www.younglife.org
Youth for Christ/USA http://www.youthforchrist.org
Youthworker Journal http://www.youthspecialties.com

SECULAR YOUTH GROUPS, CLUBS & ORGANIZATIONS

The first secular youth group organizations designed by adults for kids date back to the 1830s. However, from 1910 to 1919, some of the most significant youth organizations began – including 4-H Clubs, Boy Scouts, Camp Fire, Girl Scouts, Junior Red Cross, Junior Achievement, the YMCA Pioneers, the YWCA Girl Reserves. It's interesting to note that just as the G.I. Generation was coming of age as youth, many rapid societal changes influenced their upbringing. Today's current crop of kids have experienced a similar burst of rapid societal change. Consider the cross-generational connection between how the G.I. Generation and today's Millennial Generation seem to share a mystically linked relationship when it comes to making it through childhood:

- Both generations follow a preceding generation that caused great concern for youth – the Lost Generation born from the early 1880s to 1900 and GenXers born in the 1960s and 1970s.

- Both generations were much more favored and considered special by society vs. the generation before them.

- While parents of G.I.s were advised by the Little Mothers Leagues "Don't give the baby beer to drink!" parents of Millennials were warned by hospital maternity posters screaming "Don't shake the baby!"

- Both the 1890s and the 1990s shared in a "crisis of masculinity" given the "boy problem"[76] during both periods of time "raising cain"[77] as well as "raising boys"[78] – "real boys"[79] – became a popular parenting problem.

- The youth "gang instinct" for both generations helped build numerous adult-led youth group organizations and initiatives.

Looking at these similarities from a generational perspective, these so-called mystical links look less like interesting coincidences and more like evidence supporting the repeating cycles of generational history – continuing to turn the pages of time. Perhaps not identically, but rhythmically similar. Take the growing concern of increasing child obesity today compared to the late-1800s early-1900s. Back then: "Observers who remembered America's rural past worried that boys circa 1900 were no longer physically strong, self-reliant, and resourceful as their pioneer ancestors had been. So two special men, Ernest Thompson Seton and Daniel Carter Beard, resolved to address the disturbing and unequal situation of American boys."[80]

SCOUT'S HONOR

Seton (the first Chief Scout for the Boy Scouts of America) and Beard (the first national Scout commissioner) brought what began in England by Robert Baden-Powell to America in 1910 and started scouting. William Boyce, a publisher from Chicago actually incorporated the Boy Scouts of America following a trip to England in 1909. The story goes that he had "lost his way in a dense London fog. A boy came to his aid and, after guiding the man, refused a tip, explaining that as a Scout he would not take a tip for doing a Good Turn. This gesture by an unknown Scout inspired a meeting with Robert Baden-Powell."[81]

Robert Baden-Powell along with his sister Agnes Baden-Powell (founder of the Girl Guides) also inspired Juliette Gordon Low in 1912 to start the Girl Scouts. "For Low, founding the Girl Scouts was not some grim mission born of endless bouts with male chauvinists, but rather a joyous expression of her long-held conviction that young women should pursue any course they desired."[82] Her dream included "giving something for all the girls. She envisioned an organization that would bring girls out of their cloistered home environments to serve in their communities and experience the open air."[83]

Today, Boy Scouts and Girl Scouts in America collectively involve over six million kids and over two million adult volunteers. These values-based character-building organizations continue to instill the principals of honor, always trying to do your best, and helping other people at all times. Both organizations have intentionally developed age and developmentally appropriate versions of their programs:

Girl Scout Programs

Daisy Girl Scouts for ages 5-6
Brownie Girl Scouts for ages 6-8
Junior Girl Scouts for ages 8-11
Cadette Girl Scouts for ages 11-14
Senior Girl Scouts for ages 14-17

Boy Scout Programs

Tiger Cubs for 1st grade/age 7
Cub Scouts for 2nd-5th grades/ages 8-10
Webelos Scouts for 4th-5ht grades/age 10
Boy Scouts for ages 11-17
Varsity Scouting for ages 14-17
Venturing for ages 14-20 co-ed

They both have a similar pro-civic engagement, pro-service, G.I. Generation type message that Millennials seem to resonate with certainly more than Xers ever did:

The Girl Scout Promise	**The Boy Scout Promise**

On my honor, I will try:
    To serve God and my country,
    To help people at all times,
    And to live by the Girl Scout Law.
	On my honor, I will do my best
	    To do my duty to God and my country
	    and to obey the Scout Law;
	    To help other people at all times;
	    To keep myself physically strong,
	    mentally awake, and morally straight.

The Girl Scout Law	**The Boy Scout Law**

I will do my best to be
    honest and fair,
    friendly and helpful,
    considerate and caring,
    courageous and strong, and
    responsible for what I say and do,
and to
    respect myself and others,
    respect authority,
    use resources wisely,
    make the world a better place, and
    be a sister to every Girl Scout.
	A Scout is:
	    Trustworthy
	    Loyal
	    Helpful
	    Friendly
	    Courteous
	    Kind
	    Obedient
	    Cheerful
	    Thrifty
	    Brave
	    Clean
	    Reverent

BTWFYI: For more background on scouting in America see *On My Honor: Boy Scouts and the Making of American Youth* by Jay Mechling and *The Boy Scouts* by Robert Peterson. Boy Scouts of America http://www.scouting.org Girl Scouts of America http://www.girlscouts.org

YOUTH CAMPS AND RETREATS

Let's face it, one of the main reasons kids get involved in youth groups, clubs and organizations is for the trips, the retreats and even summer camp! It's a chance to briefly get away from home, be with friends, make new friends and learn something. Day camps and over-night resident camps have experienced record growth, with the number of day camps increasing nearly 90 percent in the past 20 years. According to the American Camping Association, there are more than 12,000 camps in the U.S. (7,000 resident camps and 5,000 day camps). Each summer more than 10 million kids participate in some kind of "camp experience." Nearly twice that many kids attend church or youth group retreats, scout outings, or some form of "camp" throughout the year. And those numbers don't even consider a growing number of camp-school partnerships taking place during the academic school day. While a majority of this century-old camp business continues to be more of a nonprofit-agency managed (approximately 8,000 camps) or a mom-and-pop, family-run, privately owned operation, handed down from generation to generation (approximately 4,000 camps) – today's camps ain't no "Hello Mudduh, Hello Fadduh"[84] kind of experience.

Kids today certainly aren't roughing it at camp like they used to. Sleepaway camps have evolved way past the rugged cabins and platform tents with no electricity or toilets. Today's camps are beyond the bunk-bed-barracks of yesterday; they're more like condos with canoes, well-designed and maintained retreat homes complete with full bathrooms and finished furniture. There's even a growing number of spas and wellness centers opening themselves up to host summer camp for kids.[85] No "bug juice" at mealtimes either. We're talking gourmet salad bars, vegetarian meal options and create-your-own-sundae stations.

But facilities alone won't do it and today camps hire teachers and counselors with specialized training and education. In the past ten years there's also been an increase in the hiring of international staff, exposing kids to different cultures and language. Some top-shelf camps maintain a camper-to-staff ratio as low as 2.5 to 1. "The bottom line is going to be about the relationships the kids develop with staff members and other children,"[86] says Jesse Scherer, a second-generation owner of Camp Eagle Hill in Columbia County, New York.

The programming kids experience and the memories they bring back after camp might surprise you. "Along with duffels of wet, dirty clothes and an assortment of cuts and bruises, the kids who leave central Michigan's SpringHill Camp every summer take with them a videotaped chronicle of their stay. Shot in the quick-edit style of MTV, the tape documents the standard activities of camp: mud fights, tetherball, tugs-of-war, horses, archery, screaming teenagers, a variety of water sports, and the occasional softball game. It also depicts a new range of activities: mountain and BMX bikes, a skate park, rappelling, something called a zip line, a winding water slide worthy of an amusement park, dramatic productions, and a rock band complete with what looks for all the world like a mosh pit."[87] The biggest attendance growth seems to surround "specialty camps" which have a narrower programming focus. Camps that go after a specific niche of experience and specialize in tennis, drama, music, golf, investing or even computers. While these camps by design have a more limited appeal than general camps do, they can also command a higher price.

Fees run on average from $200 to $400 per week for residential programs and $75 to $300 per week for day camp programs. Some of the more specialized camps and *crème de la crème* summer camps charge more than $7,000 for an entire eight-week stay. Parents are often surprised to find out that there's no government oversight of camps and perhaps assume that because kids are involved, there must be some sort of regulations in place. There are none. That's why the American Camping Association established its ACA-accreditation program to assist the public in selecting camps that meet industry-accepted and government-recognized standards.[88]

WARNING! More recently there seems to be a small but growing number of kids going to residential sleepaway camps "at ages previous generations viewed as more suited for the backyard wading pool."[89] In 1990 the average age of a residential camper was 11 years old. By 2000 it was just over nine, according the ACA. More dual-income parents looking at limited childcare options during the summer might be challenging what some consider to be a developmentally appropriate age for kids. Camps find it hard to ignore these "young adventurers" sometimes as young as five- and six-years-old, when each new wave of pee-wee campers represent potential longer-term repeat customers. "The influx at the young end is making up for a loss at the other end: By the time they reach their early teen years, most kids these days have outgrown camp and opt for adventure tours or study-abroad programs."[89] Most experts agree that around eight years old seems to be the *earliest* age when kids benefit from going to an overnight camp.

What do kids get out of going to camp? Based on research, studies and surveys from several sources – here's what kids get at camp:

- Organized camping experiences have a positive effect on an individual's "construct of self," meaning increased self-awareness, level of self-esteem, and perception of self-concept.[90]

- Developmentally appropriate challenges for skill development.

- Increased interpersonal skills development in dealing with other people, with other backgrounds, from other places. Due largely to the Internet, camps draw 20 percent of their participants from Asia, South America and Europe. What was in the past a uniquely American experience, has quickly become more international.[86]

- Highly effective alternative learning approaches – experientially based. Teaching and reaching kids in ways that traditional educational practices simply can't compete with. Perhaps that's why more and more schools are partnering with camps for year-round education and youth development. "Camp-school partnerships represent a tremendous opportunity for camps to re-establish themselves as an integral part of America's educational reform movement,"[91] suggests Peg Smith, the American Camping Association Executive Director.

- While little formal research exists and more study certainly needs to be done, some early indicators show that kids who participate in summer camp programs such as Break-Aways "appear to score higher on standardized tests than those who did not attend camp. Campers also tend to demonstrate higher levels of emotional and social development and leadership skills." In addition, the teachers who have participated in working at summer camp programs, take the many experiential learning approaches they learned at camp and bring them into their classrooms.[92]

- When school-age kids have the "summer off," researchers have found that many experience a learning loss, particularly for kids who are considered academically at risk. One student even acknowledged this and recognized camp as helping to "keep my brain going so I'm not brain dead when I get back to school."[93]

"The biggest plus of camp is that camps help young people discover and explore their talents, interests, and values. Kids who have had these kinds of camp experiences end up being healthier and have less problems which concern us all."

– Dr. Peter Scales, Senior Fellow at The Search Institute

Youth development experts like Dr. Scales and many others have long recognized the value kids get out of having a positive camp experience. Parents, teachers, youth group leaders, and camp counselors have seen first hand the profound impact camp can have on a kid's developmental growth. Yet, despite all the anecdotal evidence, research, studies and surveys from various sources, no formal nationwide research project has been conducted to "identify exactly what outcomes campers experience, and which inputs and activities are most effective in helping campers succeed."[94]

Until now: The American Camping Association, with funding from the Lilly Endowment and other partners representing the fields of camping, education, social work and youth development, will be conducting a first-of-its-kind national assessment of the impact of camps on kids. The goal is to analyze and validate "best practice" models, which will then serve as the foundation in designing effective camp programs and activities for the future.

BTWFYI: You can find out more about youth camps at:
American Camping Association http://www.acacamps.org
Association of Independent Camps http://www.independentcamps.com
Big Brothers Big Sisters http://www.bbbsa.org
Christian Camping International http://cci.gospelcom.net/ccihome/
Kids Camp Directory http://www.kidscamps.com
National Association of Christian Camps http://4dw.net/naccamps/
Jewish Community Centers Association http://www.jcca.org
National Recreation & Parks Association http://www.nrpa.org
The National Camp Association http://www.summercamp.org
YMCA Camps http://www.ymca.net
YWCA Camps http://www.ywca.org

BOOKS WORTH READING ABOUT KIDS' ACTIVITIES

Children of Fast-Track Parents: Raising Self-sufficient and Confident Children in an Achievement-Oriented World
by Andrée Aelion Brooks

The Truth About Getting In
by Katherine Cohen

Sign Me Up! The Parents' Complete Guide to Sports, Activities, Music Lessons, Dance Classes, and Other Extracurriculars
by Stacy DeBroff

Take Back Your Kids
by William Doherty

The Hurried Child: Growing Up Too Fast Too Soon
by David Elkind

High School After-School: What Is It? What Might It Be? Why Is It Important? by the Forum for Youth Investment
http://www.forumforyouthinvestment.org/comment/ostpc2.pdf

The Trouble with Perfect: How Parents Can Avoid the Overachievement Rap and Still Raise Successful Children
by Elisabeth Gutherie and Kathy Matthews

Out-of-School Time@fhrp (Harvard Family Research Project)
http://www.gse.harvard.edu/hfrp/projects/afterschool/about.html

The Gatekeepers: Inside the Admissions Process
by Jacques Steinberg

Positive Pushing: How to Raise a Successful and Happy Child
by Jim Taylor

Keeping Your Kids Out Front Without Kicking Them From Behind
by Ian Tofler and Theresa Foy DiGeronimo

WEB SITES WORTH VISITING ABOUT KIDS' ACTIVITIES

21st CCLC	http://www.ed.gov/21stcclc
4-H Council	http://www.fourhcouncil.edu
Afterschool.gov	http://www.afterschool.gov
Afterschool Alliance	http://www.afterschoolalliance.org
Afterschool Association	http://www.nsaca.org
Afterschool Now	http://www.afterschoolnow.org
Child Care Aware	http://www.childcareaware.org
Connect For Kids	http://www.connectforkids.org
Critical Hours	http://www.nmefdn.org/CriticalHours.htm
Forum for Youth	http://www.forumforyouthinvestment.org
Mom Central	http://www.momcentral.com
National Honor Society	http://www.nhs.us
Police Athletic Leagues	http://www.nationalpal.org
Student Contests/Activities	http://www.nhs.us/scaa/scaa_search.cfm
Student Councils	http://www.nasc.us
Youth Development	http://www.nydic.org

NOTES FOR CHAPTER FOUR

1. Durkin, D. (2000, June 16). Growing Up Fast. *The Washington Times*, p. 5.

2. Brady, E., & Rosewater, A. (2001, August 24). The Need To Star at 12: Kids hop on the fast track to potential athletic stardom at earlier age. *USA Today*, p. 1.

3. Naar, M. (2000). *Our Town: Youth Sports, Palm Pilots and Pilo* [Online]. Palo Alto Weekly. http://www.service.com/PAW/morgue/page4/2000_Aug_30.OURTOWN.html

4. Institute for International Sport. (2001). *Center for Sports Parenting* [Online]. University of Rhode Island. http://www.sportsparenting.org

5. Engh, F. (1999). *Why Johnny Hates Sports: Why organized youth sports are failing our children and what we can do about it*. Garden City, NY: Avery Publishing Group.

6. American Academy of Pediatrics. (2001, June). *Organized Sports for Children and Preadolescents* [Online]. http://www.aap.org/policy/re0052.html

7. Carr, C. (2000, March 8). *The Psychology of Optimal Performance in Sport, Creativity and Life*. Paper presented at the Wright State School of Professional Psychology Continuing Education Workshop, Dayton, Ohio.

8. Gold, S., & Weber, T. (2000, February 27). Inside the Machine: Youth sports in overdrive. *Los Angeles Times*, p. 1.

9. Burnett, D. (2001). *Frequently Asked Questions* [Online]. Center for Sports Parenting. http://www.sportsparenting.org/csp/csp_faq.cfm?category=resource

10. Murphy, S. (1999). *The Cheers and the Tears: A healthy alternative to the dark side of youth sports today*. San Francisco: Jossey-Bass Publishers.

11. Llewellyn, J. H. (2001). *Let 'em Play*. Marietta, GA: Longstreet Press.

12. Carr, C. (2001, September 24). Personal Communication [Email].

13. Lancaster, S. B. (2002). *Fair Play: Making Organized Sports a Great Experience for Your Kids*. New York: Prentice Hall Press.

14.   National Recreation & Parks Association. (2002). *FUN FIRST! Sports for Kids Program* [Online]. http://www.nrpa.org/story.cfm?story_id=1212&departmentID=17&publicationID=11

15.   Schreiber, L. R. (1990). *The Parents' Guide to Kids' Sports.* Boston: Sports Illustrated/Little, Brown and Company.

16.   Rodda, B. (2003). *For the Fun of it.* Wooster, OH: Wooster Book Company.

17.   Henry, T. (2002, May 19). Study: Arts education has academic effect. *USA Today.*

18.   Deasy, R. J. (2002). *Critical Links: Learning in the Arts and Student Academic and Social Development.* Washington, DC: Arts Education Partnership.

19.   Catterall, J. S. (2002, May 16). *Critical Links: Press Conference Speaker Remarks.* Paper presented at the National Press Club, Washington, DC.

20.   Brada, D., & Clemens, M. (2002). *Music USA: A Statistical Review of the Music Products Industry.* Carlsbad, CA: NAMM the International Music Products Association.

21.   Gallup. (2000). *American's Attitudes Toward Music, Music Making and Music Education* [Online]. http://www.bands.org/public/businessmedia/mediaresource/amersupmus.asp

22.   Bands of America. (2002). *High School Students, Music in Schools, Participants and Spectators* [Online]. Bands of America Inc. http://www.bands.org

23.   National Center for Education Statistics. (1992). *National Educational Longitudinal Study.* Washington, DC: Institute of Education Sciences U.S. Department of Education.

24.   The College Entrance Examination Board. (2001). *College-Bound Seniors National Report: Profile of SAT Program Test Takers.* Princeton, NJ: The College Board.

25.   Music for All Foundation. (2004). *QuickFacts and Benefits of Music and the Arts in Education and Society* [Online]. http://www.music-for-all.org/quickfacts.html

26.   Texas Commission on Drug and Alcohol Abuse. (1998). *Texas Commission on Drug and Alcohol Abuse Report.* Houston, TX.

27.   Catterall, J. S., Chapleau, R., & Iwanaga, J. (1999). *Involvement in the Arts and Human Development.* Los Angeles: The Imagination Project at UCLA Graduate School of Education and Information Studies.

28. Miller, A., & Coen, D. (1994). The Case for Music in the Schools. *Phi Delta Kappan, 75*(6), 459-461.

29. National Arts Education Research Center. (1990). New York: New York University School of Education.

30. National Center for Education Statistics. (1990). *National Educational Longitudinal Study.* Washington, DC: Institute of Education Sciences U.S. Department of Education.

31. Schlaug, G., Jancke, L., Huang, Y., & Steinmetz, H. (1994). *In vivo morphometry of interhem ispheric assymetry and connectivity in musicians.* Paper presented at the 3rd International Conference for Music Perception and Cognition, Liege, Belgium.

32. Bergonzi, L., & Smith, J. (1996). *Effects of Arts Education on Participation in the Arts.* Santa Ana, CA: Seven Locks Press.

33. National Endowment for the Arts. (2002). *The Arts in the GDP* [Online]. NEA Research Division. http://www.arts.gov/pub/Notes/78.pdf

34. National Governors Association. (2001). *The Role of the Arts in Economic Development* (Issue Brief). Washington, DC.

35. National Governors Association. (2002). *The Impact of Arts Education on Workforce Preparation* (Issue Brief). Washington, DC.

36. National Coalition for Music Education. (1995). *Fact Sheet: Arts and Jobs.* Reston, VA: MENC.

37. Americans for the Arts. (2002). *Arts and Economic Prosperity: The Economic Impact of Nonprofit Arts Organizations and Their Audiences.* Washington, DC.

38. Cherbo, J. M., & Wyszomirski, M. J. (2000). *The Public Life of the Arts in America*: Rutgers University Press.

39. Shakespeare, W. (1599). *As You Like It (Act II, Scene VII).* http://www.online-literature.com/shakespeare/youlike/

40. Chester, E. (2002). *Employing Generation Why?* Lakewood, CO: Tucker House Books.

41. Logan, G. (2003, March 5). Personal Communication [Email].

42. McSwain, M. (1999). *Millennial Markers, the Class of '99, and the Legacy of Columbine: An Interview with William Strauss* [Online]. Love Those Millennials. http://www.millennials.com/ltm/strauss.html

43. Eggen, D. (2000, June 8). The Cappies: A Star Is Born. *The Washington Post,* p. 1.

44.   Theater Students Get Their Share of the Limelight. (2002, June 23). *The New York Times*.

45.   West, K. (2002). *Why The Cappies? An Interview with a Co-Founder* [Online]. The Cappies, Inc. http://www.cappies.com/usa/start/strauss.html

46.   National Dance Education Organization. (2002). *Evolution of the Field* [Online]. http://www.ndeo.net/whoweare.htm

47.   Music Educators National Conference. (1994). *The National Standards for Arts Education: What Every Young American Should Know and Be Able to Do in the Arts*. Reston, VA: MENC.

48.   Black, S. (2001). Shall We Dance? National dance standards recognize that not all expression is verbal. *American School Board Journal, 188*(8).

49.   Herbert, D. (1998, March). Model Approaches to Arts Education. *Principal Magazine*.

50.   The Gymboree Corporation. (2003). *Gymboree Play & Music* [Online]. http://www.playandmusic.com/b2c/customer/home.jsp

51.   Kindermusik International Inc. (2003). *Kindermusik* [Online]. http://www.kindermusik.com

52.   Pope, K. (2001, March). Marketing Mozart. *Parenting, 24*.

53.   Fowler, C. (1991). Every Child Needs the Arts. In D. Dickinson (Ed.), *Creating The Future: Perspectives on Educational Change* (pp. 123-127). Aston Clinton, Bucks, UK: Accelerated Learning Systems Ltd.

54.   Richstatter O.F.M., T. (2004). *Fr. Tom Richstatter's Home Page* [Online]. http://www.tomrichstatter.org

55.   McDowell, J. (2000). *The Disconnected Generation*. Wheaton, IL: Josh McDowell Ministry/Word Publishing.

56.   Celek, T., Zander, D., & Kampert, P. (1996). *Inside the Soul of a New Generation: Insights and Strategies for Reaching Busters*. Grand Rapids, MI: Zondervan Publishing.

57.   Zoba, W. M. (1999). *Generation 2K: What Parents & Others Need to Know About the Millennials*. Downers Grove, IL: InterVarsity Press.

58.   Barna, G. (2001). *Real Teens: A Contemporary Snapshot of Youth Culture*. Ventura, CA: Regal Books.

59.   Leland, J. (2000, May 8). Searching For a Holy Spirit. *Newsweek,* 61-63.

60.   Cimino, R., & Lattin, D. (1999, April). Choosing My Religion. *American Demographics*.

61. Mueller, W. (1999). *Understanding Today's Youth Culture* (Revised ed.). Wheaton, IL: Tyndale House Publishers, Inc.

62. Cimino, R., & Lattin, D. (2002). *Shopping for Faith: American Religion in the New Millennium*. San Francisco: Jossey-Bass.

63. Roof, W. C. (1999). *Spiritual Marketplace: Baby Boomers and the Remaking of American Religion*. Princeton, NJ: Princeton University Press.

64. Gorski, E. (2002, January 26). Theology on Tap program is where everybody knows your name: Young adults talk doctrine over beer. *Dayton Daily News*, p. 2.

65. Aldersgate United Methodist Church. (2004). *Saturday Night Alive* [Online]. http://www.aldersgatealive.com

66. Mill Creek Community Church. (2004). *Church at the Movies* [Online]. http://www.millcreekcc.com/popcorn.htm

67. Moss, K. (2004, January 31). Mega-Church Takes Some Services to Big Screen. *Dayton Daily News*, p. B1.

68. North Coast Church. (1998). [Online]. http://www.northcoastchurch.com

69. Leadership Network. (2000). *Starbucks and the Video Café* [Online]. Epicenter. http://www.epicchurch.net/read.asp?cid=1079

70. Mong, C. (2002, April 28). Church tunes in with high-tech halllujahs. *Dayton Daily News*, p. 1.

71. Gregory, M. (2004, March 14). Teen Mass attracts hundreds. *Rochester Democrat and Chronicle*.

72. Cox, P. (2004, March 18). Christian club a hit with teens. *Dayton Daily News*, p. Z2.

73. Cnaan, R., & Gelles, R. (2002). *Youth and Religion: A Nation of Young Believers*. Philadelphia: University of Pennsylvania.

74. Crockett, F. (2003, June 28). Personal Communication [Interview].

75. Lawrence, R. (2000, November/December). What's the deal with youth talks? *Group Magazine*, 34-37.

76. Forbush, W. B. (1902). *The Boy Problem*. Boston: Pilgrim Press.

77. Kindlon, D. J., Thompson, M., & Barker, T. (2000). *Raising Cain: Protecting the Emotional Life of Boys*. New York: Ballantine Books.

78. Biddulph, S. (1998). *Raising Boys: Why Boys Are Different-And How to Help Them Become Happy and Well-Balanced Men*. Berkeley, CA: Celestial Arts.

79. Pollack, W. (1998). *Real Boys: Rescuing Our Sons from the Myths of Boyhood*. New York: Holt.

80. Peterson, R. W. (1984). *The Boy Scouts: An American Adventure*. New York: American Heritage.

81. Boy Scouts of America. (2003). *Founders of Scouting and the BSA* [Online]. http://www.scouting.org/factsheets/02-211.html

82. Edmondson, J. (2003, February). Scout's Honor: Juliette Gordon Low and the founding of the Girl Scouts. *Sky Magazine,* 68-71.

83. Girl Scouts of America. (2003). *Girl Scout History* [Online]. http://www.girlscouts.org/about/history.html

84. Sherman, A. (1963). *Hello Mudduh, Hello Fadduh!* [Audio]: Curtain Call Productions.

85. Higgins, M. (2003). Summer Camp for Wimps. *Wall Street Journal,* p. D1.

86. Forsman, T. (2001, June 6). Hello Muddah, Hello Fadduh! Business is booming at America's summer camps. *Business Week.*

87. Balmer, R. (2003, September). God and the water slide: Christain camping is bigger than ever, but some rituals never change. *Christianity Today,* 54-60.

88. American Camping Association. (2003). *ACA Standards Accreditation* [Online]. http://www.acacamps.org/accreditation/index.htm

89. Carton, B. (2000, August 15). Kindergarten Camp: Kids Sleepaway Camp At Even Youger Ages - Too Little to Write Home. *Wall Street Journal,* p. B4.

90. Marsh, P. E. (1999). *What Does Camp Do for Kids?* Unpublished Masters Thesis, Indiana University, Bloomington, IN.

91. O'Donnell, J. (2001). *Creating Camp-School Partnerships: A Guidebook to Success* (Online). Martinsville, IN: American Camping Association.

92. O'Donnell, J. (2004). *Camp Trends - The Changing Role of Camps: School partnerships place camps at the heart of educational reform* [Online]. American Camping Association Media Center. http://www.acacamps.org/media_center/view/php?file=camp_trends_article13.htm

93.   New York Department of Education. (2001). *Break-Aways Final Evaluation Report Second Year* (Online). New York: New York City Board of Education/American Camping Association's New York Section.

94.   American Camping Association. (2001). *Youth Development Outcomes of the Camp Experience* [Online]. http://www.acacamps.org/research/grant.htm

Inspiring Kids to be Self-Disciplined

When it comes to dealing with kids everyone would like a silver-bullet, fool-proof, this-will-always-work, one-size-fits-all kind of solution to their discipline dilemmas. That desire applies equally at home, at school, and at work. Parents, teachers, and managers demand answers to their problems. And where demand turns up, can supply be far behind? Many books line the store shelves devoted to eliminating unwanted behavior. Others offer cookbook-style approaches to dealing with *any* given situation in a step-by-step here's how-to use various punishments and/or rewards to "motivate your kids to behave." Some of these books are very good; many more are simply information overload. Today raising kids has become "an uptight, guilt-ridden affair" where a parent's "obsession with doing the perfect job is the very thing that reduces the quality of their parenting."[1]

Discipline

<u>WARNING</u>! Throughout this chapter many of the references made relate to parenting. Please don't let that "put you off" if you happen to be a teacher or manager. Much of what's shared relates directly to you as well.

When it comes to discipline, some people actually think discipline motivates kids to behave. Sorry, but that's not discipline. It's either a punishment or a bribe. Carrot and sticking kids to do what we want them to do has very little to do with discipline in the truest sense of the word. After all, "discipline" comes from the word *discipulus* which means "pupil" and *disciplina*, which means "learning." It's also very similar to the word *disciple*. And, since actions speak louder than words, perhaps the most important discipline strategy parents, teachers and managers can use is modeling – setting the example for kids with deeds as well as words.

"What you do speaks so loud that I cannot hear what you say."
– Ralph Waldo Emerson

Most of the time when we think about disciplining kids we think of either punishments or rewards. Some people take away privileges, others use a variety of time-out experiences (some good, some bad). Rather than get into the nitty-gritty of all that, let's look at discipline from a different perspective. A longer-term perspective. A bigger, broader perspective. Perhaps even a generational perspective.

PUNISHMENT VS. DISCIPLINE

One core point can't be overstressed: Punishment and discipline are *not* the same. Too many people think that punishment inspires better behavior in their kids. By making kids feel bad, humiliated and deprived of any dignity, they actually believe they're "motivating their kids" to improve behavior. How many times have you heard (or maybe even thought), "I'll show them who's in charge!" and versions thereof? Most people discipline their kids with punishment to gain control over their kids rather than teach kids how to have self-control. Punishment simply makes kids pay for the past, whereas discipline teaches kids and helps them learn for the future.

Punishment is...	Discipline is...
Something you do *to* your child	Something you do *with* your child
A reaction to a problem	A proactive way of life
Discouraging	Encouraging
Focused on blame (pay for past)	Focused on future (learn for next time)
Reinforcing external locus of control	Reinforcing internal locus of control
One tactic	Many strategies
Used to teach kids what they did wrong	Used to teach kids what they can do
Something used more as kids get older	Something instilled from infancy
More about controlling kids	More about teaching kids self-control

Now punishment does teach kids something. It just may not be what you want them to learn from the experience. More often than not what kids learn from being punished is:

A feeling of resentment – "It's not fair!" is the common phrase signaling a lack of understanding between what they did or didn't do and the punishment you've given them. "How could you do this to me!" takes it even further while trying to shift some guilt toward the punisher.

A rebellious/revengeful attitude – "I'll get you for that!" expresses a basic fighting back (the first part of "fight or flight") response.

A retreat (or flight) into either being sneakier – "Next time I won't get caught" – **or a reduced level of self-esteem**, as in: "I'm a bad person. I always get into trouble." Sometimes this can set up a self-fulfilling prophecy that reinforces itself with more punishment.

When punishment becomes the primary discipline tactic within an overly strict authoritarian household, parents react quickly and angrily to children who make poor decisions. Excessive control actually diminishes a child's development of personal responsibility. Imposing control externally, parents inadvertently create kids who are irresponsible, hostile, aggressive and rebellious. Rather than assume responsibility for their actions, kids quickly learn to blame someone else or something else to avoid the punishment. They tend to look at the system or situation as being unfair towards them. "It's not my fault!" Threats and warnings are met with manipulation and covert-like behavior.

So much for helping kids behave more constructively. Punishment too many times simply asserts control, bringing the parent-child (or teacher-student, or even manager-employee) relationship into a power struggle. At first it might seem to work, but in reality all it produces is short-term compliance, with some long-term effects we'll discuss a bit later.

GENERATIONAL PARENTING PATTERNS

During the Depression, when members of the Silent Generation were kids being raised by Lost and G.I. Generation parents, punishment was a way of life. It was a time when "because I said so" worked. "Chain of command" was alive and well. In a stressful time for American society it probably *had* to be – many families were dealing with some incredibly trying times. (If you think too much media and keeping an SUV moving is stressful, consider 25 percent unemployment in 1932, or the high-school Class of 1940 attending their senior prom as Hitler took over France in the space of a week and prepared to bomb Britain.)

A consistent and constant hierarchy of order existed in most families. "You do as you're told!" Corporal punishment was the norm in homes, and it was even applied in schools. Perhaps all this punishment and control helped create millions of adults who were resentful of how they had been raised. In this case, that would be the Silents who, by the 1950s, were helping their World War II elders raise the Boomers. What we know for sure is that – thanks to the popularity of Dr. Spock, new medicines, vaccines, and postwar prosperity – childhood grew more relaxed during the 1950s. By the time the 1970s dawned, it was "relaxed" to the point of being neglectful and chaotic! A new generation of kids, born during the "Consciousness Revolution" would enter the world during "the most virulently anti-child periods in American history."[2]

Consider parenting during the 1960s and 1970s. First of all, fewer people were even becoming parents then. Thanks in large part to the U.S. approving the sale of a new form of contraception in 1962 – "the pill." GenXers were also at that time the "most aborted generation in America history." Following the Supreme Court's *Roe v. Wade* decision in 1973, abortion was suddenly a legal option and increased 80 percent from 1973 to 1979. Divorce became commonplace. As kids, Xers would experience twice the risk of their parents getting divorced compared to Boomers and three times the risk compared to Silents. Add to this the fact that more women were entering the workforce full-time – perhaps because they were recently divorced. It's no wonder day care centers exploded across the country and latch-key kids came home by themselves. As teenagers, kids who were born in the 1960s and 1970s were committing suicide more frequently than any generation since before the turn of the century.

In *Great Expectations*, Landon Jones noted how, "In the mid-1970s, something funny happened to divorce. People were laughing about it. A comic strip names *Splitsville* began lampooning newly separated couples... Divorced characters began showing up on prime-time television more often than cowboys used to. Rhoda and Phyllis had dumped their husbands. Maude was threatening to. Meredith Baxter Birney has split from her guy on *Family*... We had come a long way, it seemed, from the day when the [CBS] network had refused to allow Mary Tyler Moore's production company to present her as a newly divorced woman instead of the bachelor girl she ultimately became."[3] A long way – in the space from 1970, when *Mary Tyler Moore* began, to middle of the same decade, when four-fifths of the 50 states had passed no-fault divorce laws!

Within families and in society overall, constant change was replacing consistency. Schools, now filled by Boom-generation teachers hostile to structure and looking for "relevance," lost public support. Twenty years later, clarifying what he called "the Why Behind Generation X," Geoffrey Holtz would write: "The grand experiments in education performed on [our generation] just may be the most outlandish and the most damaging of all those that society has attempted in recent decades."[4] Almost everything started to be negotiable and "situational." Fewer limits, fewer boundaries and an excessive need for approval – on the part of parents!

So much permissiveness – escapism on the part of adults who preferred to act like teenagers, thereby assuring that the household had no adults in it – certainly had a social price. Children raised in a permissive environment, with limits either not established or not consistently enforced, struggle to work within limits when they are. Structured situations such as in school, work and society overall create tension for kids not used to effectively operating with inherent limits. They tend to view control as being mean and/or not caring about them as individuals. Kids of permissive parents tend to be disrespectful, unmotivated and manipulative. They can be excessive and sometimes unable to draw boundaries between themselves and others. Hmmm, sounds like a lot of Boomers and Xers, you say?

Maybe so. Or maybe this is more monolithic generalization, stereotyping and pigeonholing that Paul Loeb, Claire Raines and others warn us about. Certainly not all pre-1950s parents were autocratic "take no shit" parents that ended up with overly permissive "I don't give a shit" Boomer children who then gave them cynical individualistically sarcastic "no shit" Xer grandchildren. And certainly not all 1970s parents were figureheads unable to demonstrate "tough love" because they were too distracted by their own "midlife" and other long-running personal crises.

But it certainly makes you wonder: Do parenting styles vary that much from generation to generation? What are some of the unintended consequences parents unknowingly nurture in their kids? Are we as a society simply going to keep swinging back and forth from one parenting extreme to the other? Ann Hulbert, in her book *Raising America*, researched child-rearing advice since 1900 to discover the answer – yes. From disciplined to permissive, parent-centered to child-centered, scientific to sermonizing, "each generation has produced a sort of Jekyll and Hyde, from the stern L. Emmett Holt and the empathetic G. Stanley Hall, to the doctrinaire John Watson and the child-oriented Arnold Gessell, to Benjamin Spock."[5] Even today's current best-selling parenting advice-givers represent a continuation of this historical seesaw of approaches. Consider the more child-centered T. Berry Brazelton and Stanley Greenspan, in contrast to their stricter colleagues James Dobson and John Rosemond.

"Natural joints are between generations and they are the way in which we were reared."

– Layne Longfellow

Consider how historical eras of parenting styles changed over the years from when G.I.s were kids versus when GenXers were kids. "In 1924, American parents were asked what character traits they would most like their children to develop as they grew up. There were two qualities of character above all others that parents wanted for their kids. First, strict obedience and second, loyalty to traditional institutions such as church. In 1988, The University of Michigan's Institute for Survey and Research replicated the survey, American parents responded there were two things they would like their children to develop – qualities of character. First, independence and second, tolerance of differences."[6]

Getting down to specifics: When it comes to discipline, what parenting factors are influencing kids today and where's the "sweet spot" for maximum parental effectiveness with minimal long-term negative consequences? The answers seem to be all over the map and that may or may not bode well when the proverbial "shit hits the fan."

Parenting is an incredibly complex activity that ideally adjusts in developmentally appropriate ways. Rather than cover all the specific behaviors that work or don't work individually and collectively with today's kids, let's consider the range of factors that influence discipline. I use the word *range* because there's no either-or to any of these factors. Too many people have the misconception that, if they're not overly strict with their kids, that means they're being permissive. In practice this notion fails to account for the vast space between being "hard on your kids" and "easy on your kids." Like many things in life, parenting is not a black-or-white situation. It's more of a multi-shaded spectrum of grays depending largely on the situation and the kids. And as any parent, teacher, or manager will tell you, it's always the gray areas that get you. The purpose, for the rest of this chapter, is to present you with a better light to illuminate the path that works best for you, your kids, and the situation.

WARNING! You'll find various ranges of factors presented on the following matrix of parenting approaches and overlapping styles. At first they may appear to illustrate unworkable extremes and generic polarities of possibility. (Although you may know one or two people who might try to make some extreme work for them!) Obviously people vary their approach given the circumstance of any situation and probably would find themselves somewhere in-between. Consider where you tend to find yourself most often. How about where your parents might fit into these ranges of various extremes?

The parenting approaches and style matrix

RESPONSIVENESS
+

|

-   EXPECTATIONS   +

Parental responsiveness pertains to the warmth or supportive atmosphere parents create. It means the extent that parents intentionally foster individuality, self-regulation, and self-assertion by supporting and understanding kids' individual needs and demands.[7]

Expectations can also be referred to as demandingness, level of demand or behavioral control. This includes the number of demands parents make on kids to behave, how they confront a kid who disobeys, the level of maturity expected, and the amount of supervision a parent provides.

Whether parents are very demanding (have high expectations) or not very demanding (have low expectations) of their kids and how responsive or non-responsive they are to their kids sets up a number of parenting approaches and styles.

Indulgent Lenient Permissive Parents	Involved Authoritative Parents
Uninvolved Parents	Autocratic Authoritarian Controlling Parents

RESPONSIVENESS (+ top, − bottom)

-   EXPECTATIONS   +

Indulgent parents tend to be more non-directive, lenient or permissive in their overall parenting approach. They're less demanding and very responsive, mostly acquiescing to their kids' wants and needs. They are considered by some as non-traditional and tend not to require mature behavior from their kids. Individual relationships are more important than structure. Allowing for too much self-regulation especially at an early age, their self-indulgent children become prone to an almost silver-platter kind of syndrome. Later in the kid's life, these parents avoid confrontation by simply giving in. Kids raised by indulgent parents exhibit academic-performance shortfalls in school and tend to show more behavior problems too.

Autocratic parents are much more demanding than indulgent parents – perhaps too much so. These parents tend to be highly directive with very little responsiveness towards their kids' needs, wants or even perceptions. Mostly concerned with obedience and chain-of-command, they expect their orders to be obeyed without exception or any needed explanation. Structure is more important than relationships. Thus, control and the amount exerted over kids by parents ranges from strict to permissive.

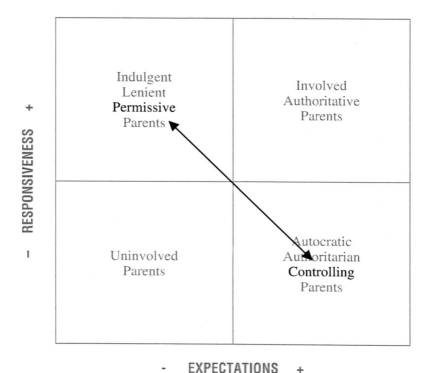

Now of course parents need to consistently demonstrate and exert *developmentally appropriate control* over their children. Normal development depends a great deal on how/when this control is managed. Starting with more when kids are young and gradually shifting to less as they head out into the world on their own as emerging adults. Two important words through all this would be consistently and gradually. The amount of control a parent would exert over a five-year-old is obviously different from a fifteen-year-old. The difference lies in the fifteen-year-old being developmentally capable of sharing perceptions (his and hopefully yours) in a given situation. Five-year-olds mostly see the world their way. Both can set up a power struggle between parent and child. Unfortunately, how parents handle power struggles when their kid is five will sometimes be the way they handle them when their kid is fifteen – they give in.

"In 99 out of a 100 power struggles between parent and a child, the child will win."

— Rudolf Dreikurs

Maybe it was all the T-shirts and bumper stickers that said "Question Authority" that caused Boomers, at least during the 1970s, to have a hard time exerting control over their Xer kids. In his book *Too Much of a Good Thing*, Dan Kindlon speculates: "The debacles of the Vietnam War, Kent State shootings, and Watergate break-in made us lose faith in our leaders. When we became parents, this attitude meant that we were often uncomfortable exerting authority over our children. We felt uneasy about setting strict limits."

− PERMISSIVE TO CONTROLLING +

Permissive parenting was not just a reaction to the "command and control" modes of the Depression and World War II. It's perhaps also the result of the increased economic growth that followed the war. "You don't raise children permissively in a world of scarcity, you raise children permissively during a period of prosperity."[6] People also went overboard interpreting and at times actually misunderstanding the words of Dr. Benjamin Spock (1903-1998), the famous "baby doctor." First published in 1946, his book *The Common Sense Book of Baby and Child Care* became the bible to many parents – moms especially – who were busy raising a brand new flock of kids America would later call "Boomers." In fact it became one of the best selling non-fiction books of all time – second only to the bible![8] It was the first parenting book that avoided excessive medical jargon and presented child-rearing ideas in a straightforward, easy to understand, practical way.

Prior to Spock's book, most parenting books (if you could find one) intimidated the average mother or father with condescendingly inaccessible medical terms. Sometimes parents were scolded to keep rigid feeding, weaning, sleeping and toilet-training schedules regardless of what they sensed their baby needed. Some books actually told parents to lock crying children in their room, avoid excessively hugging, kissing and showing too much affection to babies.

Parents of Boomers welcomed Dr. Spock's refreshingly down-to-earth book, which sought to balance the scales a bit from all the overly rigid and clinical pediatric guidance of the past. As it became popular during the late 1940s, and given the memories of a recent world war, as well as the new nuclear threats that were emerging, many parents may have felt especially protective of their young

Baby Boomers. Some critics of Spock would say the children were indulged. Looking for domestic tranquility, families ended up moving out to the suburbs. On their own, far from grandparents and a network of aunts, uncles and extended family members, "parents of America's baby boom generation turned to Spock."[9]

To be fair, few people actually read the entire book. Most parents would simply flip to the pages that interested them when presented with a particular problem (an extensively detailed index made *Baby and Child Care* an easy reference book). And Spock never deserved the negative labels that later came his way. Branded by critics as "the father of permissiveness" who single-handedly "Spock-marked" a generation of free-spirited hippies, he was actually raised in a solidly conservative New England family, went to Yale where he rowed crew and helped win an Olympic gold medal in 1924, and he even served in the U.S. Navy! Needless to say, the man knew discipline and the benefit it brought.

Throughout his book he advocated asking for respect, cooperation and politeness from children. Providing firm leadership as parents and giving children strong values. He himself thought he made it quite clear that parents should be firm and even stressed that children need standards. Dr. Spock also believed that parents needed to "respect children because they're human beings and they deserve respect, and they'll grow up to be better people."[10] Emphasizing the importance of the differences between individual babies, he suggested the need for flexibility and in general a wise, reasonable, moderate, middle ground, common sense approach.

"I didn't want to encourage permissiveness, but rather to relax rigidity" was Dr. Spock's frequent reply to the many critics who demonized him in the 1960s and 1970s. His own political activism – against the U.S. role in Vietnam and atmospheric nuclear testing, advocating the legalization of marijuana and abortion – certainly gave his critics an opening. But they overdid it, making Spock the scapegoat for all the radical youth behavior of the 1960s. Overly permissive child-rearing principles, erroneously popularized and inaccurately attributed to Dr. Spock, weren't a part of his writing at all.

At its extreme, permissiveness is freedom without any structure or order, unlimited choices with an "anything you want" kind of attitude. Kids who experience permissive parenting and/or discipline tend to grow up with an attitude that the world owes them everything. They spend most of their time manipulating others into taking care of what they want and need. Rather than being given the opportunity to develop their own capabilities and independence, they strive to avoid personal responsibility. When things go wrong, they usually blame someone else or something else.

On the other end of the parental control range is an excessively strict, overly controlling parenting style. Everything is usually about order with no freedom, no choices and 100 percent parental control (usually by edict!). At this extreme, adults are always "in charge" and become a gatekeeper for everything a kid can or can't do. There's a heavy emphasis on catching kids doing something wrong, following orders and rules.

Parents also take on the responsibility of managing too many things *for* their kids. By excessively controlling the life of their son or daughter, *self*-control never has a chance to develop within the child. Why not? Because Mom or Dad are always there to set things up, do things, take care of all the little details, make all the choices, decide everything, and prevent problems before they occur. This overly controlling parental micro-management sets their kid up to be less self-confident. "Micromanaging every detail of a child's existence so that he or she doesn't miss a thing and striving to control every variable so the child doesn't mess up and have to experience frustration or failure gives children the unspoken sense that their parents suspect that without constant help they will never be able to take care of themselves."[11]

-   UNINVOLVED TO INVOLVED   +

The range of parental involvement from uninvolved to involved factors in to discipline as well. If parents place very little demand or expectation on their kids *and* they're not responsive to or involved in their kids' lives, most of the time the response becomes "Whatever" or "I don't give a shit!" In extreme cases it even goes so far as to reject and neglect kids.

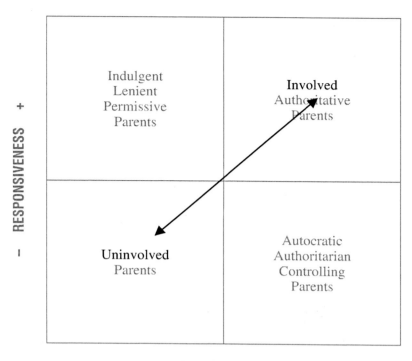

RESPONSIVENESS

+

–

Indulgent
Lenient
Permissive
Parents

Involved
Authoritative
Parents

Uninvolved
Parents

Autocratic
Authoritarian
Controlling
Parents

–   EXPECTATIONS   +

It was mentioned earlier and is worth repeating here that the most significant and important influence in a kid's life that really matters – above all others – is how much a child's parents or primary care-giving adults loved them and showed their affection towards them. If you had to pick a second most important influence that really matters, without question it would be involvement. Time after time, study after study, interview after interview, whenever you find someone who succeeds in life at any level there's always one common element that made the most difference – active parental involvement.

<u>WARNING</u>! Now if you happen to be a parent who wishes you could be more actively involved with your kids and aren't, please don't misunderstand. And don't start to feel guilty hearing that classic Harry Chapin song "Cat's in the Cradle" echoing over and over in your head. Whatever your personal circumstances might be (or may have been) with your kids, the last thing I want you to do is get all defensive right now. We've all heard enough about quality time issues with kids and quantity time issues. Research clearly shows – it's both!

Uninvolved parents sometimes get so involved in their own lives, their own careers, their own needs, that they fail to be very responsive to their kids. Plus let's face it, progress in today's world has given everyone more to do on their to do list! Too many times it's just easier for the parents to do things themselves rather than teach their kids about responsibility. Out of expediency or simply by trying to avoid the hassle, parents place few demands on their kids. Uninvolved parents tend to be less aware of what's really happening in their kid's life and because of this at times fail to be very responsive. Expectations are low across the board and kids of uninvolved parents tend to perform poorly in many areas.

Involved parents are actively interested and engaged in their kids' lives – not intrusively or restrictively. They simply operate with a high level of responsiveness as well as high expectations or demands. Being involved allows them to monitor what's really happening with their kids. They're constantly imparting clear standards for their kid's behavior and conduct – sharing in many teachable moments along the way. Discipline supports learning rather than simply punishing. Plus, by being involved with their kids, parents have lots of opportunity to model what they expect in their kid's behavior.

Involved parents have multiple opportunities to share many mini-teachable moments with their kids. Effectively sprinkling in little lessons over the course of a lifetime becomes more effective than the occasional big drawn-out lecture. Plus these teachable moments occur within the context of the immediate situation, rather than waiting until later "when you father gets home" and/or after the fact.

WARNING! Some parents are overly involved in their kid's life to the point of controlling everything they do. They set things up, organize, plan and in some cases even create everything needed for the kid. Some of the dangers of this kind of over-involvement exist in today's adult-run youth sports culture as shared earlier. To be fair, it really can be seen everywhere and anywhere that parents do too much *for* or *to* their kids – rather than *with* them. There's a vast difference between simply dropping your kid off at some youth activity and micro-managing the entire experience *for* them. Parents who are appropriately and actively involved with their kids know how to balance their involvement within developmentally appropriate parameters. They're not overly intrusive.[12]

One of the interesting factors that cuts across and influences both how involved and responsive someone is with kids pertains to their level of awareness. More than anything, kids today want people to be real, to be with them, and to relate to them in an authentically honest manner. It's hard to do that if you're not paying attention to them. Individually and collectively kids can tell when someone is either unaware or aware of what's going on with them and in their world. Today's fast-paced, 24/7, hyperlinked, hurry up, always-on world has made awareness so much more important and challenging. Everyone seems to be pulled in 40 different directions (make that 400 different directions) and paying attention to our kids, our students, and our employees would rank as the third most important influence that really matters.

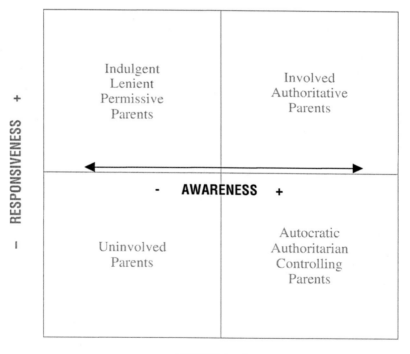

In the largest adolescent health study ever conducted in the U.S., a congressionally mandated, federally funded National Longitudinal Study on Adolescent Health, parental awareness and involvement were found to be *the* most effective remedies to dangerous teen behavior. Kids who reported a connectedness to their parents were the least likely to engage in risky behaviors that endangered their health. The study found – contrary to common misperception – that parents and *not* peers play a central role for their kids even through adolescence. The researchers also found that kids who feel connected at school – a perception of being a part of school, treated fairly by teachers, and feeling close to people at school – are also less likely to engage in risky behaviors. It's also important to note that *no* reliable links were found between kids of divorced parents, race, poverty, school size, teacher-student ratio, teacher experience, grade range of school, and students engaging in risky behavior.[13]

- HOSTILITY TO LOVE +
(Conditional acceptance to Unconditional acceptance)

Since love according to the research ranks as the most significant and important influence in a kid's life, perhaps we need to take just a second to understand the difference between conditional love (and acceptance) versus unconditional love (and acceptance). Statements parents make like "I love you when you behave like this" or "You know I love you, *but* when bring home a report card like this!" qualify love with conditional strings attached. Unqualified love is not won or lost. It isn't earned or taken away based simply on what they do or how they behave. Unconditional love has no strings attached. Sure, you may not love everything your kid does – recklessly breaking things, using bad language and the constantly messy room – but you still *love* your kid.

WARNING! This does *not* mean that you accept everything and anything your kid does. Unqualified love isn't about making everything okay. That's crossing over into permissiveness. If anything you want to love your kid so much that you establish limits, consistently maintain them and help support them in good times and in bad.

Unconditional love requires that when necessary we are crystal clear about disapproving of the actions taken, choices made, consequences resulting – but *not* the person! Most of the time when we cross that line and conditionalize our love and acceptance, it sounds something like "Mom I know you love me when I get good grades, but…" or "Dad, I know you love me when I'm sleeping, but…" Ultimately, kids need to know, feel and believe that they are more important than anything they do.

Supporting your kids unconditionally, in good times and bad, also requires that you love them enough to let them experience and sometimes even suffer the consequences of their actions in order to learn from them. Too many times in today's world we're afraid to let kids experience failure. We're so busy rescuing them from life's little misfortunes (and occasionally big misfortunes) that they never learn from their mistakes. Instead, what they learn is that someone will always be there to save them, cover for them, or take care of the mess. And, whether you intend to or not, you won't always be there for them. They need to figure things out for themselves sometimes and deal with the consequences of their choices and/or actions.

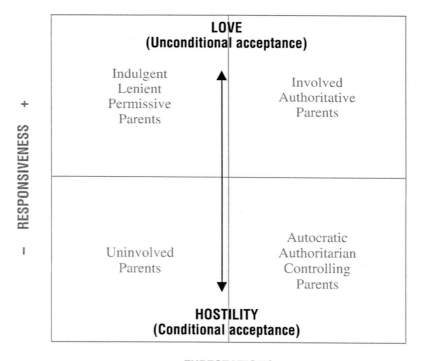

Instead of simply trying to gain temporary compliance with our kids, or control over their behavior, think of discipline (like motivation) in terms of self-discipline. Ultimately we want our children, our students and our employees to be self-motivated and self-disciplined don't we? How many times have you caught yourself thinking, "I'm sick and tired of telling these kids what to do and when to do it!" While at the very same time kids are thinking, "I'm sick and tired of being told what to do and when to do it!" How do we get them, in the words of Nike®, to "just do it!" To behave. To respond appropriately. To think before they act. To be responsible, respectful and resourceful.

THE SWEET SPOT FOR SELF-DISCIPLINE

So where's the sweet spot in all these various ranges of factors that influence discipline? How can anyone dealing with kids today find the balancing point that yields the greatest effectiveness both now in the short term while setting them up for success in the long term?

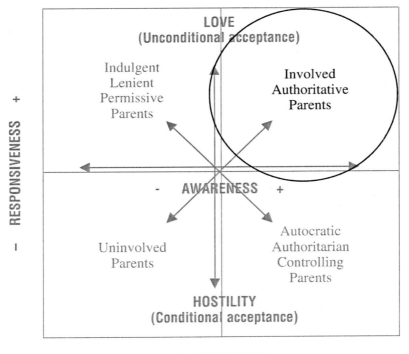

Involved parents who maintain a highly responsive, authoritative parenting approach – with unconditional love as well as high expectations – and who actively stay aware of what's going on with their kids create the optimal conditions to develop self-motivated kids who are self-disciplined. This more balanced style of parenting logically uses a high level of love, responsiveness, awareness, expectations/demands and involvement. Families of involved authoritative parents operate in an almost democratic manner where everyone gets involved at appropriate levels. I say almost because it's important parents maintain ultimate "veto power" (like that of a President) or have the final say like that of a benevolent dictator when it comes to (and *only* when it comes to) situations which may affect the well-being of younger family members.

There *is* a difference between being *authoritative* and being an *authoritarian*. It may all sound like semantics, but authoritative parents present expectations not demands upon their kids in a firm and respectful way. Authoritative parents are kind and firm at the same time. They maintain their own dignity and their kid's dignity by avoiding hostility.

Some parents are very kind and too many times have difficulty being firm, which usually leads to excessive permissiveness. This kind of wishy-washy back-and-forth kindness to firmness causes kids to become manipulative and avoid responsibility. Other parents are firm without kindness, which usually leads to excessive strictness. Overly strict *authoritarian* behavior incites kids to rebel and/or defy. *Authoritative* parents however use firmness *with* kindness while expecting their kids to cooperate, learning boundaries within an unconditionally loving relationship. There's a constant balance of empathy *with* consequences minus any anger or hostility.

Involved authoritative parents understand that the three most significant and important influences in a kid's life are:

1. How much a kid's parents or primary care-giving adults love them and show their affection towards them.

2. Parental involvement.

3. Parental awareness.

Without getting too touchy-feely regarding the words *love* and *affection*, it's easy to see how these same three influences could be appropriately brought into the classroom and on the job. Perhaps think of the term *positive regard*. When students know their teacher cares about them and for them, gets involved with them and is aware of what's going both in class as well as out of class in their life – that students are more motivated to learn! When employees know their boss, supervisor or upper management cares about them and treats them as meaningful contributors to the enterprise, actually works with them versus just demanding work from them, and pays attention to the employee's ideas, perspective, needs, wants and concerns – employees are more motivated to work!

Hopefully you're thinking "well that just makes sense!" Sure all parents would say "of course I love my kids!" All teachers would say "of course I love my class!" All employers would say "of course I care for my employees!" And of course they *all* would. But actions speak louder than words. Consistency also counts in good times and in bad. This isn't just about what we do and say when our kids behave, when the class acts appropriately, or when employees are really working hard. It's also about when they don't, or aren't, or haven't been. If all you do is conditionalize and/or qualify these three significant influences – then the best you can expect both short term and long term are inconsistently mixed results. When it comes to motivation, everything becomes a game of "hit or miss" leaving you constantly wondering "what makes these kids kick?"

Parents, teachers, and managers end up bouncing all over the various ranges of factors that influence discipline and/or behavior. They try to get more involved in their kid's life. Yet as activity increases with age and brothers or sisters get more involved in stuff – they can't keep up. Teachers try to create a collaborative learning environment where kids are actively engaged with them. Yet as more and more states start mandating standardized testing as well as other academically skewed accountability practices, kids are forced to "sit down, shut up and fill in the bubble sheet!" Managers try to get their employees more committed to collaborating and contributing in meaningful ways. Yet as labor unions make demands, HR requirements increase, and management demands fewer people do more for less, employees are "covering their butts" and getting "burned out."

The 123s of encouraging self-discipline

Based on the many ❑ ABCs of motivating kids today – which were shared in the very first book of our series *What Makes Kids KICK* – and given what we've already presented in this book, here are a few ✔ 123 steps to take if you want to encourage kids to KICK IT IN with self-discipline.

✔ **Offer choices within defined parameters** – Kids respond to choices more positively than demands. Be sure the choices are appropriate to the situation and developmental level of the child.

✔ **Talk less and ask more** – Questions help you gain understanding. Too many times we want to go into our lecture about this or that and kids already have them numbered. Getting a kid's perception may be more helpful than simply imposing your own perception upon them.

✔ **Avoid anger** – "The reason I'm so angry is because I love you!" yelled at the top of your lungs doesn't always convey the intended message. Modeling hostility around kids teaches them that the way to get what you want is to get mad.

✔ **Set clear limits** – Only when kids have clear limits defined ahead of time can they develop the autonomy-learning skill of operating within those limits.

✔ **Establish high standards** – Involved authoritative parents know how to establish reasonable, developmentally appropriate expectations and high standards for their kids. Because they're involved, they know what their kids can handle as well as what best fits the situation.

✔ **Consequences (two types)** – Kids learn self-discipline best when they understand and foresee various consequences for their behavior, choices and decisions. *Natural consequences* occur as a direct result of doing or not doing something. If you forget your coat on a cold day, you're cold. If you don't remember to bring your lunch, you're hungry or perhaps forced to figure something out so you won't be. *Logical consequences* occur or are required in situations such as when you spill your milk – you clean it up.

Or perhaps parental intervention is called for because allowing a natural consequence to occur wouldn't be smart. For example, a natural consequence to not brushing your teeth would be cavities. But *that* might be a bit extreme cause-and-effect lesson with kids. So most parents would have a logical consequence to stop doing whatever you're doing (i.e. playing with friends) and go brush your teeth. Notice how logical consequences are obvious, related, reasonable, respectful (of both child and parent) and overall reveals a lesson that helps kids understand what they need to do.

✔ **Provide clear feedback** – Specifically related to the behavior, effective feedback separates the act from the actor or the art from the artist. It's informational, constructive, and encourages further self-reflection by the child. It's not just saying "Nice job!" It's providing deeper and clearer comments such as "Wow! Look how you used all those shades of blue in painting the sky. How did you do that?"

✔ **Time-out for kids** – When used appropriately, time-out gives kids a chance to develop their own ability to self-regulate behavior. Too many times however time-out has simply become a lame strategy to get kids out of an angry parent's hair or a form of forcible isolation imposed on kids who must remain in solitary confinement. For a more positive approach to time-out check out Jane Nelson's *Positive Time-Out and 50 Ways to Avoid Power Struggles in the Home and the Classroom.*

✔ **Time-out for you** – The first step to dealing with anything is to be calm. This might be one of the most simple and important tips to remember. Too bad that, in the heat of the moment when it comes to discipline, it's often easier said than done. It mostly comes down to this: Do take care of yourself so your kids don't wear you down to the snapping point.

✔ **Let kids fail sometimes** – It's hard to learn from your mistakes if everyone fixes everything for you, rescues you from failure, and covers the consequences of your actions with "it's okay, I'll take care of that, let me do it." Dealing with failure and mistakes constructively is a part of life. Whenever developmentally appropriate (and safe), allow kids to fail as well as to learn from that failure.

✔ **Help kids reflect** – Both successes and failures can teach kids a great deal, but only if we help kids distill the wisdom to be gained in the process. Guide kids through the reflective process of "What did they experience? What choices and/or actions on their part contributed to the success or failure?" Most importantly, "What did they learn from the experience and how will knowing this influence what they do in the future?"

✔ **Consistency with flexibility** – Parents who consistently discipline within the sweet spot of high responsiveness, high expectations, high awareness, high involvement, and with lots of unconditional love, fare better than most. Sure, sometimes they're flexible when appropriate. On occasion, they might even "permissively" give in. Sometimes they might even controllingly, autocratically put their foot down. (That's why you may have noticed the sweet spot did cross over the line a bit on page 139.)

✔ **Spend time not money** – In today's world many parents do it, buying their kid something to make up for the lack of time they've been able to spend with them. Maybe the guilt that parents feel eases in doing so, but eventually kids see right through "the buyoff" – and use it as a source of manipulation to get what they want. In so doing, we inadvertently teach a lesson that "things to get" are more important than "time together."

✔ **Develop responsibility by giving responsibility** – It's hard to learn about being responsible if you're never given any real responsibility. It's also hard to know what your kid is capable of if you're not involved enough to know what's developmentally appropriate for them within various situations. Overly permissive and indulgent parents sabotage this by doing things for their kids that they can do themselves. Overly controlling autocratic parents make kids do things they're not ready to do on their own and then punish them when they fail.

✔ **Examples speak louder than words** – That old grandmother's curse – "I hope some day you grow up and have kids just like *you*" – tends to come true in many cases because we end up being parents just like them. Not always, but let's face it: The most powerful parenting examples you ever saw were not in books or on TV; they were your own parents. You may have even said while growing up, "I'll never…" and yet your actions are doing one thing, while your words say another. Guess which one wins out in terms of influence with your kids? That old saying "do as I say, not as I do" just doesn't cut it.

✔ **Follow through with firmness, dignity and respect** – Second only to consistency, follow-through creates many problems when *not* followed through.

✔ **Show unconditional love** – Love your kids for who they are not what they do. Show respect and dignity at all times.

✔ **We are a family** – Create an environment where everyone in the family feels accepted "as they are" and for "who they are" regardless of what they do. Show kids that you love them despite their mistakes and that if anything, mistakes are opportunities to learn and grow.

✔ **Have fun with your kids** – Social scientists have found that when kids play with their parents, it eases some of the stress kids feel – *especially* as they get older.[13] Stop the world and have some fun with your kids. Whether it's simply a "family game night"[14] playing a board game or getting outside for some fun, play is what William Doherty calls "the great leveler in parent-child relationships."

✔ **Give more encouragement than praise** – Yes, there is a difference! Encouragement expresses confidence in and appreciation of someone, not just what they did:

Encouragement	Praise
You did it!	That's very good!
I appreciate your help!	You get an 'A' today!
You're fun to be with!	Good job!
I admire your efforts!	I'm so proud of you!

Two problems with most praise is that it's usually a conditional judgment focused mainly on a person's performance – so much for unconditionlizing our love. And it's usually never specific enough to count as feedback that's helpful (i.e. What was "very good"? An "A" for what?). Encouragement is more about the person while praise is more about what they did.

Many people lump affirmation, encouragement, praise, positive reinforcement and all the other related terms into one category. Let's get ultra-clear with our vocabulary here – not splitting psycholinguistic hairs, but just to define which words mean what. Performance-based words of approval aren't an expression of unconditional love. By their very nature they're conditional. The phrase "Good job!" is conditional. It's evaluatively based on our judgment, rather than theirs.

Before I skate any further out onto thin ice, please rest assured that nothing's wrong with encouraging and supporting kids. "Encouragement is focused on the enjoyment your child experiences when doing an activity. Praise is focused on the outcome of a task."[16] Encouragement is more *process*-focused, praise is more product- or result-focused.

Praise also tends to relate to an attribute kids can't take credit for, such as beautiful blond hair, gorgeous blue eyes, and "you're so pretty." All of us know a few praise junkies who were manipulated their whole life via verbal rewards and now constantly depend upon other people's opinions of their work to get them though the day. They lack the self-assessment skills needed to determine the quality of their work. We need kids in this world who can think for themselves and learn how to assess what they do, and how they do, so they can improve doing it!

Ultimately the home serves as the first school for every kid. Parents are their first teachers. Your perception influences your level of motivation, attitude, and even behavior. Fostering a child's perception of personal control over their environment significantly helps kids to become self-disciplined, self-regulated and self-motivated.

During the years prior to entering school, kids begin to formulate their own understanding of cause and effect. Through all the various experiences they have, what they've identified and analyzed as being significant in causing those experiences to happen – and the generalized cumulative resulting perception they end up with – uniquely dominates their frame of reference. Their perception becomes their reality: They either see themselves as destiny's plaything, to be tossed around the world throughout their life with little or no power to really affect what happens to them. Or they have a strong sense of having influence and power over the events in their life, believing that they can choose to respond in a number of ways to deal with a particular circumstance.

When kids are simply managed with discipline or conditional praise, we eliminate the developmental opportunity to nurture their own abilities to self-assess, self-regulate, learn self-control and become self-disciplined because we're always doing it *for* them or *to* them. What's worse, it reinforces a more externally oriented motivational perception within kids and influences their own understanding that "the world's out to get them" so "get what you can while you can." This sets up a classic case of carrot-and-sticking the rest of that kid's life.

Kids who develop their own abilities to self-assess, self-regulate, learn self-control – and who actually become self-disciplined – realize the world is theirs and that we're all willing to work *with* them. Parents, neighbors, youth group leaders, coaches, teachers, and even bosses are all involved with kids maintaining a highly responsive, authoritative style with unconditional love as well as high expectations, actively staying aware of what's going on, and creating the optimal conditions to develop self-motivated kids who KICK IT IN!

BOOKS ABOUT DEVELOPING SELF-DISCIPLINE IN KIDS

No More Misbehavin'
by Michele Borba

Kids Are Worth It! Giving Your Child the Gift of Inner Discipline
by Barbara Coloroso

Raising a Responsible Child
by Don Dinkmeyer, Sr. and Gary McKay

The Parents Handbook
by Don Dinkmeyer, Sr., Gary McKay and Don Dinkmeyer, Jr.

Children: The Challenge
Discipline Without Tears
New Approach to Discipline: Logical Consequences
by Rudolf Dreikurs

How To Talk So Kids Will Listen & Listen So Kids Will Talk
by Adele Faber and Elaine Mazlish

I Swore I'd Never Do That!
by Elizabeth Fishel

Teaching Children Self-Discipline at Home and at School
by Thomas Gordon

Love & Limits: Achieving a Balance in Parenting
by Ronald Huxley

Between Parent and Child
Between Parent and Teenager
by Haim Ginott

Raising a Self-Starter
Raising Happy Kids
by Elizabeth Hartley-Brewer

Punished by Rewards
Unconditional Parenting
by Alfie Kohn

Setting Limits
by Robert MacKenzie

Discipline Without Stress Punishments or Rewards
by Marvin Marshall

Raising Children Who Think for Themselves
Raising Everyday Heroes: Parenting Children to be Self-Reliant
Hearing is Believing: How Words Can Make or Break Our Kids
by Elisa Medhus

Positive Discipline
Positive Time-Out
by Jane Nelsen

Positive Discipline A-Z
by Jane Nelsen, Lynn Lott and H. Stephen Glenn

The Parent's Toolshop
by Jody Johnston Pawel

The Discipline Book
by William Sears and Martha Sears

Parenting Guide to Positive Discipline
by Paula Spencer

Our Last Best Shot:
Guiding Our Children Through Early Adolescence
by Laura Stepp

Do Your Kids Know You Love Them?
by Fred Streit and Beatrice Krauss

The Secret of Parenting: How to Be in Charge of Today's Kids
From Toddlers to Preteens Without Threats or Punishment
by Anthony Wolf

WEB SITES ABOUT DEVELOPING SELF-DISCIPLINE IN KIDS

http://www.aacap.org/publications/factsfam/discplin.htm

Developing Capable People http://www.capabilitiesinc.com

Discipline Without Stress	http://www.disciplinewithoutstress.com
Dr. Bill & Martha Sears	http://www.askdrsears.com
Dr. Spock	http://www.drspock.com
Effective Discipline	http://www.stophitting.com
Family Life	http://ianrpubs.unl.edu/family/
Thomas Gordon Training	http://www.gordontraining.com
Healthy Parenting Today	http://www.ehealthyparenting.com
Love & Logic	http://www.loveandlogic.com
Kids Are Worth It	http://www.kidsareworthit.com
Alfie Kohn	http://www.alfiekohn.org
Dr. Elisa Medhus	http://www.drmedhus.com
Parent's Handbooks	http://www.parentshandbooks.org
Parent's Toolshop	http://www.parentstoolshop.com
Parenting Toolbox	http://parentingtoolbox.com
Positive Discipline	http://www.positivediscipline.com
Positive Discipline Assoc.	http://www.posdis.org
Positive Parenting	http://www.positiveparenting.com
Prevent Child Abuse	http://www.preventchildabuse.org
Project NoSpank	http://www.nospank.net
Talk With Your Kids	http://www.talkingwithkids.org
STEP Parenting Program	http://www.agsnet.com/parenting.asp

NOTES FOR CHAPTER FIVE

1. Guarendi, R. N. (1986). *You're a Better Parent Than You Think!* New York: Fireside.

2. Howe, N., & Strauss, W. (1991). *Generations: The History of America's Future 1584 to 2069.* New York: William Morrow and Company, Inc.

3. Jones, L. Y. (1980). *Great Expectations: America and the Baby Boom Generation.* New York: Ballantine Books.

4. Holtz, G. T. (1995). *Welcome to the Jungle: The Why Behind 'Generation X'.* New York: St. Martin's Griffin.

5. Schiff, S. (2003, April 27). Raising America: Because I Said So. *New York Times.*

6. Longfellow, L. (1993). *Generations of Excellence: Why Our Changing Values Add Value* [Video]. Prescott, AZ.

7. Baumrind, D. (1991). The Influence of Parenting Style. *Journal of Early Adolescence, 11*(1), 56-95.

8. CNN Interactive. (1998, March 16). *Famed Pediatrician Dr. Spock dies at age 94* [Online]. CNN. http://www.cnn.com/US/9803/16/obit.dr.spock/

9. Maier, T. (1998, March 30). Everybody's Grandfather: Dr. Spock raised the baby boom generation and changed America. *U.S. News & World Report.*

10. Spock, B. (1946). *The Common Sense Book of Baby and Child Care.* New York: Duell, Sloan & Pearce.

11. Rosenfeld, A., & Wise, N. (2000). *Hyper-Parenting: Are You Hurting Your Child by Trying Too Hard?* New York: St. Martin's Press.

12. Barber, B. K. (2002). *Intrusive Parenting: How Psychological Control Affects Children and Adolescents* (1st ed.). Washington, DC: American Psychological Association.

13. Resnick, M. D. (1997). Protecting Adolescents from Harm: Findings from the National Longitudinal Study of Adolescent Health. *Journal of the American Medical Association, 278,* 823-832.

14. Stepp, L. S. (2001, July 2). Joining In the Family Fun. *Washington Post.*

15. Hasbro. (2001). *Family Game Night Campaign* [Online]. http://www.hasbro.com/familygamenight/

16. Greenspon, T. S. (2002). *Freeing Our Families from Perfectionism.* Minneapolis, MN: Free Spirit Publishing.

Organizations & Research Sources

This list is by no means "everyone and anyone" who works with kids, helps kids, knows kids, are advocates for kids, has resources available in dealing with, living with, teaching and learning with, managing and working with, or marketing and selling to kids. But it's a good start. The resources listed here are included because of their high-quality content, real-world relevance and practical application value. It's stuff you can use! Many times these resources will have their own list of references and links taking you even further. Be open-minded as you review the various resources. Parents and teachers can learn a great deal from the media, managing and marketing sources. Likewise, business professionals, managers and even marketers can gain a great deal of insight from the parenting/family, school and health sources.

<u>WARNING</u>! If you happen to come across a resource that you don't personally see any value in and/or agree with – please simply skip it. Don't discount the positive value of the entire list just because of one or two you find fault with or that personally offend you because of a particular stance they may take on a particular issue.

Obviously due to a constantly changing world this list was out-of-date and incomplete seven seconds after it was researched and typed up. If you would like a more up-to-date listing, simply visit http://www.whatmakeskidskick.com

RESOURCE LIST TABLE OF CONTENTS

Parenting/Family..155
School..160
Health 166
Research and Statistics 168
Culture..172
Politics, Activism, Community 176
Media..180
Violence 182
Addiction and Substance Abuse...184
Sex, Teen Pregnancy and STDs 188
Runaway, Homeless & Missing Children..................................190
Suicide Prevention 191
National Youth Organizations & Clubs.....................................192
Managing Kids..193
Marketing to Kids 194

Parenting/Family

The Alliance for Children and Families
11700 West Lake Park Drive
Milwaukee, WI 53224-3099
800-221-3726
http://www.alliance1.org

The Alliance for Children and Families is an international membership association representing more than 350 private, nonprofit child- and family-serving organizations. Contains facts, figures and information on how families can become more engaged in schools and communities.

■■■■■■■■■■■■■■■■■■■■■■■■■■■■■■■■■■■■■■

Center for Parent/Youth Understanding
P.O. Box 414
Elizabethtown, PA 17022
800-807-CPYU
http://www.cpyu.org

The Center for Parent/Youth Understanding is a nonprofit organization committed to building strong families by serving to bridge the cultural-generational gap between parents and teenagers. CPYU helps parents, youthworkers, educators and others understand teenagers and their culture so that they will be better equipped to help children and teens navigate the challenging world of adolescence.

■■■■■■■■■■■■■■■■■■■■■■■■■■■■■■■■■■■■■■

Council on Contemporary Families
http://www.contemporaryfamilies.org

The Council on Contemporary Families (CCF) is a nonprofit organization founded in 1996 by a diverse group of family researchers, mental health and social work practitioners, and activists. Their goal is to enhance the national conversation about what contemporary families need and how these needs can best be met. Articles, resources, bibliography and links.

■■■■■■■■■■■■■■■■■■■■■■■■■■■■■■■■■■■■■■

Developing Capable People
http://www.capabilitiesinc.com

Developed by Stephen Glenn, the Developing Capable People program has an outstanding reputation in helping parents identify the strategies and develop the methods needed to help kids grow into capable people. Workshops are available.

Facts for Families
by the American Academy of Child and Adolescent Psychiatry
3615 Wisconsin Avenue NW
Washington, D.C. 20016-3007
202-966-7300
http://www.aacap.org/publications/factsfam/index.htm

The AACAP developed Facts for Families to provide concise and up-to-date information on issues that affect children, teenagers, and their families. The AACAP provides this important information as a public service and the Facts for Families may be duplicated and distributed free of charge as long as the American Academy of Child and Adolescent Psychiatry is properly credited and no profit is gained from their use.

▪▪▪▪▪▪▪▪▪▪▪▪▪▪▪▪▪▪▪▪▪▪▪▪▪▪▪▪▪▪▪▪▪▪▪▪▪

Family Communications, Inc.
4802 Fifth Avenue
Pittsburgh, PA 15213
412-687-2990
http://www.fci.org

From the producers of Mister Rogers' Neighborhood, Family Communications focuses on strengthening the relationships between children, their families, and the community of people who support them. Helping to nurture those relationships is the core of their work. The web site has information for parents and educators of preschool and young elementary age kids.

▪▪▪▪▪▪▪▪▪▪▪▪▪▪▪▪▪▪▪▪▪▪▪▪▪▪▪▪▪▪▪▪▪▪▪▪

Family Life 1st/Putting Family First
http://www.puttingfamilyfirst.org

Family Life 1st/Putting Family First is a group of citizens building a community where family life is an honored and celebrated priority. Balance has become gravely out of whack for many families of all social classes, and retrieving family life requires a public, grass roots movement generated and sustained by families themselves.

▪▪▪▪▪▪▪▪▪▪▪▪▪▪▪▪▪▪▪▪▪▪▪▪▪▪▪▪▪▪▪▪▪▪▪▪

Focus on the Family
P.O. Box 3550
Colorado Springs, CO 80935-3550
800-232-6459
http://www.fotf.org

This nonprofit organization, founded by Dr. James Dobson, produces his nationally syndicated radio programs and offers books, resources and research on the family.

Hyper-Parenting
http://www.hyperparenting.com

This site for the book by Dr. Alvin Rosenfeld and Nicole Wise, Hyper-Parenting explains why it is better – in the short and long run – for parents and kids alike to slow down, do less, and generally turn the volume down on family life. This site has tips to avoiding the Hyper-Parenting trap as well as a discussion board.

■ ■

Love and Logic Institute, Inc.
2207 Jackson Street
Golden, CO 80401-2300
800-588-5644
http://www.loveandlogic.com

This philosophy of raising and teaching children allows adults to be happier, empowered, and more skilled in their interactions with children. Love allows children to grow through their mistakes. Logic allows children to live with the consequences of their choices. Love and Logic is a way of working with children that puts parents and teachers back in control, teaches children to be responsible, and prepares young people to live in the real world, with its many choices and consequences. Many great articles and links to books as well as parenting/teaching resources!

■ ■

National Black Child Development Institute
http://www.nbcdi.org

Supports and develops programs, workshops, and resources for African-American children in the areas of health, education, welfare, and parenting. Excellent information and resources.

■ ■

National Center for Fathering
P.O. Box 413888
Kansas City, MO 64141
913-384-4661
http://www.fathers.com

Founded in 1990 by Dr. Ken Canfield, the National Center for Fathering conducts and shares research, articles and resources for Dads.

■ ■

National Children's Coalition
1095 Market Street, Suite 611
San Francisco, CA 94119
510-444-6074
http://child.net

Lots of articles to view for kids, teens, and parents. Good resource for parents because many topics are available.

National Directory of Children and Youth Family Services
14 Inverness Drive East, Suite D144
Englewood, CO 80112
800-343-6681
http://www.childrenyouthfamilydir.com

This is a national directory for youth and family services and claims to be the most comprehensive guide for professionals who help troubled youth.

■■■■■■■■■■■■■■■■■■■■■■■■■■■■■■■■■■■■■■

National Fatherhood Initiative
101 Lake Forest Boulevard, Suite 360
Gaithersburg, MD 20877
301-948-0599
http://www.fatherhood.org

They are trying to restore responsible fatherhood through public education. The organization's site includes advice for Dads, a catalog of fathering resources, tips from other fathers and a list of links to other organizations.

■■■■■■■■■■■■■■■■■■■■■■■■■■■■■■■■■■■■■■

National Parenting Association
444 Park Avenue South, Suite 602
New York, NY 10016
212-679-4004
http://www.parentsunite.org

The National Parenting Association is working to make parenting a higher priority in both the private lives of people and on the public agenda nationally. This nonprofit, non-partisan organization founded in 1993 provides resources, references and current issue related insights to parenting.

■■■■■■■■■■■■■■■■■■■■■■■■■■■■■■■■■■■■■■

The National Parenting Center
800-753-6667
http://www.tnpc.com

This web site offers several pamphlets in their On-line Adolescence Reading Room on communicating with pre-teens and teens. It also hosts more than 100 chat rooms for parents on the challenges of parenting and offers links to other web sites.

■■■■■■■■■■■■■■■■■■■■■■■■■■■■■■■■■■■■■■

National Safe Kids Campaign
1301 Pennsylvania Ave. NW, Suite 1000
Washington, DC 20004-1707
202-662-0600
http://www.safekids.org

Great site used to prevent unintentional injury to children. Items include car seats, poison, fire, firearms, toys, etc. Good resource for safety conscious parents.

PACER Center
8161 Normandale Boulevard
Minneapolis, MN 55437-1044
952-838-9000
http://www.pacer.org

Parent Advocacy Coalition for Educational Rights Center helps parents with
children with disabilities. Contains many helpful categories such as resources with
links, projects, legislation, employment strategies, info on emotional behavioral
disorders, etc. Very helpful site.

■ ■

Positive Discipline
by Empowering People, Inc.
P.O. Box 1926
Orem, UT 84059-1926
800-456-7770
http://www.positivediscipline.com

Positive Discipline is based on the philosophies of Alfred Adler and Rudolf Dreikurs
who believed that all human beings have equal rights to dignity and respect. All
Positive Discipline methods are non-punitive and non-permissive. They are "kind"
and "firm" at the same time. Kind, because that shows respect for the child (and for
the adult). Firm, because that shows respect for what needs to be done. Lots of
wonderful articles!

■ ■

Alfred P. Sloan Family Center on Parents, Children & Work
1155 East 60th Street
Chicago, IL 60637
773-256-6352
http://www.sloanworkingfamilies.org

The Alfred P. Sloan Family Center on Parents, Children & Work at the University of
Chicago was established to examine issues facing contemporary working families.
Focuses on how parents who are working full-time manage the conflicting demands
of work and family. Many research findings, papers and materials available.

■ ■

Talking With Kids About Tough Issues
355 Lexington Avenue
11th Floor, New York, NY 10017
800-CHILD-44 (800-244-5344)
http://www.talkingwithkids.org

A joint project of the Henry J. Kaiser Family Foundation and Children Now, this
booklet encourages parents to explore their own values and beliefs in order to better
communicate them to their children. Topics covered include HIV/AIDS, sex and
sexuality, violence, drugs and alcohol.

Weekly Reader
200 First Stamford Place
Stamford, CT 06912
800-446-3355
http://www.weeklyreader.com

Contains parent section with great articles concerning diverse areas of child raising. Also links to educational topics of current interests and news.

■ ■

Youth and Child Resource Net
P.O. Box 72174
Oakland, CA 94612
http://www.child.net/childco.htm

Lots of links and articles about children. Great resource on parenting with many articles about education.

School

ACT
2201 N. Dodge Street
Iowa City, Iowa 52243-0168
319-337-1000
http://www.act.org

ACT is an independent, not-for-profit organization that provides assessment, research, information, and program management services in the broad areas of education and workforce development. Creators of the ACT test.

■ ■

Afterschool.gov
http://www.afterschool.gov

Good information on federal resources that support children and youth during out-of-school hours.

■ ■

American Homeschooling Association
P.O. Box 3142
Palmer, Alaska 99645
800-236-3278
http://www.americanhomeschoolassociation.org

The American Homeschool Association (AHA) is a service organization sponsored in part by the publishers of Home Education Magazine. The AHA was created in 1995 to network homeschoolers on a national level. Current AHA services include an on-line news and discussion list which provides news, information, and resources for homeschoolers, media contacts, and education officials.

Character Counts!
by the Josephson Institute of Ethics
4640 Admiralty Way, Suite 1001
Marina del Rey, CA 90292-6610
310-306-1868
http://www.charactercounts.org

The Josephson Institute of Ethics is a public-benefit, nonpartisan, nonprofit
membership organization founded to improve the ethical quality of society by
advocating principled reasoning and ethical decision making. The Character Counts
youth education initiative is a project of the Institute.

■ ■

Character Education Guide
3450 Sacramento Street, Suite 619
San Francisco, CA 94118
800-359-KIDS
http://www.goodcharacter.com

Character Education guide and free resources for teachers. Subcategories include
teaching guides for all grades, character in sports, opportunities for students to
practice good character, web sources, discussions, and links to key character
education organizations. Good site for teachers!

■ ■

The College Board
45 Columbus Avenue
New York, NY 10023-6992
212-713-8000
http://www.collegeboard.com

The College Board is a national nonprofit membership association whose mission is
to prepare, inspire, and connect students to college and opportunity. Founded in
1900, the association is composed of more than 4,200 schools, colleges, universities,
and other educational organizations. Each year, the College Board serves over three
million students and their parents, 22,000 high schools, and 3,500 colleges through
major programs and services in college admission, guidance, assessment, financial
aid, enrollment, teaching and learning. Creators of the SAT and PSAT.

■ ■

Communities In Schools
277 South Washington Street, Suite 210
Alexandria, VA 22314
800-CIS-4KIDS (800-247-4543)
http://www.cisnet.org

This nationwide independent network champions the connection of needed
community resources with schools to help young people learn, stay in school, and
prepare for life.

Education Commission of the States
700 Broadway, Suite 1200
Denver, CO 80203-3460
303-299-3600
http://www.ecs.org

The Education Commission of the States is an interstate compact created to improve public education by facilitating the exchange of and promote the development of educational policy based on available research and strategies.

▪ ▪

FairTest: The National Center for Fair & Open Testing
342 Broadway
Cambridge, MA 02139
617-864-4810
http://www.fairtest.org

The National Center for Fair & Open Testing is an advocacy organization working to end the abuses, misuses and flaws of standardized testing and ensure that evaluation of students and workers is fair, open, and educationally sound.

▪ ▪

Higher Education Research Institute
UCLA Graduate School of Education
3005 Moore Hall Box 951521
Los Angeles, CA 90095-1521
310-825-1925
http://www.gseis.ucla.edu/heri/heri.html

The Institute serves as an interdisciplinary center for research, evaluation, information, policy studies and research training in postsecondary education. HERI's research program covers a variety of topics including the outcomes of postsecondary education, leadership development, faculty performance, federal and state policy, and educational equity.

▪ ▪

Institute for Educational Leadership
1001 Connecticut Avenue NW, Suite 310
Washington, DC 20036
202-822-8405
http://www.iel.org

Their mission is to improve education by empowering people with knowledge, applications, and positive vision. Site contains both programs and publications including a section called "School Leadership for the 21st Century Initiative."

Institute for Research and Reform in Education
http://www.irre.org

IRRE has creative yet practical initiatives to improve the life chances of children and youth, especially those in low-income communities. Building on best practices and wide-ranging research, IRRE applies a theory of change approach to help communities and schools plan and evaluate their work. IRRE has publications and relevant resource rich materials for the fields of education, youth development and community change.

■ ■

LD On-Line
2775 South Quincy Street
Arlington, VA 22206
703-998-2600
http://www.ldonline.org

Fabulous place for parents of Learning Disabled children. Contains information for parents and teachers, is up-to-date, and contains multiple categories.

■ ■

The National Association for the Education of Young Children
1509 16th Street, NW
Washington, DC 20036-1426
800-424-2460
http://www.naeyc.org

The NAEYC is the nation's largest and most influential organization of early childhood educators and others dedicated to improving the quality of programs for children from birth through third grade. Many resources and developmentally appropriate information for parents and teachers.

■ ■

National Association of Secondary School Principals
1904 Association Drive
Reston, VA 20191-1537
703-860-0200
http://www.nassp.org

NASSP is the largest organization of school leaders in the country representing more than 36,000 middle level and senior high school principals. Resource rich with links to NASSP-sponsored student activities groups such as the National Honor Society®, National Junior Honor Society®, National Association of Student Councils®, National Association of Student Activity Advisers®, Middle Level Student Activity Advisers Association®.

National Center for Education Statistics
1990 K Street NW
Washington, DC 20006
202-502-7300
http://nces.ed.gov

NCES is the primary federal entity for collecting and analyzing data that are related to education in the U.S.

■ ■

National Home Educational Network
P.O. Box 41067
Long Beach, CA 90853
http://www.nhen.org

The National Home Education Network exists to encourage and facilitate the vital grassroots work of state and local homeschooling groups and individuals by providing information, fostering networking and promoting public relations on a national level.

■ ■

National Home Education Research Institute
http://www.nheri.org

NHERI, nonprofit research and educational organization makes available for public purchase many print, audio, and video productions ranging from basic bottom-line fact sheets about homeschooling to more technically sophisticated academic reports.

■ ■

National School Safety Center
141 Duesenberg Drive, Suite 11
Westlake Village, CA 91362
805-373-9977
http://www.nssc1.org

NSSC serves as a clearinghouse for current information on school safety issues, maintaining a resource center with more than 50,000 articles, publications and films.

■ ■

Parent Teacher Association
330 North Wabash Avenue, Suite 2100
Chicago, IL 60611
800-307-4PTA (800-307-4782)
http://www.pta.org

The National PTA is the oldest and largest volunteer association in the United States working exclusively on behalf of children and youth.

SchoolMatch
5027 Pine Creek Drive
Westerville, OH 43081
614-890-1573
http://www.schoolmatch.com

Launched in June of 1995, SchoolMatch is the school research and database service firm that specializes in rating schools (K-12) using auditable data for the parent and corporation.

■ ■

School Psychology Resources On-line
http://www.schoolpsychology.net

Huge glossary of learning disabilities, disorders, etc. along with other information. This is a good place for a parent or teacher to begin researching a problem. Disorders include ADHD, autism, anxiety disorder, and others.

■ ■

U.S. Department of Education
400 Maryland Avenue, SW
Washington, DC 20202-0498
800-USA-LEARN (800-872-5327)
http://www.ed.gov

A storehouse of statistics on safe and drug-free schools, education, libraries, financial aid, and all things educational.

■ ■

ThinkQuest
by the Oracle Help Us Help Foundation
http://www.thinkquest.org

Encourages the advancement of education through the use of technology. Hosts internet competitions, a library of educational web sites created by students, teachers, and conferences.

■ ■

Who's Who Among American High School Students and
Who's Who Among America's Teachers
by Educational Communications, Inc.
1701 Directors Blvd., Suite 920
Austin, TX 78744
512-440-2300
http://www.eci-whoswho.com

Since 1970 they have polled the attitudes and opinions of Who's Who students and teachers on timely issues in their annual surveys.

Young Adult Library Services Association
American Library Association
50 East Huron
Chicago, IL 60611
800-545-2433
http://www.ala.org/yalsa/

Library site that contains book reviews with areas specializing in kids and teens.

Health

The Allergy and Asthma Network/Mothers of Asthmatics, Inc.
2751 Prosperity Avenue, Suite 150
Fairfax, VA 22031
800-878-4403
http://www.aanma.org

Lists publications, reports, products and up-to-date information on asthma.

▪▪

American Academy of Child and Adolescent Psychiatry
3615 Wisconsin Avenue NW
Washington, D.C. 20016-3007
202-966-7300
http://www.aacap.org

Provided as a public service to aid in the understanding of developmental behavioral and mental problems in children.

▪▪

The American Lung Association
61 Broadway, 6th Floor
New York, NY 10006
212-315-8700
http://www.lungusa.org

Uses cartoon character Bronkie: The Dinosaur with Asthma to teach about asthma. Presented by the American Lung Association along with many other great links, references and facts.

▪▪

Centers for Disease Control and Prevention
1600 Clifton Road
Atlanta, GA 30333
404-639-3311
http://www.cdc.gov

If you're looking for statistics and information on health issues this site is it. The site features a search engine and an extensive list of links to other sites. There's a section on Adolescent and School Health at http://www.cdc.gov/HealthyYouth/index.htm

Change Your Mind About Mental Health
by the American Psychological Association
750 First Street NE
Washington, DC 20002-4242
877-495-0009
http://www.apahelpcenter.org

Learning acceptance towards getting mental health help when needed. Sponsored by the American Psychological Association.

■ ■

drDrew.com
36 West Colorado Boulevard, Suite 5
Pasadena, California 91105
http://www.drdrew.com

Made popular by Dr. Drew's work with MTV, his web site has information from doctors and health institutions, as well as comments and stories from celebrities and other on-line community members.

■ ■

Dr. John Grohol's Mental Health Page
http://www.psychcentral.com

An index for psychology, support, and mental health issues, resources, and people on the Internet, this site includes a glossary of information, articles and essays, book reviews, live chats, and a hotline..

■ ■

KidsHealth
Nemours Center for Children's Health
P.O. Box 269
Wilmington, DE 19899
http://www.kidshealth.org

KidsHealth.org is devoted to providing health information for parents, teens, and kids. Created by the medical professionals at the Nemours Foundation, KidsHealth has information on newborn health concerns, gun safety for children, the effects of divorce, infections, behavior & emotions, food & fitness, surgeries, and growing up healthy.

■ ■

Sleep Information/National Heart, Lung & Blood Institute
Building 31, Room 5A52
31 Center Drive MSC
Bethesda, MD 20892
http://www.nhlbi.nih.gov/health/prof/sleep/index.htm

Good sleep information for youth and adults from health care professionals. Covers disorders and lists additional resources.

USDA/ARS Children's Nutrition Research Center
at Baylor College of Medicine
1100 Bates Street
Houston, TX 77030
http://www.bcm.tmc.edu/cnrc/

The Children's Nutrition Research Center (CNRC) is dedicated to defining the
nutrient needs of children, from conception through adolescence, and the needs of
pregnant women and nursing mothers. Scientific data from the Center enables health
care providers and policy advisors to make dietary recommendations that will
improve the health of today's children and that of generations to come.

Research and Statistics

ADOL
The Adolescence Directory On-line
http://education.indiana.edu/cas/adol/adol.html

Site contains articles of diverse concerns such as teen violence, mental health, health
risks, and also a section for teens only. It also contains information for counselors
and also a teacher talk forum. This electronic guide of information on adolescent
issues is maintained by the Center for Adolescent Studies at Indiana University.

■ ■

Alliance for Childhood
P.O. Box 444
College Park, MD 20741
301-513-1777
http://www.allianceforchildhood.net

A network of individuals working together for the well being of children. Great
information and research related to children's issues such as questioning the impact
of technology on kids, the importance of play and others.

■ ■

American FactFinder
by the U.S. Census Bureau
Washington, DC 20233
301-457-4608
http://factfinder.census.gov

On the Internet since March 1999, American FactFinder revolutionizes the way the
Census Bureau publishes decennial results. American FactFinder allows the Census
Bureau to disseminate more data to more users faster.

ChildStats
http://www.childstats.gov

This is the official site for the Federal Interagency Forum on Child and Family
Statistics. It offers easy access to federal and state statistics and reports on children
and their families, including: population and family characteristics, economic
security, health, behavior and social environment, and education.

■ ■

Child Trends
4301 Connecticut Avenue NW, Suite 100
Washington, DC 20008
202-362-5580
http://www.childtrends.org
http://www.childtrendsdatabank.org

Child Trends, Inc. is a nonprofit, nonpartisan research organization that studies
children, youth, and families through research, data collection, and data analysis.

■ ■

CYFERNet
Children, Youth and Families Education Research Network
612-626-1111
http://www.cyfernet.org

CYFERNet is a service of the Cooperative Extension System and offers research
information about children, parents, families, and community.

■ ■

Family Research Council
801 G. Street, NW
Washington, DC 20001
202-2100 or 800-225-4008
http://www.frc.org

Lots of "culture facts" and resources regarding family, current issues, state and
national statistics.

■ ■

FirstGov
http://firstgov.gov

This site is the World Wide Web information portal for the United States Federal
Government. FirstGov is intended to be the first-stop resource to find any
government information on the Internet, with topics ranging from kids and families
to money and benefits to science and technology - and everything in between. The
directory is subject-divided and provides state and local government links as well.

The Future of Children
300 Second Street, Suite 200
Los Altos, CA 94022
650-948-7658
http://www.futureofchildren.org

The Future of Children is published twice annually by The David and Lucile Packard Foundation. The primary purpose of The Future of Children is to disseminate timely information and research on major issues related to children's well-being.

▪▪▪▪▪▪▪▪▪▪▪▪▪▪▪▪▪▪▪▪▪▪▪▪▪▪▪▪▪▪▪▪▪▪▪▪▪▪▪

Institute for Youth Development
P.O. Box 16560
Washington DC, 20041
703-471-8750
http://www.youthdevelopment.org

IYD is a non-partisan, nonprofit organization that promotes a comprehensive risk avoidance message to youth for five harmful risk behaviors that are inextricably linked: alcohol, drugs, sex, tobacco and violence. IYD believes that children and teens, provided with consistent and sound messages, are capable of making positive choices to avoid these risk behaviors altogether, especially if they are empowered by strong parent and family connections. Their web site is designed for both professionals in the field of youth development and for mothers, fathers, and teens looking for current information and advice.

▪▪▪▪▪▪▪▪▪▪▪▪▪▪▪▪▪▪▪▪▪▪▪▪▪▪▪▪▪▪▪▪▪▪▪▪▪▪▪

Kids Count
The Annie E. Casey Foundation
701 St. Paul St. Baltimore, MD 21202
410-547-6600
http://www.aecf.org/kidscount/index.htm

Tracks the status and well being of children nationally and state by state.

▪▪▪▪▪▪▪▪▪▪▪▪▪▪▪▪▪▪▪▪▪▪▪▪▪▪▪▪▪▪▪▪▪▪▪▪▪▪▪

Monitoring the Future:
A Continuing Study of America's Youth
http://www.monitoringthefuture.org

The Monitoring the Future Study is funded by research grants from the National Institute on Drug Abuse. MTF is conducted at the Survey Research Center in the Institute for Social Research at the University of Michigan. This is a continuing study that monitors the habits and lifestyle of American youth. A good site for keeping up-to-date on today's youth.

National Clearinghouse on Families & Youth
P.O. Box 13505
Silver Spring, MD 20911-3505
301-608-8098
http://www.ncfy.com

Site contains a library on youth issues, forums, and an outreach program that
provides support and funding information.

■■■■■■■■■■■■■■■■■■■■■■■■■■■■■■■■■■

National Youth Development Information Center
1319 F Street NW, Suite 601
Washington, DC 20004
877-NYDIC-4-U (877-693-4248)
http://www.nydic.org

Contains evaluations of youth programs, research, directories, statistics, funding,
etc. Promotes positive growth and attitudes. Excellent source of information on
youth development as well as related topics.

■■■■■■■■■■■■■■■■■■■■■■■■■■■■■■■■■■

Search Institute
615 First Avenue NE, Suite 125
Minneapolis, MN 55413
800-888-7828
http://www.search-institute.org

Search Institute is an independent, nonprofit organization committed not only to
contributing to the knowledge base about youth, but also committed to translating
high-quality research on children and youth into practical ideas, tools, services, and
resources for families, neighborhoods, schools, organizations, and communities.

■■■■■■■■■■■■■■■■■■■■■■■■■■■■■■■■■■

State of Our Nation's Youth by the Horatio Alger Association
99 Canal Center Plaza
Alexandria, Virginia 22314
703-684-9444
http://www.horatioalger.com/pubmat/surpro.htm

The State of Our Nation's Youth analyzes the varying types and levels of family and
peer support American youth receive, their outlook on numerous issues from
education to social attitudes, and what these students see as the biggest obstacles in
their lives as opposed to obstacles perceived by adults and educators.

■■■■■■■■■■■■■■■■■■■■■■■■■■■■■■■■■■

University of Michigan's Document Center/ Statistical Resources on the Web
http://www.lib.umich.edu/govdocs/stats.html

Site offers a huge amount of categories for finding statistics. There are easy to use
icons for choosing topics, and a left-hand scrolling menu that contains numerous
categories. Great for research.

The Urban Health Initiative
7900 East Greenlake Drive North, Suite 302
Seattle, WA 98103-4850
206-616-3637
http://www.urbanhealth.org

Their purpose is to promote ideas that work. Information is available on after school programs, early childhood intervention, child abuse and neglect, reading, substance abuse, teen pregnancy and youth violence prevention.

▪ ▪

Youth Attitude Tracking Study
by the Defense Manpower Data Center
U.S. Department of Defense
http://www.dmdc.osd.mil/yats/

The annual Youth Attitude Tracking Study (YATS) has, since 1975, collected information from American youth vital to the Department of Defense and the individual military Services.

Culture

Alloy, Inc.
West 26th Street, 11th Floor
New York, NY 10001
212-244-4297
http://www.alloy.com

Alloy.com is one of the web's largest and most dynamic destinations for girls. Fashioned as a virtual mall with all the social trappings of teen-hood, Alloy.com invites girls to interact, browse and connect.

▪ ▪

ASPIRA Association, Inc.
1444 Eye Street NW, Suite 800
Washington, DC 20005
202-835-3600
http://www.aspira.org

ASPIRA is the only national nonprofit organization devoted solely to the education and leadership development of Puerto Rican and other Latino youth. The ASPIRA Association promotes the empowerment of the Puerto Rican and Latino community by developing and nurturing the leadership, intellectual, and cultural potential of its youth so that they may contribute their skills and dedication to the fullest development of the Puerto Rican and Latino community everywhere.

Bolt
http://www.bolt.com

Bolt is one of the Internet's most popular hangouts for high school and college students. Using cutting-edge communication tools, Bolt gives kids the power to speak their mind on whatever they want, from kissing to current events, from the SATs to the latest CDs. With substantial content written by kids, Bolt is one of the largest on-line communities of kids.

■ ■

Children's Express
1101 14th Street NW, Third Floor
Washington, DC 20005
202-737-7377
http://www.cenews.org

Children's Express is an international nonprofit media organization, founded in 1975, that produces stories by reporters (ages 8 to 13) and editors (ages 14 to 18) for adult print, broadcast, and interactive media. A Pulitzer Prize nominee, CE has received Emmy, Peabody and Casey awards for outstanding journalism.

■ ■

The City Kids Foundation
57 Leonard Street
New York, NY 10013
http://www.citykids.com

Focuses on teaching youth-to-youth communication skills to aid in problem-solving and decision making processes. Principles include youth communication, multicultural bridge building, and safe spaces.

■ ■

FreeZone (A division of The Gale Group)
730 North Franklin, Suite 706
Chicago IL 60610
312-573-3800
http://www.freezone.com

FreeZone was one of the first community sites on the Internet and is one of the only kids' sites that is 100 percent monitored and screened by trained adult employees. Kid-driven content has made FreeZone one of the most popular Internet sites for kids ages 8 to 14.

■ ■

The Gallup Organization
901 F Street, NW
Washington, D.C. 20004
202-715-3030
http://www.gallup.com

Under their Gallup Poll News service they cover Education and Youth issues.

Generation-Y Amarillo Globe-News
P.O. Box 2091
Amarillo, TX 79166
806-376-4488
http://www.generation-y.com

Generation-Y is an on-line "youth" edition of the Amarillo Globe-News written by teens for teens.

■ ■

Great Transitions
Carnegie Corporation of New York
437 Madison Avenue, New York, NY 10022
212-371-3200
http://www.carnegie.org/sub/pubs/reports/great_transitions/gr_exec.html

This report represents the culmination of the Carnegie Council on Adolescent Development's ten years of research on the adolescent experience in contemporary culture. The site contains a synthesis of "the best available knowledge and wisdom about adolescence in America."

■ ■

In the Mix (PBS Television Show)
114 E. 32nd Street Suite 903
New York, NY 60016
212-684-3940
http://www.IntheMix.org

Single theme programs of important issues – reality TV for kids.

■ ■

Kids Space Foundation
http://www.kids-space.org

Their mission is to use the Internet to foster literacy, artistic expression, and cultural tolerance and understanding. This is a web site where kids can go and write stories and draw pictures.

■ ■

Look-Look, LLC
6685 Hollywood Boulevard
Hollywood, CA 90028
323-856-5555
http://www.look-look.com

Look-Look.com is a self-described "24-hour culture cam" a global network of 10,000+ youth correspondents, respondents, and photojournalists who report on their own culture. It is said to be "the most credible resource on the study of global youth ages 14-30. They offer an on-line, real-time research and information service focused on global youth culture.

Millennials Rising
http://www.millennialsrising.com

Hosted by Neil Howe and William Strauss the authors of Millennials Rising, this
site provides a serious discussion forum on Millennial issues. Contains discussion
forums, essays and links.

■ ■

TakingITGlobal
19 Duncan Street, Suite 505
Toronto, ON M5H 3H1 Canada
416-977-9363
http://www.takingitglobal.org

TakingITGlobal.org is a global online community, providing youth with inspiration
to make a difference, a source of information on issues, opportunities to take action,
and a bridge to get involved locally, nationally and globally. Membership is free of
charge and allows you to interact with various aspects of the web site, to contribute
ideas, experiences, and actions.

■ ■

Yo! Youth Outlook
660 Market Street, Room 210
San Francisco, CA 94104
415-438-4755
http://www.youthoutlook.org

YO! is a monthly newspaper by and about young people, which also syndicates
articles to newspapers across the U.S. YO! connects young people with each other
and gives adults a window into the constantly changing cultures of youth. This
project of the Pacific News Service (PNS), an international network of writers,
scholars and journalists, has a high profile with Bay Area readers via its weekly
column in the San Francisco Examiner.

■ ■

Youth Today
1200 17th St., NW, 4th Fl.
Washington, DC 20036
202-785-0764
http://www.youthtoday.org

A nonprofit organization dedicated to helping people help youth. American Youth
Work Center and Youth Today Newspaper publishers.

Politics, Activism, Community

America's Promise
909 North Washington Street, Suite 400
Alexandria, VA 22314-1556
703-684-4500
http://www.americaspromise.org

America's Promise has created a diverse and growing alliance of nearly 500 national organizations, which make large-scale national commitments to mobilize people from every sector of American life to build the character and competence of our nation's youth.

▪ ▪

Campus Compact
Brown University
P.O. Box 1975
Providence, RI 02912
401-867-3950
http://www.compact.org

A national coalition of college and university presidents committed to the civic purposes of higher education. Campus Compact promotes community service that develops students' citizenship skills and values, encourages collaborative partnerships between schools and communities, and assists faculty who want o integrate public and community engagement into their teaching.

▪ ▪

CIRCLE: The Center for Information & Research on Civic Learning & Engagement
School of Public Affairs
University of Maryland
College Park, MD 20742
301-405-2790
http://www.civicyouth.org

Since 2001, CIRCLE has conducted, collected, and funded research on the civic and political participation of young Americans. Wonderful working papers, fact sheets and reports on youth voting, civic education, trends, and demographics.

▪ ▪

Connect for Kids (By The Benton Foundation)
950 18th Street NW
Washington DC 20006
202-638-5770
http://www.connectforkids.org

Connect for Kids, an award-winning multimedia project of the Benton foundation, helps adults make their communities better places for families and children. The Web site offers a place on the Internet for adults – parents, grandparents, educators, policymakers and others – who want to become more active citizens, from volunteering to voting with kids in mind.

Do Something
423 West 55th Street, 8th Floor
New York, NY 10019
http://www.dosomething.org

Since its founding in 1993, Do Something has helped inspire and empower millions
of young people to be leaders who measurably strengthen their communities.

■ ■

Freedom Channel
1233 20th St., NW, Suite 302
Washington, DC, 20036
202-785-5920
http://www.freedomchannel.com

Select from 3,000+ political videos from hundreds of candidates for President,
Senate, House and Governor. Watch issue videos from the candidates and from
special interest groups. There's also a comprehensive free archive of campaign
television ads.

■ ■

The Innovation Center for Community & Youth Development
6930 Carroll Avenue, Suite 502
Takoma Park, MD 20912-4423
301-270-1700
http://www.theinnovationcenter.org

Lots of fresh ideas and experiential learning focused on bringing youth, adults,
organizations and communities together. Many materials designed to engage both
young and old creating new partners for positive change in the way youth
development takes place.

■ ■

Millennial Politics
http://www.millennialpolitics.com

From the authors of the book *Millennial Manifesto*, this web site offers an extensive
list of resources, organizations and links to other web sites.

■ ■

The National Mentoring Partnership
1600 Duke St., Suite 300
Alexandria, VA 22314
703-224-2200
http://www.mentoring.org

This site is about helping people to become mentors, to receive a mentor, and to
teach people to become better mentors. They help schools and communities to build
and/or strengthen their programs through additional training, support, and
awareness.

National Network for Youth
http://www.nn4youth.org

This organization works to empower youth, to strengthen families, to teach about healthy alternatives, to teach about diversity, to network and coordinates a National Youth Leadership Institute.

■ ■

The New Voters Project
http://www.newvotersproject.org

The New Voters Project is a nonprofit organization dedicated to increasing voter turnout among citizens age 18-24.

■ ■

Teen Power Politics
http://www.teenpowerpolitics.com

A site to support Sara Jane Boyers book with the same title, it has GREAT links to many organizations and resources at http://www.teenpowerpolitics.com/tpp_ref.html

■ ■

What Kids Can Do, Inc.
P.O. Box 603252
Providence, RI 02906
401-247-7665
http://www.whatkidscando.org

A site designed to inspire powerful learning with public purpose, you'll find student work as well as voices shared, research involving student learning and resources.

■ ■

United States Student Association
1413 K St. NW 9th Floor
Washington, DC 20005
202-347-8772
http://www.usstudents.org

Founded in 1947, USSA is a recognized voice for students on Capitol Hill, in the White House, and at the Department of Education. USSA works on building grassroots power among students to expand access to education at the federal, state and campus level.

■ ■

Youth-e-Vote
http://www.youthevote.net

Presented by http://www.election.com and http://www.freedomchannel this site was the first national registration and on-line voting in America. More than one million K-12 students participated in its historic on-line unofficial 2000 presidential election.

Youth and Social Policy
3815 Walnut Street
Philadelphia, PA 19104-6179
215-898-2229
http://www.ssw.upenn.edu/crysp/

The Center for Research on Youth and Social Policy works to bring about positive social change by improving the way human services are developed, delivered, and evaluated. CRYSP seeks to have a major impact on the issues and systems affecting vulnerable populations, particularly children, while promoting social justice and social change through applied research, planning, and technical assistance.

■ ■

Youth Initiative
Open Society Institute
400 West 59th Street
New York, NY 10019
212-548-0600
http://www.soros.org/initiatives/youth

The Youth Initiative aims to develop the analytical, research, and self-expression skills that young people need to think critically about their world and to engage actively in the U.S. democracy.

■ ■

Youth Serve America
1101 15th Street, NW, Suite 200
Washington, DC 20005
202-296-2992
http://www.servenet.org

A central clearinghouse for youth who wish to serve their communities through volunteer work.

Media

Arbitron
142 West 57th Street
New York, NY 10019-3300
212-887-1300
http://www.arbitron.com

Arbitron, an international media research firm, conducts and publishes informative studies, delivering insights into the way today's consumers use radio and other media, how their lifestyles affect their media and consumer behavior and what the future holds for the media around the world. Best of all, these studies are freely available and ready to download.

■ ■

Center for Media Literacy
4727 Wilshire Blvd., #403
Los Angeles, CA 90010
323-931-4177
http://www.medialit.org

The Center for Media Literacy is dedicated to a new vision of literacy for the 21st century: the ability to communicate competently in all media forms, print and electronic, as well as to access, understand, analyze and evaluate the powerful images, words and sounds that make up our contemporary mass media culture.

■ ■

Center for Research on the Effects of Television
Ithaca College
119 Williams Hall
Ithaca, NY 14850-7290
607-274-1324
http://www.ithaca.edu/cretv/

CRETV has two components: an archive of television content and a research lab conducting studies of the content of television and its effects on viewers. The archive reflects a representative sample of American television. Analyses of the content can be used to document the nature of television (its structure, the content of programs and commercials) and to trace changes that occur over time. This information can subsequently be used to study the psychology of television – its effects on different types of viewers, how viewers comprehend and respond to the content they see, and the role television plays in the psychological development across the life span. The CRETV lab is also available on a content basis to test children's understanding of specific TV content and effectiveness of media literacy techniques.

Children Now
1212 Broadway, 5th Floor
Oakland, CA 94612
510-763-2444
http://www.childrennow.org

Children Now is a nonpartisan, independent voice for children, working to translate
the nation's commitment to children and families into action. Recognized nationally
for its policy expertise and up-to-date information on the status of children, media,
health and welfare, Children Now uses communications strategies to reach parents,
lawmakers, citizens, business, media and community leaders, creating attention and
generating positive change on behalf of children.

▪ ▪

Concerned Children's Advertisers
2300 Yonge Street, Suite 804
P.O. Box 2432
Toronto, ON M4P 1E4 CANADA
416-484-0871
http://www.cca-canada.com

A nonprofit organization of 26 Canadian companies, advertisers, broadcasters and
agencies who market and advertise products and services to children and their
families. CCA strives to combine marketing to children with the social responsibility
of caring for children. Resources for organizations, parents, teachers and kids.

▪ ▪

Directory of Media Literacy Organizations and the Media Literacy Review
University of Oregon
Eugene, OR 97403-1215
541-346-3405
http://interact.uoregon.edu/MediaLit/HomePage
http://interact.uoregon.edu/MediaLit/mlr/home/index.html

It is the goal of the Media Literacy On-Line Project to make available to educators,
producers, students, and parents, information and resources related to the influence
of media in the lives of children, youth, and adults. It contains an alphabetical listing
and links to dozens of media literacy groups and organizations worldwide. If you are
concerned about what children and teens are watching, log onto this site maintained
by the Media Literacy Project at the University of Oregon.

▪ ▪

National Institute on Media and the Family
606 24th Avenue South, Suite 606
Minneapolis, MN 55454 USA
888-672-5437
http://www.mediaandthefamily.org

Evaluates TV programs, computer and video games, and movies. Site contains free
family resources and ideas for educators. Particularly helpful are the tools families
can use to evaluate their media habits and health.

Parents Television Council
707 Wilshire Boulevard, Suite 1950
Los Angeles, CA 90017
213-629-9255
http://www.parentstv.org

They want parents to join together to increase the demand for family appropriate programming. They review all the TV shows by giving a summary and also by providing a rating for sex, language, and violence. It's updated every week. A project of the Media Research Center, the site includes up-to-date suggestions for family-friendly viewing, suggestions on how to influence television programming, a family guide to prime time television, and lots of research and analysis.

■ ■

Pew Internet & American Life Project
1100 Connecticut Avenue NW, Suite 710
Washington, DC 20036
202-296-0019
http://www.pewinternet.org

The Pew Internet & American Life Project creates and funds original, academic-quality research that explores the impact of the Internet on children, families, communities, the work place, schools, health care and civic/political life.

■ ■

TV-Turnoff Network (formerly TV-Free America)
1601 Connecticut Avenue NW #303
Washington, DC 20009
202-518-5556
http://www.tvturnoff.org

Founded in 1994, TV-Turnoff Network is dedicated to the belief that we all have the power to determine the role that television plays in our own lives. Rather than waiting for others to make "better" TV, we can turn it off and reclaim time for our families, our friends, and for ourselves. TV-Turnoff Week is a grassroots project that works. More than 65 national organizations, including the American Medical Association, the National Education Association, and the American Academy of Pediatrics, support or endorse TV-Turnoff Week.

Violence

Center for Effective Collaboration and Practice
1000 Thomas Jefferson Street NW, Suite 400
Washington, DC 20007
888-457-1551
http://www.air.org

This site is from the American Institutes for Research and lists LOTS of reference places related to violence prevention.

Family Research Library
126 Horton Social Science Center
University of New Hampshire
Durham, NH 03824-3586
603-862-1888
http://www.unh.edu/frl/

The Family Research Laboratory (FRL) has devoted itself primarily to understanding family violence and the impact of violence in families. It offers comprehensive literature reviews, new theories, and methodologically sound studies. Researchers at the FRL pioneered many of the techniques that have enabled social scientists to estimate directly the scope of family violence. These efforts have brought international recognition to the FRL.

■ ■

Join Together
441 Stuart Street
Boston, MA 02116
617-437-1500
http://www.jointogether.org

Focus is primarily gun violence and substance abuse. Current articles are available.

■ ■

National Resource Center for Safe Schools
101 SW Main, Suite 500
Portland, OR 97204
800-268-2275 or 503-275-0131
http://www.safetyzone.org

Contains topics that are personal, such as how to handle a bully, as well as technological (bomb threat pamphlet). One can access both research material as well as practical advice. Very comprehensive on the subject.

■ ■

Parents and Teachers Against Violence in Education (PTAVE)
P.O. Box 1033
Alamo, CA 94507-7033
925-831-1661
http://www.nospank.net

A resource for students, parents, educators, health care professionals, policymakers, and everyone who believes that children's optimal development occurs in nurturing, violence-free environments and that every child has the right to grow and learn in such an environment.

Report-it.com Inc.
P.O. Box 163
Oakdale, NY 11769-0163
631-218 1980
http://www.report-it.com

An anonymous student tipline and helpline that's working together with the education community to help keep schools safe. Confidential reporting system for violence in school.

■ ■

Violence Prevention Program
Physicians for Social Responsibility
1101 14th Street Northwest, Suite 700
Washington, DC 20005
202-898-0150
http://www.psr.org

PSR's Violence Prevention Program is building a national Violence Prevention Network of physicians, public health professionals, PSR staff and supporters working to reduce firearms and domestic violence.

■ ■

Warning Signs: Youth Anti-Violence Initiative
American Psychological Association
Washington, DC
800-268-0078
http://www.apahelpcenter.org/featuredtopics/feature.php?id=38

This project is a partnership between the American Psychological Association and MTV. Pertains to warning signs of violence and stopping violence before it happens.

Addiction and Substance Abuse

Al-Anon and Alateen
Al-Anon Family Group Headquarters
1600 Corporate Landing Parkway
Virginia Beach, VA 23454
757-563-1600
http://www.Al-Anon-Alateen.org

Provides hope and help for families and friends of alcoholics.

■ ■

The American Academy of Child and Adolescent Psychiatry
3615 Wisconsin Avenue NW
Washington, DC 20016-3007
202-966-7300
http://www.aacap.org/publications/factsfam/index.htm

The AACAP developed Facts for Families to provide concise and up-to-date information on issues that affect children, teenagers, and their families. The AACAP provides this important information as a public service and the Facts for Families may be duplicated and distributed free of charge.

▪▪▪▪▪▪▪▪▪▪▪▪▪▪▪▪▪▪▪▪▪▪▪▪▪▪▪▪▪▪▪▪▪▪▪▪

Anorexia Nervosa and Related Eating Disorders
http://www.anred.com

An organization that provides information about anorexia nervosa, bulimia nervosa, binge eating disorder, compulsive exercising, and other less well-known food and weight disorders. Material includes details about recovery and prevention.

▪▪▪▪▪▪▪▪▪▪▪▪▪▪▪▪▪▪▪▪▪▪▪▪▪▪▪▪▪▪▪▪▪▪▪▪

CDC's Tobacco Info-Youth Page Tips 4 Kids
Centers for Disease Control and Prevention
4770 Buford Highway, NE
Atlanta, GA 30341-3724
800-CDC-1311 (800-232-1311)
http://www.cdc.gov/tobacco/tips4youth.htm

Contains information about the hazards of smoking and how to quit. Links to other sites.

▪▪▪▪▪▪▪▪▪▪▪▪▪▪▪▪▪▪▪▪▪▪▪▪▪▪▪▪▪▪▪▪▪▪▪▪

Cocaine Anonymous
3740 Overland Avenue, Suite C
Los Angeles, CA 90034-6337
310-559-5833
http://www.ca.org

12-Step Program for cocaine addiction. Includes on-line help, publications and literature.

▪▪▪▪▪▪▪▪▪▪▪▪▪▪▪▪▪▪▪▪▪▪▪▪▪▪▪▪▪▪▪▪▪▪▪▪

D.A.R.E. America
http://www.dare.com

D.A.R.E., now operating in 80% of all school districts around the country and reaching over 36 million young people, is the most extensive substance abuse prevention delivery system in the country.

▪▪▪▪▪▪▪▪▪▪▪▪▪▪▪▪▪▪▪▪▪▪▪▪▪▪▪▪▪▪▪▪▪▪▪▪

Do It Now Foundation
P.O. Box 27568
Tempe, AZ 85285-7568
480-736-0599
http://www.doitnow.org

America's Drug Information connection, this site contains updated publications, interviews, catalogues, etc.

Drug-Free Resource Net
Partnership For A Drug-Free America
405 Lexington Avenue, Suite 1601
New York, NY 10174
212-922-1560
http://www.drugfreeamerica.org

Created and maintained by the Partnership for a Drug-Free America, this site offers a complete and accurate compilation of information about substance abuse. Included are a comprehensive database on drugs and help for parents. Contains information for all ages and includes advice for parents. Extremely comprehensive.

■ ■

Eating Disorder Recovery On-line
Tucson, Arizona
520-323-3734
http://www.edrecovery.com

Contains information, programs, and services for people with eating disorders. Includes an on-line quiz to help determine signs and symptoms.

■ ■

Marijuana Anonymous
P.O. Box 2912
Van Nuys, CA 91404
800-766-6779
http://www.marijuana-anonymous.org

12-step program for quitting marijuana use. Includes on-line help, publications and literature.

■ ■

Narcotics Anonymous
P.O. Box 9999
Van Nuys, California 91409
818-773-9999
http://www.wsoinc.com

They have literature, services and assistance to aid people addicted to narcotics regardless of where they live. Very comprehensive resource.

■ ■

National Center for Tobacco-Free Kids
1707 L Street NW, Suite 800
Washington, DC 20036
202-296-5469
http://tobaccofreekids.org

Contains information on anti-smoking initiatives both nationally and globally. Easy access to articles such as targeting women and big tobacco's tempting of children. Contains a state-by-state listing of policies and procedures concerning smoking.

The National Center on Addiction and Substance Abuse
at Columbia University
633 Third Avenue, 19th floor
New York, NY 10017-6706
212-841-5200
http://www.casacolumbia.org

CASA is organized around four divisions: Health and Treatment Research and
Analysis, Policy Research and Analysis, Program Demonstration and
Communications. CASA's policy research encompasses the effects substance abuse
and addiction have on many of our nation's most serious social problems. They
assess what works in prevention, treatment and law enforcement. Lots of research
and resources.

▪ ▪

NCADI for Kids Only
National Clearing House for Alcohol and Drug Information
11426-28 Rockville Pike, Suite 20
Rockville, MD 20852
800-729-6686
http://www.health.org

NCADI is one of the largest federal clearinghouses, offering more than 500 items to
the public, many of which are free of charge.

▪ ▪

National Council on Alcoholism and Drug Dependence
12 West 21st Street
New York, NY 10010
212-206-6770
http://www.ncadd.org

Organization is trying to fight stigma attached to alcoholism and drug abuse. Site
contains information for both parents and children. Good brochures that address
specific communication problems. The NCADD provides education, information,
help and hope in the fight against alcohol and drug addictions. Filled with substance
abuse related definitions, facts, overviews, parent information, resources, press
releases, etc.

▪ ▪

National Institute on Drug Abuse
U.S. Department of Health and Human Services
6001 Executive Boulevard, Room 5213
Bethesda, Maryland 20892-9651
301-443-1124
http://www.nida.nih.gov

Contains separate sections for Health professionals, parents, teachers, and students
with information on drugs, drug use, and current research on illicit drugs. Includes a
long list of links to other related substance abuse sites.

Sex, Teen Pregnancy and STDs

Advocates For Youth
1025 Vermont Avenue NW, Suite 200
Washington, DC 20005
202-347-5700
http://www.advocatesforyouth.org

Covers how to talk about STDs, HIV/AIDS, teen pregnancy, and positive, educational television viewing. Lots of resources, links and a "teen scene" area.

■ ■

American Social Health Association
P.O. Box 13827
Research Triangle Park, NC 27709
919-361-8400 or 800-227-8922
http://www.ashastd.org and http://www.iwannaknow.org

The American Social Health Association is recognized by the public, patients, providers and policy makers for developing and delivering accurate, medically reliable information about STDs.

■ ■

Campaign for Our Children
120 West Fayette Street, Suite 1200
Baltimore, MD 21201
410-576-9015
http://www.cfoc.org

CFOC produces ad campaigns encouraging parent-child communication and sexual abstinence among teens. The CFOC web site hosts areas with information for parents and teens.

■ ■

Department of Health and Human Services
Office of Adolescent Pregnancy Programs
4350 East West Highway, Suite 200 West
Bethesda, MD 20814
301-594-4004
http://www.dhhs.gov

Contains family planning information and state-by-state programs, legislation and grants in the areas of adolescent pregnancy.

■ ■

It's Your Sex Life
The Kaiser Family Foundation
2400 Sand Hill Road
Menlo Park, CA 94025
888-BE-SAFE-1 (888-237-2331)
www.itsyoursexlife.org

A guide to safe and responsible sex. Contains links to other web sites and also lots of different hot line numbers for people who may be in a crisis situation.

■ ■

National Abstinence Clearinghouse
801 East 41st Street
Sioux Falls, SD 57105
888-577-2966
http://www.abstinence.net

The National Abstinence Clearinghouse is an alliance of nationally known educators formed to promote the appreciation and practice of sexual abstinence. The NAC provides a resource center that distributes information on abstinence programs, curricula and information.

■ ■

The National Campaign to Prevent Teen Pregnancy
1776 Massachusetts Avenue NW, Suite 200
Washington, DC 20036
202-478-8500
http://www.teenpregnancy.org

This group's aim is to prevent teen pregnancy and child poverty by providing education to teens, parents, and public, by enlisting the help of the media, and by encouraging public discussion to build common ground. Site contains tips for parents and teens, as well as a state by state guide.

■ ■

Not Me, Not Now
39 West Main Street, Room 204
Rochester, NY 14614
877-603-7306
http://www.notmenotnow.org

Not Me, Not Now was launched in 1994 as a multifaceted abstinence-only campaign to reduce the teen pregnancy rate. An advertising campaign serves as the centerpiece of Not Me, Not Now. The campaign, which features teens, communicates the consequences of teenage pregnancy.

■ ■

Planned Parenthood
810 Seventh Avenue
New York, NY 10019
800-669-0156 or 800-230-PLAN (800-230-7526)
http://www.ppfa.org and http://www.teenwire.org

Founded in 1916, Planned Parenthood is the world's largest and oldest voluntary family planning organization.

Sex, Etc.
Rutgers University School of Social Work
536 George Street
New Brunswick, NJ 08901-1167
732-932-7126
http://www.sexetc.org

Provided through Rutgers University, this site by teens for teens is very cool. Designed to appeal to teens in terms of graphics/layout etc., it's very honest and graphic. Their philosophy is based on the fact that schools teach too little too late.

■ ■

Sexuality and Education Council of the U.S. (SIECUS)
130 West 42nd Street, Suite 350
New York, NY 10036-7802
212-819-9770
http://www.siecus.org

Their position is that sexuality is a natural and healthy part of living and advocates making responsible choices. Includes information for parents, teens, media, religious institutions, lawmakers, etc. They also have a school health education clearing house and library service.

Runaway, Homeless & Missing Children

Covenant House
346 West 17th Street
New York, NY 10011
800-999-9999
www.covenanthouse.org

In addition to food, shelter, clothing and crisis care, Covenant House provides a variety of services to homeless youth including health care, education, vocational preparation, drug abuse treatment and prevention programs, legal services, recreation, mother/child programs, transitional living programs, street outreach and aftercare. Also includes articles for parents on how to talk to teens.

■ ■

Family and Youth Services Bureau
National Clearinghouse on Families & Youth
P.O. Box 13505
Silver Spring, MD 20911-3505
301-608-8098
http://www.acf.dhhs.gov/programs/fysb/

The Family and Youth Services Bureau (FYSB) is a Federal agency dedicated to supporting young people and strengthening families. The Bureau does so by providing runaway and homeless youth service grants to local communities; the Bureau also funds research and projects.

InterNetwork for Youth
4411 SE Clinton Street
Portland, Oregon 97206-1621
503-319-5251
http://www.in4y.com

A national directory of runaway and many other youth service agencies.

■ ■

National Center for Missing and Exploited Children
Charles B. Wang International Children's Building
699 Prince Street
Alexandria, Virginia 22314-3175
The United States of America
703-274-3900 or 800-THE-LOST (800-843-5678)
http://www.missingkids.org

They are a resource center of missing children. Includes a section about school
safety and information on how to protect a child from being stolen in the first place.
Contains hotline for people who need assistance and a search database.

■ ■

Suicide Prevention

The American Psychiatric Association
1400 K Street NW
Washington, DC 20005
888-357-7924
http://www.psych.org/public_info/teenag~1.cfm

The American Psychiatric Association is a medical specialty society recognized
worldwide. Its 40,500 U.S. and international physicians specialize in the diagnosis
and treatment of mental and emotional illnesses and substance use disorders.

■ ■

Children's Safety Network
National Injury and Violence Prevention Resource Center
Education Development Center Inc.
55 Chapel Street
Newton, MA 02458-1060
617-969-7101 ext. 2207
http://www.edc.org/HHD/csn/

Has a "Youth Suicide Prevention Fact Sheet" packet available as well as additional
resources and technical assistance to parents, teachers, child health agencies and
other organizations seeking to reduce unintentional injuries and violence to children
and adolescents. They are one of four Children's Safety Network Resource Centers
funded by the Maternal and Child Health Bureau of the U. S. Department of Health
and Human Services.

Suicide Prevention Advocacy Network USA
5034 Odious Way
Marietta, GA 30068
888-649-1366
http://www.spanusa.org

SPANUSA promotes advocacy by raising awareness and creating political will to develop and fund a first-ever National Strategy for Suicide Prevention.

National Youth Organizations & Clubs

BTWFYI: Rather than attempt to list every national youth organization and club in the U.S. (which could create a phonebook size publication itself!), here are some directories that can point you in the right direction...

Directory of American Youth Organizations
(by The National Youth Development Information Center)
1319 F Street NW, Suite 601
Washington, DC 20004
877-NYDIC-4-U (877-693-4248)
http://www.nydic.org/dayo.html

This searchable on-line directory contains over 500 adult-sponsored national organizations that enroll millions of American children and teenagers in groups, troops, teams, and clubs.

■ ■

Global Youth ACTION Network
211 E. 43rd St., Suite 905
New York, NY 10017
212-661-6111
http://www.youthlink.org

The Global Youth ACTION Network is a collaboration among youth and youth-serving organizations to share information, resources and solutions to promote greater youth engagement.

■ ■

YouthTree USA
http://www.youthtreeusa.com

Search this directory to find youth and family programs and services locally and nationwide. It has one of the most comprehensive internet directories of programs, services, and resources promoting the healthy development of youth (K-college students) and families.

Managing Kids

Claire Raines Communications
222 Milwaukee Street
Denver, CO 80206-0500
303-322-0474
http://www.generationsatwork.com

A co-author of Generations at Work, Claire's web site if filled with useful
information and ideas on how to manage across generational lines.

▪ ▪

LifeCourse Associates
9080 Eaton Park Road
Great Falls, VA 22066
516-624-0043
http://www.lifecourse.com

LifeCourse Associates is a growing consulting group inspired by the generational
discoveries of Neil Howe and William Strauss, whose collected work lends order,
meaning, and predictability to national trends. They serve companies, government
agencies, and nonprofits. The LifeCourse Method blends social science and history
to put managers in charge of their personal and institutional futures. No one who
works with LifeCourse need ever again confuse the analysis of generations with
pop-culture trivia and mere demographic data.

▪ ▪

Teenage Workforce Solutions, Inc.
5933 South Highway 94, Suite 204
St. Charles, MO 63304
877-736-7535
http://www.thepeoplesolution.com

Authors of "The Teenage Worker Retention and Motivation Study."

▪ ▪

Workforce.com
c/o ACC Communications, Inc.
245 Fischer Avenue B-2
Costa Mesa, CA 92626
714-751-1883
http://www.workforce.com

Workforce.com provides free access to the largest database of
HR content on the internet updated daily. Thousands of articles, tips, assessments,
links, forms, sample policies, and other tools.

Marketing to Kids

360 Youth
10 Abeel Road
Cranbury, NJ 08512
609-655-8878
http://www.360youth.com

360 Youth, the media and marketing arm of Alloy, Inc. integrates the assets and
experience of the largest and strongest college and teen marketing companies
including MarketSource Corporation, CASS Communications, Alloy, Market Place
Media and others to provide sales and marketing solutions targeting young adults.

■ ■

American Demographics
470 Park Avenue South, 8th Floor
New York, NY 10016
212-545-3600
http://www.americandemographics.com

Magazine covering consumer trends and demographic information for business.
Web site has many articles, links and references.

■ ■

Bra!n Camp
271 Madison Avenue, Suite 200
New York, NY 10016
212-545-9559
http://www.braincamp.com

Bra!nCamp is the only high-level, cross-media conference specifically geared to
major players in children's entertainment.

■ ■

Cheskin
255 Shoreline Drive, Suite 100
Redwood Shores, CA 94065
650-802-2100
http://www.cheskin.com

A strategic market research and consulting firm, the company has consistently
recognized the signs of change and evolved in response. They pioneered the use of
ethnographic techniques and contextual observation. GREAT featured studies
available at http://www.cheskin.com/think/thinking.html

Grunwald Associates
1793 Escalante Way
Burlingame, CA 94010
650-692-3100
http://www.grunwald.com

Grunwald Associates publishes seminal industry research on children and the Internet. Their national survey, Children, Families and the Internet 2000, examines children's Internet use from home and school. The National School Boards Association is our survey partner. Partial underwriting was provided by Children's Television Workshop, along with Microsoft.

■ ■

The Generational Imperative, Inc.
1343 Fleming Street
Cincinnati, OH 45206
513-221-1973
http://www.genimperative.com

TGI is a research-driven consulting firm that researches, analyzes, and presents generational dynamics to its clients in order to strengthen their marketing, advertising, employee recruiting, retention, loyalty and productivity.

■ ■

KidzEyes
c/o C&R Research Services, Inc.
500 N. Michigan Avenue, Suite 1331
Chicago, IL 60611
312-828-9200
http://www.kidzeyes.com

For over 20 years, C&R researchers have pioneered and enhanced new techniques for talking with children of all ages, from preschoolers through teens in both qualitative and quantitative settings. They interview thousands of children (parents, too) each year to address wide ranging issues.

■ ■

KidScreen
366 Adelaide Street West, Suite 500
Toronto, Ontario M5V 1R9 Canada
416-408-2300
http://www.kidscreen.com

A resource filled with lots of updated information about reaching kids through entertainment, KidScreen focuses on the converging worlds of children's entertainment, marketing and merchandising. A publication of Brunico Communications.

KidsMarketing, Inc.
22471 Aspan Street
Suite 205F
Lake Forest, CA 92630
949-206-9688
http://www.kidsmarketing.com

GREAT site with lots of research, editorial marketing analysis, and talk back areas.
Subscription required for full access.

■ ■

Kid Power Xchange/IQPC
150 Clove Road
P.O. Box 401
Little Falls, NJ 07424-0401
800-882-8684
http://www.kidpowerx.com and http://www.iqpc.com

Kid Power Xchange Conferences are presented by the International Quality &
Productivity Center (IQPC). By providing accurate, objective and up-to-date
developments and trends, IQPC enables organizations to remain competitive and
profitable. They recognize the value of face-to-face forums, and strive to make each
conference a valuable learning experience, allowing attendees to receive a maximum
return on investment.

■ ■

Understanding Youth™
Strategy by Brunico Communications, Inc.
366 Adelaide Street West, Suite 500
Toronto, Ontario M5V 1R9 Canada
416-408-2300
http://www.understandingyouth.com

You'll find via both the web site and the event, lots of valuable insight into who's
thinking what about kids today – marketing to them and selling to them. You can
even view presentation slides from the event and read many special reports on youth
marketing.

■ ■

Yankelovich
101 Merritt 7 Corporate Park
Norwalk, CT 06851
203-846-0100
http://www.yankelovich.com

The Nickelodeon/Yankelovich Youth MONITOR™ study combines Yankelovich's
knowledge of consumers with the kidsmarts of youth experts at Nickelodeon.
Together they have delivered a powerful research tool to understand the potential of
kids – a growing group of influencers, consumers and future customers. They have
tracked how youth trends and attitudes have changed since previous Youth
MONITOR waves - some as far back as 1988.

Youth University
by WonderGroup
312 Plum Street, Suite 1000
Cincinnati OH 45202
513-357-2950
http://www.wondergroupinc.com

Youth University is a monthly e-mail newsletter with news, views and inside scoops about today's kids, tweens and teens put out by WonderGroup a full-service marketing agency.

■ ■

Youthopia
440 Eglinton Avenue East, Suite 902
Toronto, Ontario, Canada M4P 1M2
416-545-0367
http://www.youthopia.com

Web site has youth marketing news, youth trends and information on today's youth.

■ ■

the Zandl Group
270 Lafayette Street
New York, NY 10012
212-274-1222
http://www.zandlgroup.com

Provides trend analysis, consumer research and marketing direction for businesses and organizations that need to reach the 82 million young adults, teens and tweens in the U.S.

■ ■

Zillions (by Consumer Reports)
http://www.zillions.org

Zillions purpose is to help kids make informed and independent consumer decisions, and to develop consumer literacy that will serve them and society throughout their lives. It aims to help young people question and evaluate products and services; build financial literacy and manage their resources with knowledge and forethought; think critically about advertising and other media messages; grasp broader family and community values inherent in consumerism; and define themselves in terms of who they are, not what they own. A Research Team of 40 classes also takes part in taste tests and other research projects for Zillions On-line reports. There is also an area for teachers who want lesson plans, guides, additional research/reference information and teaching tools to help kids 8 and up evaluate products, see through ad hype, be money smart and think for themselves.

42nd Street (the musical), 94
4-H, 104
9/11, 51, 85
A&E, 33, 44
ABC News, 72
Abilities *or* Ability, 147, 28, 143
Abortion, 124, 132
Academic
	Achievement, 83, 85, *see* Grades
	Academic enrichment, 62
	Honors, 87
	Performance shortfalls, 129
Acceptance, 11, 137-139
Accidental teen deaths, 18
Accountability practices, 141
Achievement, 83-89,
	Attitudes about, 78, 111
	Pressure to, 19
	see Academic Achievement
	and Grades
Adolescence *or* Adolescent, 13, 80-
	81, 137
	Early adolescence, 149
	Late adolescence, 80
	see Teen(s) *or* Teenager(s)
Adu, Freddy, 76
Adult-led, Adult-organized,
	8, 61, 77-78, 89, 104, 133-135
Affection, 131, 134, 140-141
Affirmation, 146
Affluence, 17, 21-23, 31, 38
African Americans, 4-5, 11-12
	see Black households
After-school, 8, 27, 53, 62, 77, 111
AIBO, 49, 72
Alcohol, 52, 87
Aldersgate United Methodist
	Church, 117
Allowance(s), 24-29, 38
American Academy of Pediatrics,
	51, 77, 81
American Camping Association,
	106, 108-110
Appreciation, 145
Aquarius, 93-94
Arbor, Ann, 42
Arts, 75, 83-88, 90-91, 94-98
Assessments, 95
	see Self-assessment, 146
Assets, 30-31, *see* Search Institute
AT&T Wireless, 64
At-Home Mothers, 14

Atlantic Monthly, 45
Auerbach, Stevanne, 34, 37, 44
Authoritarian parents, 99, 123, 129-
	130, 134, 136, 138-140
Authoritative parents, 129-130, 134,
	136, 138-140, 142, 147
Autocratic parents, 129, 144
Awdry, Reverend W., 60
Baby Boom Generation
	see Boomer Generation
babyGap, 32
Baden-Powell, Agnes *or* Robert, 105
Baldwin, Bruce, 23, 39
Band, 85
Bands of America, 86, 88, 114
Barna, George, 99, 102-103, 116
Barney & Friends, 57, 73
Barones (*Everybody Loves Raymond*),
	6
Bear in the Big Blue House, 57, 73
Beard, Daniel Carter, 105
Behavior, 10, 81-84, Chapter Five
Benidt, Steve, 32
Benson, Peter, 13, 15
Berkeley, Busby, 94, 118
Between the Lions, 59, 74
Bible, 98, 103, 131
Bigelow, Bob, 82
Birney, Meredith Baxter, 125
Black households, 5, 11-12
Black, Susan, 95, 116
Blackwell, Kenneth, 9, 15
Blue-collar, 57
BMW, 31
BMX bikes, 107
Bob the Builder, 56, 73
Boomer Generation
	as parents, 18-19, 23, 126, 131
	as teachers, 125
	as kids *or* teens, 27, 35, 124,
	influence of, 38, 92-93, 102
	parents of, 125, 131-132
Borba, Michele, 148
Bosak, Susan, 67
Boy Scouts of America, 61, 104-106
Boyce, William, 105
Bradys (*The Brady Bunch*), 6
Brazelton, T. Berry, 42, 126
Breakfast Club (the movie), 94
Broadband access, 37
Brooks, Andrée Aelion, 111
B.T.W.F.Y.I., ix

Bundys (*Married... With Children*), 6
Burnett, Darrell, 79-80, 113
Burnout, 17, 20
Burns, James MacGregor, v
Business Week, 45, 74, 118
Butler, Barbara, 33, 44
Cabbage Patch Kids, 35
Cable television, 48
Camp Fire USA, 104
Camping *or* Camps, 106-110
Capitol Steps, 90-91
Cappies, 91-92, 94
Care Bears, 60, 74
Carlson, Barbara, 69
Carlson, Karen, 69
Car-pooling, 49
Carr, Chris, 78, 80, 113
Carrot and sticking kids, 2, 122, 147
Carton, Barbara, 108, 118
Catholic, *see* Religion
CATO Institute, 43
Catterall, James, 83-84, 114
CBS, 50, 125
CCD *or* Confraternity of Christian
    Doctrine, 98
Celek, Tim, 99, 116
Cell phone, 48, 64-65
Channel One, 26
Chapin, Harry, 134
Character, 126-127
Charitable giving, 29
Charter schools, 11
Chase, Chevy, 93
Cheerleading, 62
Cherry, Conrad, 99
Chester, Eric, 89, 115
Chicago Archdiocese, 100
Child abuse, 9, 78, 150
Child care, 112
Child death rates, 18
Child development, 18, 40, 78
Child poverty rate, 7
Childhood
    Disappearance of, 51
    Evolution of, 19, 69, 104, 124
    Room décor, 31
    Parents spoiling, 18, 21, 39, 47
Childhood obesity, 37
Child-rearing, Chapter Two
Choices, 20, 26, 103, 132-133, 137-
    138, 142, 144
Choir, 85

Chores, 24-30, 98
Christian, 60, 98-100, 102, 110
Christianity Today, 103
Church, 99-103, 107, 127
Cimino, Richard, 101, 116-117
Citizen(s) *or* Citizenship, 19, 24,
Civics, 95
Civil rights, 11, 15
Civility, 57
Class, 63, 86-87, 95, 97, 141
Classroom(s), 109, 141, 143
Cleaver, Theodore "Beaver", 8
Cleavers (*Leave It to Beaver*), 3, 6
CNN, 12, 51, 151
Cognitive growth *or* development 34,
    83-85
Cohen, Katherine, 111
Collaboration, 84, 85, 141
College, 18, 62-63, 86,
    Admissions, 20, 90, 111
    Campus, 3, 25, 63, 99
    College graduation, 63
    Entrance examinations, 114
    Scholarships, 79
    Sports, 78-79
    Students, 28, 48
Coloroso, Barbara, 39, 148
Columbine High School, 90-91, 115
Communication, 48-49, 63
Communities *or* Community,
    3-4, 13, 22, 62, 90-91, 97, 105
Community service, 75, 102
Competence, 82, 84
Competition *or* Competitive
    17, 19, 76, 78, 81-82
Computer(s), 19, 35, 48-49, 60, 68-69,
    89, 108
Conditional acceptance, 137-141
Conditional judgment, 145
Conditional reasoning, 84
Confidence, 59, 82, 145
Conflict-resolution, 84
Confraternity of Christian Doctrine *or*
    CCD, 98
Consequences, 24, 84, 126-127, 137-
    138, 140, 142-143, 148
Consistency, 125, 141, 144-145
Constructive, 56, 124, 143
Consumer(s) *or* Consumeristic,
    1, 17, 28, 31, 38, 87
Consumption, 30
Contraception *and* "the pill", 124

Contributing *or* Contribution,
6-7, 25, 27, 30-31, 90, 141, 144
Control, 80, 122-139
Self-, 66, 78, 84, 133, 146-147
Coontz, Stephanie, 13
Cooperation, 78, 89, 132, 140
Copestick, Joanna, 33
Corecurricular classes, 97
Cornucopia Kids, 23, 39
Corporal punishment, 124
Corwin, Donna, 69
Cosmic Bowling, 37
Cost of children, 31, 44
Council of Chief State School
Officers, 85, 97
Counseling *or* counselors,
2, 107, 110
Counseling, 78-79
Covey, Stephen, 22, 39
Crary, David, 11, 16
Crayola Crayons, 35
Creative-arts programs, 91
Cricket Communications, 65
Crisis Era, 50
Critical Links, 83-84, 114
Crockett, Frank, 102, 117
Cronkite, Walter, 51
Cross-generational, 12, 104
Culture *or* Cultural, 1, 10, 19, 23, 38,
40, 51, 53, 80, 86, 93-95, 99,
107, 135
Curfew, 65
Dad(s), 4-6, 18-19, 21, 27-28, 30, 37,
48, 59, 61-63, 133, 138,
see Father(s)
Dance education, 95-96
Data, x
Day care, 8, 20, 125
Deasy, Richard, 83, 114
DeBroff, Stacy, 111
Deci, Edward, v
Decision(s), 10, 20, 22, 32, 123, 142
DeFrain, John, 68
Democratic, 140
Demographic shifts, 11
Demographic(s) *or* Demography,
6, 12, 88
Depression, The Great, 5, 124, 131
Desegregation, 11
Developmentally appropriate, 25,
36-37, 82, 105, 108-109, 127,
130, 135, 142-144

Developmentally inappropriate, 62,
68, 76
Developmental
Differences, 63
Level of the child, 142
Opportunity, 147
Stages, 49
DiGeronimo, Theresa Foy, 111
Diller, Phyllis, 3
Dinkmeyer, Jr., Don, 148
Dinkmeyer, Sr., Don, 39, 148
Dinner, 21
Discipline, 2, 39, 78, 84, 86, 95,
Chapter Five
Discipline vs. Punishment, 122
Disney, 55-56, 73
Diversity, 6, 10-11, 59, 107
Divorce, 5-6, 14, 67, 124-125
Dobson, James, 126
Doherty, William, 13, 22, 39, 62, 69,
74, 111, 145
Dora the Explorer, 58, 73
Downloading songs, 90
Dr. Toy, 34, 37-38
Drama education, 83, 85, 89-90, 108
Dreikurs, Rudolf, 130, 148
Drop-outs, 87
DSL, 48
Dual-income households, 5, 7-8
Dupere, Marne, 32
DVDs, 10
Dyer, Wayne, 23, 39
Dysfunctional, 6
Economic Impact of Nonprofit Arts, 115
Education, 6, 11, 18, 21, 28, 35, 55,
78, 82-90, 95-98, 103, 107, 109-
110, 125
Ehrensaft, Diane, 18, 39, 42
Elaine Mazlish, 148
Elementary school, 6, 48, 63, 76-79
Elkind, David, 13, 42, 111
Ellington, Duke, 2
Email, 37, 48, 64, 67
Emerson, Ralph Waldo, 34, 122
Emerson, Sasha, 32
Emotion(s) *or* Emotional, 23, 34, 49,
52, 57, 62, 77, 85, 109
Empathy, 60, 84, 140
Employee(s), 124, 136, 139, 141
Encouragement, 145-146
Engagement, 84, 106
Engh, Fred, 82, 113

Entitlement attitude, 25-27
Erikson, Erik, 19
Espeland, Pamela, 13
Excessive control, 123
Excessive permissiveness, 140
Excessive strictness, 140
Expectation(s), 18, 34, 77, 96, 128-
    140, 142, 144, 147
Experiential activities, 103
Extended family, 7, 9, 67, 132
External locus of control, 123
Extracurricular programs, 97
Faber, Adele, 148
Fact(s), x
Family, *see* Chapter One
Farley, Christopher, 11, 15
Father(s), 6, 8-9, 23, 41, 131-132,
    135, *see* Dad(s)
FCC, 64
FDA, 52
Feedback, 65, 143, 145
Fellowship of Christian Athletes, 99
Female-headed family, 7
Fishel, Elizabeth, 13, 148
Fisher-Price, 35
Follow-through, 145
Fong, Stacy, 32-33
Forum for Youth Investment, 111
Fowler, Charles, 97, 116
FOX, 50, 62
FranklinCovey, 63, 74
Frantic Family Syndrome, 62, 74
Fridstein, Stanley, 31
Friend(s) *or* Friendship(s), 2, 4, 21,
    29, 57-60, 66, 78-80, 86, 91, 98,
    102-103, 106, 143
Funk, Gary, 82
G.I. Generation *(born 1900-mid 20s±)*,
    4, 8, 94, 104, 106, 124
Galbraith, Judy, 13
Gallup Organization, 86, 114
GameBoy, 37
GapKids, 32
Generational yearning, 50-51
Generational continuity, 35
Generational disorientation, 99
Generational parenting patterns, 124
Generational theory, 92
GenXers *(born in the 1960s-70s±)*,
    98, 104, 124-126, 131
    as parents, 18-19, 23, 50
    as teachers, 125

as kids *or* teens, 20, 35, 98, 124
    influence of, 32, 75, 99, 106
    parents of, 104, 126, 131
Gessell, Arnold, 126
Ginghamsburg United Methodist
    Church, 101
Ginott, Haim, 148
Girl Scouts of America, 61, 104-106,
    118
Glenn, H. Stephen, v, 7, 23, 39, 43, 149
Goals 2000, 95
Godbey, Geoffrey, 49, 72
Goldner, Brian, 35
Gordon, Thomas, 148
GPA, 63
GPS (global positioning satellite), 64-
    65
Grades, 65, 86-87, 90, 138
Grading Grown-Ups, 10, 14-15
Grammys, 91
Grandkids, 5, 67, 126
Grandparents, 4-6, 14, 30, 67, 132
Greenspan, Stanley, 126
Greenspon, Thomas, 146, 151
Gregorsky, Frank, v
Group Magazine, 103, 117
Guarendi, Raymond, 121, 151
Gutherie, Elisabeth, 111
Gymboree, 97, 116
Hair (the musical), 93-94
Hall, G. Stanley, 126
Hall, Linda, 82
Hancock, Jim, 8, 39
Hardy, Andy (movies), 94
Hart, Betsy, 19, 42
Hartley-Brewer, Elizabeth, 148
Hartzell, Mary, 40
Harvard Family Research Project, 111
Hasbro, 35, 151
Healy, Jane, 69
Herbert, Doug, 96, 116
Hertz, David, 32
High school, 29, 48. 63, 82, 90, 99
Hine, Thomas, 8
Hispanic kids, 5, 11
Hochschild, Arlie, 18, 39
Hoffman, Edward, v
Holt, L. Emmett, 126
Holtz, Geoffrey, 125, 151
Horizontal socialization, 8
Hostility, 137-140, 142
Houlihan, Thomas, 85

Howard, Clark, 29
Howe, Neil, v, 8, 92, 151
Hulbert, Ann, 39, 126
Hustedt, Jason, 69
Huxley, Ronald, 148
Huxtables (*The Cosby Show*), 6
Hyperactivity, 62
Hyper-Parenting, 18, 40-47, 70, 151
Hypothesis, x
IKEA, 32
Income
    Dual-income, 5, 7-8, 108
    Household, 1, 22, 25, 31, 88
    Inequality, 7, 22, 43
    Kids, 24-30, *see* Allowance(s)
Independence *or* Independent, 33,
    127, 133
Indulgent parents, 129, 144
Industrial Revolution, 6
Infant mortality rates, 18
Information overload, 20, 121
Inspire *or* Inspiration, vii
Instant messaging (IM), 48, 64
Intellectual skills, 19
Internal locus of control, 123
Internet, 1, 9, 37, 48, 50, 64, 109
Intrusive Parenting, 151
Involved authoritative parents,
    129-142
Job(s), 7-8, 24-29, 88, 90, 121, 141
Jones, Landon, 125, 151
Jordan, Mick, 77
Joyce, William, 59, 73
Julian, Alexander and Meagan, 32
Junior Achievement, 104
Jupiter Communications, 37
K-12 schooling, 18, 95
Kaiser Family Foundation, 42, 72
Kampert, Patrick, 99, 116
Kellogg, Susan, 13
Kennedy, John, 4
Kent State shootings, 131
Kimball-Baker, Kathleen, 13, 39
Kindermusik, 97, 116
Kindlon, Dan, 13, 39, 131
King, Larry, 51
Kohn, Alfie, v, 23, 43, 148, 150
Kornhaber, Arthur, 67
Krauss, Beatrice, 149
Kropp, Paul, 40
Lancaster, Scott, 82
Lapware, 19, *see* Computer(s)

Latino, 11, 58
Lattin, Don, 101, 117
Lauren, Ralph, 32
Lautzenheiser, Tim, v, 88
Lawrence, Mike, 33
Leaders *or* leadership, 85, 89, 102,
    109-110, 131-132, 147
LeapFrog *or* LeapPad, 34, 44
Leffert, Nancy, 13
Lego, 34, 45
Leland, John, 99, 102, 116
Letterman, David, 93
Levin, Diane, 35
Levitt, Abraham *or* Levittown, 4
Life course, 38
Lilly Endowment, 110
Limited Too, 32
Limits, 53-55, 67, 81, 88, 125, 131,
    137, 142, 148-149
Lincoln Logs, 35
Literacy, 84
Little League baseball, 76
Llewellyn, Jack, 80, 113
Locus of control, 123
Loeb, Paul, 126
Logan, Gloria, 89-90
Logical consequence, 24, 142-143, 148
Logrippo, Ro, 33
Longfellow, Layne, 126-127, 151
Longman, Phillip, 31, 44
Lost Generation, 104
Lott, Lynn, 149
Low, Juliette Gordon, 105, 118
Lutheran Brotherhood, 15
MacKenzie, Robert, 149
Mackey, Lori, 24, 43
Manipulation, 123, 144
Mann, Horace, 6
Marketers *or* marketing, 7, 34-36, 38,
    52, 63-65, 87, 97, 100
Marshall, Marvin, 149
Masculinity (crisis of), 104
Matrix of parenting approaches, 128
Matthews, Kathy, 111
Mature behavior, 129
McDowell, Josh, 99, 116
McGowan, Mickey, 35
McGregor, Jena, 27, 43
McKay, Gary, 39, 148
McSwain, Michael, 91
Mechling, Jay, 106
Medhus, Elisa, 149

Media business, 50
Media Education, 70, 73
Media, 2, 20, 42, *see* Chapter Three
MENC, 88, 115-116
Merrill Lynch, 26, 43
Middle class, 6, 43
Middle school, 93, 98
Mill Creek Community Church, 100
Millennial culture, 93-94
Miller, Dennis, 3, 15
Milton Chen, 61
Mindstorms, 34, 45
Minority children, 11
Mintz, Steven, 13
Money, 23-30, 33, 40, 144
Moore, Mary Tyler, 125
Moral, 60
Moroney, Tom, 82
Mom(s) *or* Mother(s), 4-6, 14, 18-21,
    25, 36-37, 61-63, 76, 131-133, 138
Motivation, 28,, 78-79, 83-85, 139,
    141, 146-147
Motorola, 64
Mozart effect, 97, 116
Mr. Rogers' Neighborhood, 56
Mueller, Walt, 100, 117
Murphy, Jane, 61, 69
Murphy, Shane, 80, 83, 113
Music, 19, 21, 61, 83-88, 111
Music USA, 114
Naar, Mike, 77, 113
National Alliance for Youth Sports,
    81, 83
National Arts Education Research
    Center, 115
National Assessment of Educational
    Progress, 95
National Dance Education
    Organization, 96, 116
National Endowment for the Arts,
    85, 88, 98, 115
National Football League, 81
National Governors Association, 87-
    88, 115
National Institute of Mental Health, 51
National Recreation & Parks
    Association, 81, 110, 114
National Youth Sports Safety
    Foundation, 79
Natural consequence, 24, 142-143
NBC, 50
Neighborhood, *see* Chapter One, 55

Neiheisel, Tom, 34
Nelsen, Jane, 7, 22, 39, 143, 149
New York Times, 91
Nextel, 64
NFL, 76, 81
Nick Jr., 56
Nickelodeon, 26, 56, 73
Nike, 21, 139
Nintendo, 37
North Coast Church, 101, 117
Northern Virginia Theater Alliance, 91
Nostalgia, 13, 35
Obesity, 37, 53, 72, 104
Oppenheim Toy Portfolio, 37-38, 44
Oppenheim, Joanne, 34, 36-38, 44
Oppenheim, Stephanie, 34, 36-37
Oppenheimer, Todd, 69
Orange Furnishings & Home Design, 32
Orchestra, 85, 92
Organized sports, 76-83
Osborne, Larry, 101
Over-scheduling, 8, 18, 47, 61-63, 66,
    68, 75-76, 135
Owen, David, 30
Ozzie and Harriet, 6
Pace of life, 49
Pagers, 48, 64-65
Palm Pilots, 63, 113
Panasonic, 64
Parents *and* Parenting, Chapter Two
Parental involvement, 78, 133-134,
    140
Parenting Deficit, 72
Parenting Magazine, 24, 41
Parenting patterns, 124
Parenting approaches *and* style, 128
Pastrana, Travis, 76
Pawel, Jody Johnston, 149
Pawlowski, Cheryl, 53, 69, 72
PBS, 50, 55-56, 90
Perception of personal control, 146
Perfectionism, 151
Performance-based approval, 146
Permissive parenting, 125-139, 144
Persistence, 78, 84-85
Personal responsibility, 24, 123, 133
Peterson, Robert, 105-106, 118
Pew Research Center, 101
PGA Tour, 76
Plato, 56
Play-Doh, 35
PlayStation, 37

Pleasantville (the movie), 51
Plymouth-Canton Educational Park
    (High School), 89
Polls, x
Positive discipline, 149-150
Positive reinforcement, 146
Postman, Neil, 51, 69
Postmodern, 47, 99-102
Pottery Barn for Kids, 32
Poverty, 7, 22, 28, 137
Powell, Colin, 9
PowerPoint, 100
Powerpuff Girls, 59, 74
Practice *and* Theory, viii
Praise, 49, 145-147
Preschool, 8, 18, 25, 36, 48, 63-65
Pressure, 19-20, 36, 63, 77, 80-81
Project NoSpank, 150
Pseudo-extended family, 9
Psycholinguistic(s), vii, 146
PTA, 61, 81
Punishment vs. Discipline, 122
Punishments, 121-122, 149
    see Discipline
Radio Flyer wagons, 35
Raines, Claire, 126
Razor Scooters, 37
Real World, 94
Recreation, 55, 79, 81-83, 110
Red Cross, 104
Relational deprivation, 100
Religion *or* Religious
    Catholic, 9, 98-103
    Education, 98
    Ministries, 101
    Prayer, 99-100
    Spiritual, 60, 98-102
    Sunday school, 98
    Youth groups, 98
Research, x
Responsibility, 24-27, 31, 52-53,
    123, 133, 135, 140, 144
    see Personal Responsibility
Responsiveness, 128-140, 144
Rewards, 29, 55, 90, 121-122, 146,
    148-149
Richstatter, Tom, 98, 116
Risk-taking, 84
Risky behavior, 137
RoBOt, 49, *see* AIBO
Robinson, John, 49, 72
Rodda, Bob, 83

Roe v. Wade, 124
Roehlkepartain, Jolene, 13, 15
Rolie Polie Olie, 58-59
Rosemond, John, 62, 74, 126
Rosenfeld, Alvin, 18, 40, 42, 69, 151
Rubik's Cube, 35
Safe sex, 52
Sagwa, 59, 73
SAT, 85, 87, 114
Satellite dishes, 48, 50
Saturday morning TV, 52-53, 56, 60
Saturday Night Alive, 100, 117
Saturday Night Live, 93
Scales, Peter, 109-110
Scherer, Jesse, 107
Scouting, 79, 105-106, 118
Search Institute, 9-10, 14-15, 109
Sears, Martha and Bill, 41, 149-150
Secular youth groups, 104
Self-assessment, 143, 147-146
Self-confidence, 78, 84-85
Self-control, 66, 78, 84, 122-123, 133,
    147
Self-discipline, 78, 139, 142, 148,
    150, *see* Chapter Five
Self-esteem, 78, 87, 109, 123
Self-fulfilling prophecy, 123
Self-motivated, 139-140, 146-147
Selleck, George, 83
Sesame Street, 56
Seton, Ernest Thompson, 105
Sex, 52-53, 72-73
Shakespeare, 89, 115
Shrinky Dinks, 35
Siegel, Daniel, 40
Silent Generation *(born mid-1920s-early 40s±)*,
    93, 124-125
Silly Putty, 35
Simon *and* Simon2, 35, 42-43
Simpsons, 6
Singer, Dorothy, 57
Singer, Jerome, 61
Single-parent households, 7
SkyTel, 64
Slaughter, Michael, 101
Sleep habits, 18, 42
Slinkys, 35
Small, Meredith, 40
Smith, Peg, 109
Smith, Ronald, 83
Smoll, Frank, 83
Soccer moms, 77

Social change, 6
Social divide, 11
Social development, 34, 109
Social interaction, 34, 37, 80, 84-85
Socioeconomic(s), 19, 28, 87-88
Sony Corporation, 37, 49, 72
SouthBrook Christian Church, 102
Spanking, 150
Spencer, Paula, 149
Spock, Benjamin, 41, 124-126, 131-
    132, 150
Sports, 76-83, 87
Sports Illustrated, 114
SpringHill Camp, 107
Sroufe, Gerald, 85
St. James Parish, 100
St. Leonard's College, 98
Stanfield, Rochelle, 12, 16
Stanley, 58
Starbucks, 117
Strategy *and* Tactics, viii
Statistics, x
Stearns, Peter, 40
Steege, Gwen, 33
Steinberg, Jacques, 111
Stepfamily, 14
Stepp, Laura, 149
Stereotyping, 126
Steuer, Fay, 69
Stinnett, Nick, 68
Strauss, William (Bill), v, 8, 90-94, 115
Streit, Fred, 149
Stress, 13, 17, 20, 22, 28, 62, 75, 90,
    145, 149-150
Studies, x
Suburbs, 4, 92, 132
Summer camp, 62, 106-110
Surveys, x
Tactics *and* Strategy, viii
Talbots Kids, 32
Tan, Amy, 59
Tapscott, Don, 49, 69
Taylor, Betsy, 40
Taylor, Jim, 111
T-Ball leagues, 76
Teachable moments, 135
Teacher(s), 6-9, 20, 53, 84-85, 97,
    122, 127, 137, 141, 147
Teacher-student ratio, 137
Team-oriented *or* Teamwork, 86, 89,
    92-93, 96
Teaneck High School, 11

Technology, 21, 34-35, 45, 89, 92
    see Chapter Three
Teen death rates, 18
Teenage Research Unlimited, 26, 64
Teen(s) *or* Teenager(s), 8, 12-13, 26-
    28, 38, 41, 43, 86, 90-94, 102,
    107, 125, 148
TeenTalk, 62, 74
Teeth brushing, 143
Telephone, 3, 48, 52
Teletubbies, 56, 73
Television
    Addiction, 53, 69-70, 80
    Cable, 48
    Commercials, 52-53
    Programming, 51-61, 68
    Rating system, 54
    Sitcoms, 6, 34
Test(s) *or* Testing, 62-63, 85-86, 90,
    95-96, 109, 141
Theatre, 89-95, *see* Drama education
Theory, x
Theory *and* Practice, viii
Thomas the Tank Engine & Friends,
    60, 74
Thompson, Jim, 83
Time Bind, 18, 39
Timex, 64
Tinkertoys, 35
Title IX, 95
Tobacco, 87
Toddler play-dates *or* groups, 19, 62
Toddlers, 18-19, 36, 56, 65, 149
Toffler, Alvin, 20
Tofler, Ian, 111
Toilet-training, 131
Tonka trucks, 35
Toys, 31-37
Trapper-Keepers, 63
Trophy kids, 31, 44
True Love Waits, 99
Tucker, Karen, 61
TV, *see* Television
Tweens, 44
Tyon, Ty, 76
U.S. Census Bureau, 1, 4, 7, 22
Unconditional acceptance, 137-139
Unconditional love, 140, 144-147
Under-connected, 66
Uninvolved parents, 129-139
UPN, 50
USA Today, 26

Values, 1, 10, 60, 105, 109, 132
V-chip rating system, 54
Vegetarian, 107
VeggieTales, 60, 74
Verizon Wireless, 64
Vertical socialization, 8
Viacom International, 73
Vietnam War, 131
Violence, 51-54, 59, 71
Volunteer, 75, 77, 98
Washington Post, 91
Wasssssup, 52
Watergate break-in, 131
Watson, John, 126
Wattenberg, Ben, 12
WB, 50
WebMD, 72
Westheimer, Dr. Ruth, 52
White, Burton, 23, 40
Wilkersons (*Malcolm in the Middle*), 6
Win-at-all-costs, 77
Winn, Marie, 69
Wise, Nicole, 18, 40, 69
Wolf, Anthony, 149

Woods, Tiger, 76
Workforce *or* workforce preparation,
    87-88
Working kids, 27
World War II, 3-4, 6, 124, 131
Wright State University, 113
Wurman, Richard Saul, 22, 43
Xbox, 37
Xer Generation, *see* GenXers
Yahoo, 64, 71
Yahooligans, 71
Yanlelovich, 26
YMCA of the USA, 74
YMCA Pioneers, 104
Youth development, 109-110, 112
Youth for Christ/USA, 103
Youth group leaders, 102, 110, 147
Youth groups, 98-107, 110, 147
Youth sports, 76-83
Yo-Yos, 35
YWCA Girl Reserves, 104
Zander, Dieter, 99, 116
Ziff, Anne, 25
Zoba, Wendy, 99, 116

Fran Kick knows *What Makes Kids KICK!* He's been speaking to them, working with them, counseling them, teaching them and reaching them since 1986. During this time his unique perspective on what it takes to teach people to motivate themselves has been shared with thousands of students, teachers, parents and organizations.

Fran presents over one hundred programs every year across the U.S. to thousands of college/university, high school and junior high/ middle school students, plus the many people who work with them. In addition, he works with association, convention and corporate organizations who are actively engaged in teaching and reaching kids. Fran speaks at many state, regional and national conferences and has consulted with numerous schools, companies and organizations.

Fran's previous writing has appeared in numerous state and national educational publications. The U.S. Department of Education's Office of Educational Research and Improvement's ERIC/CAPS Clearinghouse published Fran's work entitled, *The Self-Perceptions of Self-Concept and Self-Esteem* and selected it for inclusion for the *Resources in Education Index*. He authored the student leadership series *KICK IT IN & TAKE THE LEAD!* and co-authored *Portfolios Across the Curriculum and Beyond* published by Corwin Press, Inc. He has his B.A. in Education and a M.A. in Educational Psychology.

For further information about Fran Kick, his programs, materials, and additional resources, check out http://www.kickitin.com.

Each chapter from every book in this series is also available as a print-disabled portable document format (PDF) read-only file. With so many resources cited and web sites provided, a PDF file enables you to quickly point-and-click your way much easier than typing in a URL. Plus, with the latest version of Adobe's Acrobat® Reader® you can find and search for terms, people and references even faster. It's the perfect computer companion to have at your fingertips for finding what's in the book and what's on the web.

BTWFYI: If you purchased the print edition of this book and did not receive the PDF edition, go visit http://www.whatmakeskidskick.com and simply use coupon code: WMKKHPDF for a special discount.

Virtually anyone – including MS-DOS, Linux®, Macintosh®, Solaris™, SUN®, and Microsoft® Windows® system users – can view a PDF file. If you do not have the latest version of Adobe's Acrobat® Reader® you can download the software for free from the Adobe web site…

http://www.adobe.com/products/acrobat/readstep2.html

Adobe®, the Adobe® logo, and Adobe Acrobat® Reader® are all registered trademarks of Adobe Systems Incorporated. All other trademarks are property of their respective owners.

ORDER FORM

BILLING & SHIPPING ADDRESS

Name		
Title/Position		
Organization		
Address		
City	State	ZIP
Phone		
Fax		
Email		

ORDER INFORMATION		Qty.	Total
What Makes Kids KICK	$27.50 each		
What Makes Kids KICK @ HOME	$27.50 each		
Sales Tax (Non-exempt Ohio orders)			
Shipping (U.S. orders add $4.95 International orders add $9.95)			
TOTAL AMOUNT =			

METHOD OF PAYMENT

❑ Check Enclosed (U.S. Funds. No C.O.D. orders accepted)

❑ Purchase Order Enclosed (U.S. Organizations only)

❑ MasterCard Credit Card

❑ Visa Credit Card

Credit Card Number

*Last 3 digits printed on the back of card.

Expires (mm/yy)   Card Code*

X

Signature

DISCOUNTED, AUDIO, AND E-BOOK VERSIONS AVAILABLE AT WWW.KICKITIN.COM

Please mail this order form with payment to: Instruction & Design Concepts
411 Maple Springs Drive, Centerville, OH 45458-9232 USA

WMKKHPBK-2005

DISCARD

What Makes Kids KICK

The first book in this series is designed as a compass of thought for working with today's postmodern kids. It provides a framework through which to view and explore the many influences and inspirational factors affecting the Millennial Generation (born 1980-2000±).

What Makes Kids KICK @ HOME

The second book in the series builds on the overall framework provided in the first book. It details what inspires kids specifically at home while providing pragmatic parenting steps that you can take to reach them, teach them and lead them.

What Makes Kids KICK @ SCHOOL (to be released)

The third book focuses on what inspires kids specifically at school. Motivating kids in the classroom to become self-directed learners requires more than just grades, smiley-face stickers, privilege points, test scores and diplomas. Inspiring a love of life-long learning might be more important for kids today than at any other time in history.

What Makes Kids KICK @ WORK (to be released)

The fourth book of the series takes a look at what inspires kids working on the job. How can you get kids to care about more than just making a buck? This book brings a roadmap of approaches you can use to help today's Millennial Generation KICK IT IN as they enter the workforce.

For more information about the entire series check out:

http://www.whatmakeskidskick.com